Jailing the Johnston Gang

Jailing the Johnston Gang

Bringing Serial Murderers to Justice

BRUCE E. MOWDAY

Published by Barricade Books Inc.
185 Bridge Plaza North
Suite 308-A
Fort Lee, NJ 07024
www.barricadebooks.com

Library of Congress Cataloging-in-Publication Data
Mowday, Bruce.
Jailing the Johnston gang : bringing serial murderers to justice /
by Bruce E. Mowday
p. cm.
ISBN 978-1-56980-363-9
1. Serial murders--United States. 2. Serial
murderers--United States. I. Title.

HV6245.M69 2008
364.152'32092275--dc22
2008045270

ISBN 13: 978-1-56980-363-9
ISBN 1-56980-363-3

10 9 8 7 6 5 4

Manufactured in the United States of America

DEDICATION

J*ailing the Johnston Gang* is dedicated to everyone involved in protecting the public's safety. Members of law enforcement make many sacrifices to do their sacred duty and they all should be recognized for their dedication.

CONTENTS

Foreword   *9*
Acknowledgments   *13*
Introduction   *17*

1 The Murder of Robin Miller   23
2 The Investigation Intensifies   33
3 Early Investigations   45
4 Master Plan   59
5 Criminal Roots   73
6 Death of Jackie Baen   83
7 "Hit Man" Cooperates   93
8 Three Murder Victims   109
9 Pieces of the Puzzle   121
10 Murder Charges Lodged   137
11 A Year of Investigations   147
12 Trial Preparations   167
13 The Ebensburg Murder Trial   185
14 Bruce A. Johnston Sr.'s Trial   213
15 Escape and More Murders   235
Index   253

FOREWORD

In the mid-1970s, when I was appointed an assistant United States attorney in Philadelphia, I was green as grass and pig-ignorant. My job as a federal prosecutor was to aid in the investigating, indicting, and trying bad guys who break federal laws. I didn't know what I didn't know and I lived in fear that I would mess up preparing or trying a case and let some felon run free. Fortunately, along with this powerful new job came a powerful new resource: the FBI. My right arm. My investigative army. My mentors.

As the government's lawyer, I was supposed to guide and direct the FBI agents' investigative efforts as we worked to build cases. In fact, in scores of my early cases, it's fairer to say that they guided me, suggesting strategies, interpreting evidence, telling me what we needed to prove and basically looking out for me. I had enough sense to be grateful. Still, it wasn't until I got better as a prosecutor that I realized how good these guys really were.

Before I entered federal law enforcement, I regarded the FBI as an "it," a thing. A bureau. An institution. A gray territory populated by a self-contained, faceless, humorless, relentless army with flat-tops and bad-fitting suits. My mental mythology still smacked of the "G-men," of self-righteous Elliott Ness clones wielding enormous power in relative secrecy.

And now that I'm years out of law enforcement, I'm disappointed that in the news, in the movies, and in pop literature I often see the FBI depicted in equally stereotypic and perhaps even more unflattering images: arrogant, turfy, secretive, myopic, inept, conspiratorial or even shady. It seems that every dammed summer detective thriller I pick up features some lone-wolf private investigator or long-suffering local police grunt, simply trying to get a little elbow room to single-handedly solve The Big Case while fending off the FBI's invariable attempts to grab the investigation, steal the glory, feather its nest, protect higher-ups, and demean every other branch of law enforcement.

This was not the FBI I got to know up close and personal. As I learned to work with FBI agents (rather than "use" them), I saw firsthand both the remarkable breadth and depth of their investigative skills and the facility with which they collaborated with other law enforcement agencies and entities. Yes, the territorial boundaries were clear (as clear as the legal boundaries between federal, state, and local jurisdiction had to be), but the border crossings were open and helpful.

The individual agents with whom I had the privilege to work were, by and large, remarkable people: selfless, generous with their time and patience, exceptionally determined and unbelievably thorough…and yes, collaborative. In my experience, their willingness to share information, resources, and glory with other law enforcement agencies was a norm, not an exception. I'm sure every stereotype can be supported with war stories and horror stories, but my experience contains precious little to support the picture of a supercilious, self-aggrandizing agency or of power-grabbing FBI agents.

That was one reason I was pleased when Bruce Mowday told me it was time to tell the full, Byzantine story of the investigation and eventual conviction—by state prosecutors—of the notorious Johnston brothers of southeastern Pennsylvania. By the time the full investigative machine was up and running; and oh, how we were running, a federal prosecutor with the immense power of the federal grand jury subpoena was co-strategizing with county district attorneys. FBI agents, state troopers, local police, and even the odd private citizen were working hand-in-glove, an implacable army working scores of fronts and hundreds of leads. There was a lot of work to go around, and fortunately the case's resolution allowed a lot of credit to go around, too. Such is true justice.

This book tells the astonishing tale of the Johnston brothers and the efforts to end a bizarre criminal empire operating among the bucolic farms of Pennsylvania and Maryland.

In one sense, it was just another ever-expanding major case investigation that eventually consumed four years and millions of taxpayer dollars. Yet, as I lived it over the course of those years, the story often seemed like a sort of hillbilly soap opera, with improbable personalities, daily twists and turns in the plot, new characters popping up and existing characters disappearing—sometimes abruptly. The tale's power to grip and fascinate has not dimmed in succeeding decades. I remember the story vividly, and after reading this book, you will too.

Douglas Richardson
Penn Valley, Pennsylvania, 2007

ACKNOWLEDGMENTS

Jailing *the Johnston Gang* is a writing project that has been in the works for almost three decades. The period of time between the completion of the investigation and the publication of this book might seem long but the years allowed reflection to place the investigation into proper context. A book written immediately after the murder trials would have not been as complete.

Every member of the law enforcement community that worked on the case, along with the attorneys and judges, needs to be acknowledged. If they were mentioned in this book or not, they were part of the team and deserve recognition. My special thanks goes to the more than twenty members of the law enforcement team that have in the past few years taken the time to sit down with me to be interviewed and recall, sometimes painfully, incidents connected with the investigation of the murders.

A special thank you goes to David Richter, the lead FBI agent on the case, and Thomas Cloud, one of the lead investigators of the Pennsylvania State Police. After departing their agencies, Dave and Tom eventually became partners in an investigative agency, Cloud, Feehery & Richter, Inc., based in West Chester, Pennsylvania. While having a meeting with them one day, I mentioned that I thought the investigative story of the Johnston murder cases had not been adequately told. They concurred and readily agreed to actively participate in the research of this book. Besides sitting for hours of interviews, they used their contacts to set up interviews with other members of the law enforcement community and former members of the Johnston gang. They also took time to review the draft of the text.

Two other members of the team, former Chester County Assistant Attorney Dolores Troiani and former Chief of Chester County Detectives Charles Zagorskie, were generous with their time and assistance. They spent hours talking to me about the case and providing me with valuable background material. Justice William H. Lamb, former Pennsylvania Supreme Court Justice and District Attorney of Chester County, found time during his busy schedule for an interview. Two former members of the Philadelphia branch of the United States Attorney's office, Walter Batty and Douglas Richardson, need to be acknowledged. Doug wrote the foreword to this book.

Current and former law enforcement officers sitting for interviews included Gabe Bolla, Joseph Carroll, J. R. Campbell, James MacElree, Larry Dampman, Michael Carroll, Paul Yoder, Ray Solt, and Thomas Frame. Former Chester County Commissioners Earl Baker and Robert Thompson both provided me with information and sat for interviews.

My wife, Katherine M. Harlan, is a fine proofreader and has greatly helped with the text. She is meticulous and has saved me from making many glaring errors. The organization of material for any book is critical and Christine Yurick aided in this endeavor for *Jailing the Johnston Gang*.

The research for this book began during the actual investigation and trials of the Johnston brothers. As a reporter for the *Daily Local News* in West Chester, Pennsylvania, I spent more than two years of my professional life trailing the investigative team from courtroom to courtroom and to several counties in Pennsylvania following the legal proceedings. I was out at nights when the bodies of the Johnstons' murder victims were unearthed. My most memorable days as a reporter were during the reporting of these murder cases and my editor, Bill Dean, and colleagues at the *Daily Local News* offered support during those days. I've included some of my personal stories in this book. All of the work had a downside as I missed a lot of time with my then young daughters, Melissa and Megan.

One interview I didn't get to do was with Chester County Common Pleas Court Judge Leonard Sugerman, who more than ably presided over the Johnston cases. Judge Sugerman, known for his brilliant legal mind, died before the latest round of interviews commenced.

I thank everyone who aided in the research and writing of this book.

Bruce E. Mowday
Uwchlan Township, Pennsylvania
September 2007

INTRODUCTION

Today, members of federal law enforcement agencies struggle to trust each other and share vital information to fight our nation's enemies. They harbor petty rivalries. Those in charge of such agencies should review what many professionals in the world of law enforcement consider to be the foremost example of cooperation among multiple departments: the investigation that resulted in the conviction of the mass murderers of the Johnston gang.

The murders committed by the Johnstons created national headlines but not the type associated with other sensational murder cases. "If this case had taken place in New York City, it would have received nation-wide headlines for months. The importance of this case has been underplayed," said Jack Levin, a noted author on criminal conduct and professor at Northeastern University.

Bruce A. Johnston Sr. was called the most notorious criminal in the history of Chester County, a county with history dating to the founding of the United States.

Countless hours were exhausted on congressional hearings and investigations, not to mention millions of taxpayers' dollars, to determine what federal agency knew what piece of information before the fatal attacks of September 11, 2001, on New York City and Washington, D. C., and the crash of a hijacked plane in Pennsylvania. In our blame-oriented society, the days after September 11 were spent in pointing fingers at agencies that might have possessed significant information that if shared would have prevented the national tragedy. Efforts stemming from those terrorist attacks to bring federal intelligence and law enforcement agencies under a unified umbrella organization have not been totally successful. These agencies still highly value their independence.

The story of the investigation, prosecution, and incarceration of the murderous members of the Johnston gang is one of investigative teamwork never before seen in Pennsylvania and many believe, never experienced in the United States. This story is a lesson for modern-day law enforcement officials: Cooperation among professional organizations pays the highest dividends.

Justice William H. Lamb, the prosecutor of the murder cases who later served on the Pennsylvania Supreme Court, said, "It should be memorialized." Other attorneys and police officers called the investigation the high points of their professional careers. Joseph Carroll, who did legal research on the case and now is the district attorney of Chester County, said the Johnston case was the most important one of his career.

Those departments taking part in the murder investigations were the United States Attorney General's Office, the Federal Bureau of Investigation, the Pennsylvania State Police, the Chester County District Attorney's Office, the Chester County Detective's Office, Maryland State Police, Delaware State Police, and a myriad of local Pennsylvania, Delaware, and Maryland police departments.

This is not to say that the investigation was perfect. In the beginning, before the Johnston gang turned violent, members of the Pennsylvania State Police at the Avondale barracks had to argue with superiors for resources. The gang members would frustrate police by creating an excessive amount of paperwork and hiring expensive and talented legal representation to keep them out of prison. As manpower was limited, overtime was needed and worked but not always paid. During one stakeout a state police official told investigators they would be paid only if they caught the Johnstons in the act of committing a crime and an arrest was made. If they didn't apprehend the criminals, they wouldn't be paid.

Some of the same interdepartmental rivalry that exists today was present during the Johnston investigation. All of the attorneys and investigators directly involved in the case said everyone was an equal no matter where they were employed. One state policeman, Gabe Bolla, said his captain was the "biggest thorn in the side" of the investigators. "His attitude was that we were the state police and no one was going to tell us what to do," Bolla recalled.

The captain's attitude wasn't infectious. David Richter, the lead FBI agent on the case, was known as "Trooper Dave." Richter said, "I don't know if there is a better cooperation between law enforcement in Pennsylvania than this case. Everyone is extremely proud of the contribution he made and he should be. I read that the FBI doesn't share information and isn't cooperative but from all of my years in the FBI, from Albany to Charlotte to Philadelphia, every agent, with few exceptions works with local law enforcement. You can't exist without working with local and state police. That image of the FBI is just not accurate." Chester County Detective Larry Dampman said many thought he was a state trooper. "We worked together," said former Chester County Detective Mike Carroll. "It didn't matter who you were working with, you just worked."

The team worked 24 hours a day, seven days a week for more than two years. The effort took a personal toll on some in the form of alcoholism and some marriages suffered. Bolla said his wife, after one of his long absences, lined up his children so they could be reintroduced to him.

The Johnston gang has not faded from the minds of those in the Delaware Valley, the area west of Philadelphia. A few years ago one of the Johnston brothers, Norman, escaped from state prison and was on the loose for weeks before being captured. As the massive manhunt was conducted in the southern portion of Chester County, the area where many of the Johnston victims were murdered, residents in the affluent countryside locked their doors and sightings of Norman Johnston drove people to the safety of their homes.

The Johnston brothers, leaders of the gang, were convicted of multiple murders. Bruce A. Johnston Sr. was serving six life sentences for six murders when he died in prison. His younger brothers, Norman and David, are behind bars and each is serving four consecutive life sentences.

The Johnstons are suspected of being involved in other murders. Information obtained for this book from a former gang member has led to the reopening of one cold case murder. At least one of the Johnston brothers is suspected of taking part in the murders of Kennett Square policemen Richard Posey and William Davis, executed by a sniper as they exited their vehicle outside their police station early one November morning.

Two of the Johnston brothers have been suspects and one former gang member said one of the brothers admitted being beside Ancell Hamm when Hamm fired the fatal bullets and another brother was driving a getaway car. Hamm was convicted of those killings and is serving a life imprisonment term. The cold-blooded murders of policemen Davis and Posey are integral parts of the Johnston story.

This book is a reminder that evil exists in the world and that the workings of criminal minds can't be diagnosed by applying common sense. The mortal sin of a Johnston gang member was to cooperate with police. Even Johnston blood relatives had to adhere by the non-snitch rule. The first victim, Gary Wayne Crouch, was murdered because he was a snitch. Three members of the Johnston's Kiddie Gang, including Bruce A. Johnston Sr.'s stepson, were murdered after they were subpoenaed to appear before a federal grand jury. Bruce A. Johnston Sr.'s son, Bruce A. Johnston Jr., was marked for death after he began cooperating with local, state, and federal investigators. An attempt was made on Johnston Jr.'s life and his girlfriend, Robin Miller, was killed. Johnston Jr. began talking after his father raped Miller.

After the two separate murder trials were completed and the Johnston brothers were placed behind prison bars, an attempt was made to write a book of the murders but more than one publisher insisted the book wouldn't sell because no one was a hero. A movie, *At Close Range*, was made in the 1980s but the Hollywood version tried to make Johnston Jr. a sympathetic character. The script was so fictionalized that the Chester County law enforcement community was offended and refused to cooperate with the filming. The movie was scheduled to be shot on location in Chester County but after receiving the cold shoulder the movie crew moved to Tennessee.

There are heroes. Douglas Richardson, who was an assistant United States attorney involved in the prosecution of the case and the author of the foreword to this book, said, "The forces of justice are the heroes."

Truly, the heroes in this mass murder were the members of the law enforcement team, the forces of justice. The law enforcement team brought Chester County's most notorious criminal, Bruce A. Johnston Sr., to justice and put out of business his vicious gang of criminals that for decades murdered, assaulted, raped, and robbed citizens throughout Chester County and many areas of the United States.

CHAPTER ONE

The Murder of Robin Miller

Late on a warm midsummer's night a teenage couple returned to the girl's rural farmhouse home after a date at Hersheypark. Hershey, a central Pennsylvania town, is home to Hershey Foods and known far and wide as Chocolate town.

In many ways the teenage couple was typical of most its age. The two believed they were worldly and experienced, they believed they were self-sufficient and only needed each other to be happy. In other ways they were completely opposite of their peers. They certainly weren't innocents. The young man, just nineteen years old, was a criminal who had served time in prison. The fifteen-year-old girl was known for a streak of wildness. She disobeyed her mother and ran away from home to be with her boyfriend. Also, the girl's relationship with her boyfriend directly led to her being raped.

And, most teenagers don't have a price on their heads.

The girl's home was in East Nottingham Township in southern Chester County, Pennsylvania, near the Maryland border. The driveway leading from Forge and Union Square roads to the farmhouse is a long one. The couple's yellow

Volkswagen Rabbit, with its headlights glowing, made the vehicle an isolated and inviting target during the early morning hours of Wednesday, August 30, 1978.

Slowly, the car traversed the cindered driveway running between the cornfields and stopped near a cluster of maple trees. Inside the car the girl began to gather her belongings, including a handbag purchased for her that day by her boyfriend of less than a year.

Robin Miller's choice of a beau was not a popular one with her family, especially her mother Linda Miller. After her daughter ran away from home to be with Bruce Alfred Johnston Jr., Linda Miller decided it was futile to try to separate the young couple. Rather than alienate her daughter, Linda Miller allowed them to live together in the farmhouse along with her other children.

Miller and Johnston Jr. first met when Robin was dating a friend of Johnston Jr. Less than a year later they had plans to marry after Robin's sixteenth birthday in July 1979.

JOHNSTON JR. WOULD do about anything to be with Robin. Less than two weeks earlier Johnston Jr., a convicted thief, had been incarcerated in Chester County Farms Prison. A joint federal and state investigative team was talking to Johnston Jr. concerning criminal activity involving his father, uncles, other relatives, boyhood friends, and an array of vicious criminals and petty thieves. For almost two decades the Johnston gang had terrorized and victimized citizens throughout the Brandywine Valley of Pennsylvania and Delaware, the eastern seaboard of the United States and beyond.

In mid-August Johnston Jr. told investigators he would cooperate and testify before a federal grand jury sitting in Philadelphia only if he could be set free and be with Robin Miller. Revenge was also on the mind of Johnston Jr. While incarcerated at Chester County Farms Prison Johnston Jr. received a letter from Miller. The letter detailed how Johnston Sr. and another gang member offered to take Miller to see Johnston Jr. in prison. Robin Miller began the trip but never made it to the prison. The two men gave Robin Miller whiskey, took her to a hotel and raped her. Johnston Jr. was out to get even with his father. He would cooperate with police and break the Johnston family's most sacred covenant: never cooperate with the police, especially against family.

Johnston Jr. was brought before Chester County Common Pleas Court Judge Leonard Sugerman in a closed court session on August 17, 1978. Judge Sugerman enjoyed a sterling judicial reputation. His judicial rulings were golden. One decision involving the burden of proof in civil cases changed Pennsylvania law. His ruling was upheld by the United States Supreme Court after a state appellate court had decided Judge Sugerman had made a wrong decision.

Judge Sugerman handled most of the pre-trial hearings and the two murder trials involving the Johnston gang. At the conclusion of the August 17 court session Johnston was on his way to being released from prison and seeing Robin. All he had to do was post nominal bail of $1.

Judge Sugerman said he never intended to have Johnston Jr. free on the streets and he only lowered bail to facilitate a transfer of Johnston Jr. from Chester County Farms Prison to Lancaster County Prison, where a case against Johnston Jr. was pending. Law enforcement officials believed Johnston Jr.'s life was in danger at Chester County Prison because of his cooperation with police. The influence of the young thief's father reached inside the prison walls. Johnston Jr. was transferred to Lancaster County Prison where he had to complete serving time for a probation violation. Johnston Jr. was given time served and released. Johnston Jr. had attained his goal; he was once again with Robin.

Law enforcement officials wanted to put Johnston Jr. in the Federal Witness Protection Program but Johnston Jr. refused, believing, he later said, he would be housed in a motel room with policemen and wouldn't be able to smoke marijuana. After returning to Robin Miller it wasn't long before his father, Bruce A. Johnston Sr., started calling Miller's house, looking for his son. Johnston Jr. had Robin Miller tell his father that he was still in prison. Johnston Jr. also received word from a relative that Johnston Sr. would give him $12,000 if he would just stop cooperating with police. In the meantime, Johnston Jr. changed his mind about federal protection and asked for help. Johnston Jr. made the decision on the day he went to the amusement park in Hershey.

Robin Miller's mother and other family members had departed for a vacation in Virginia a day before Robin's date with Johnston Jr. at Hersheypark. The young couple set off in the afternoon for hours of rides and Hershey's chocolates. Late in the evening the couple made the 60-mile drive from the park to Miller's home, near the Mason-Dixon Line that separates Pennsylvania from Maryland. The Miller family lived in part of the farmhouse and Hazel Sturges lived in the other half of the home. The rural landscape was dotted with working farms, including mushroom farms. The closer Miller and Johnston got to the empty Miller homestead that night, the less likely they would see traffic on the isolated back country roads.

The couple had a welcoming party. For hours two men waited in a field close to the Miller home. They spent time smoking cigarettes, talking, waiting, and carefully preparing their weapons for their deadly task.

Johnston Jr. pulled the Volkswagen into the driveway and made his way to the Miller farmhouse. The two men silently slipped from the field and readied their pistols as they crept to the car. After the car stopped Miller hesitated before opening the door. She wanted her new handbag and other items from Hersheypark. Johnston Jr. put on the interior light and began to open his door.

Gunshots broke the silence of the night.

Johnston Jr., the police informant, was the target of the assassins. Shot after shot was fired into the vehicle and Johnston Jr. was struck eight times; bullets found their mark and entered his head, his torso, and other parts of his body. "It stunned and dazed me," Johnston Jr. said of the shooting. "I staggered hearing shots in rapid succession and feeling pain but I didn't know from where they first fired. I guess I staggered around a little bit, and I fell in the car." Johnston Jr. fell with his head between the car seats. He looked up to see Miller sitting upright. "She screamed," he said. "I told her to get down. I thought I saw a little red mark down at her jaw, and she got out of the car and ran into the house."

The two paid killers, confident that their contract was fulfilled, retreated from the driveway, making good in their escape.

Robin Miller, the young girl in love with the wrong boy, was struck once in the chin. The wound would prove fatal. Minutes later Johnston Jr. cradled the body of his young lover while sitting on their bed. "I was trying to help her breathe. It didn't look like she was breathing," Johnston Jr. said. He called police telling them the assassins were still firing. The shooting had stopped but Johnston Jr. thought the police would arrive quicker if they believed the murderers were still at the house.

Sturges, who shared the farmhouse with the Miller family, was watching television when she heard what she believed to be fireworks. "I didn't pay any attention to them," Sturges said. She did remember seeing a man running across the yard.

A neighbor, James Joncs, recalled being awakened by screams but at first thought the noise came from wild cats.

Jones said he heard at least three gunshots. Jones told a newspaper reporter that he heard a car driving away in a southerly
direction toward Route 272 and Maryland.

An ambulance arrived at the Miller farmhouse at approximately 12:45 AM. Fifteen minutes later Miller, who was only
weeks away from entering high school, was pronounced dead
on arrival at the Southern Chester County Medical Center
in nearby Jennersville. Miller's Oxford Intermediate School
principal, Kenneth Woodward, said following the shooting,
"I knew her very well, and I liked her." Johnston Jr. was admitted to the same hospital in critical condition. He received
gunshot wounds to his head, neck, shoulder, chest, stomach,
arm, elbow, and back. Miraculously within days he recovered
sufficiently to become a participant in the Federal Witness
Protection Program. He was relocated to a small town in
Wisconsin, far from the shooting, his father, and other Johnston gang members.

PENNSYLVANIA STATE POLICEMAN Truman Joseph
Clary, who had been on the force five years, was on duty at
the Avondale barracks when he received Johnston Jr.'s call
at 12:34 AM. "He stated he was shot, that his girlfriend was
shot and he requested the police and an ambulance," Clary
later testified. "He stated she was unconscious, lying on the
floor, and could we please hurry, and that they were still
shooting."

Clary and Trooper Bernard Dickerson immediately responded to the call and were on the scene within 15 minutes.
Already, there was activity at the Miller home as the original
call was routed through Chester County's fire board radio
system, alerting the law enforcement and emergency services
communities. An ambulance was in the driveway and another state policeman, Raymond Bunjo, was talking to Johnston

Jr. The ambulance crew and Oxford policeman John Slauch were inside the Miller residence. Within minutes the ambulance, containing Miller and Johnston Jr., along with Officer Slauch, was on their way to the hospital in Jennersville.

Bunjo and Slauch had arrived at the shooting scene almost simultaneously. Bunjo walked to the porch where a light was shining. The interior of the farmhouse was also lit. "Bruce Johnston Jr. came walking out of the door," Bunjo said. "He was holding his right hand against his chest. There was blood all over his shirt. He was bleeding from the arm. There was blood on his forehead. The first words he said to me was, 'Robin is shot, help her.'"

Bunjo, Slauch and Johnston Jr. went to the upstairs bedroom where Miller was on the bed. Slauch found a weak pulse. Slauch, who had been a member of the Oxford police force less than two months, recalled seeing a wound near Miller's chin and blood in her mouth. As Bunjo went to call for an ambulance, one from Oxford arrived.

As the ambulance pulled away from the Miller residence Clary's next calls were to Lieutenant Richard Weimer, who was in charge of the Avondale barracks, and Trooper Thomas Cloud, one of the main investigators for years of the Johnston gang. Additional state policemen and law enforcement officers from the nearby borough of Oxford were arriving by the minute.

Cloud remembers being called at home and rushing to the hospital. "I knew Johnston Jr. was shot a number of times," Cloud said. "I was thinking about a deathbed statement." Cloud also called the barracks seeking to have police dispatched to the residences of the Johnston brothers Norman, David, and Bruce Johnston Sr., to see if they were at home.

One of the first persons Cloud contacted was Federal Bureau of Investigation agent David Richter. "We were out

working for the next 30 hours," Richter, the lead FBI agent
on the case, recalled.

Chester County Detective Larry Dampman was dispatched to the scene by his lieutenant, Michael Cotter.
Dampman reported, "There were bloodstains and bullet
holes inside the auto, and two bullets were found outside the
car in the driveway. Near the steps of the porch was a blood-
covered pocketbook with bloodstains leading from the auto
to the house. Inside of the house were bloodstains going up
the stairs to the second floor and into a bedroom believed to
be Robin Miller's room. There was a large amount of blood
on the bed."

The Miller farmhouse and property were meticulously
searched for evidence. Chester County Detective Sergeant
Michael Carroll took impressions of tire tracks found leading from a field near the home. As the evidence was gathered
and the crime scene secured and photographed, the majority
of the law enforcement officers went to the Avondale barracks for their next assignments in the murder investigation.
Weimer asked Carroll to call in more members of the county
detectives and Anthony Massorotti and Jacob DeBoard were
ordered to respond to the crime scene. Weimer needed the
extra manpower because the police were going to search for
members of the Johnston gang and Johnston family to see if
any could be tied to the shootings.

A search of the property found two .38 caliber projectiles,
wad cutters. The projectile portion of the wad cutter has a flat
nose and usually is made of a cheaper material than other am-
munition. Wad cutters are used for target shooting since they
are cheaper and can cut through target paper and accurately
show the location hit. Even though less powerful than other
bullets, wad cutters can still cause serious bodily damage.

Two purses were discovered at the shooting scene containing eye glasses, a memo pad, a Dentyne gum pack, hair

brushes, a container of rouge, eye makeup, nail clippers, a bottle opener, and a plastic bag that contained a substance that resembled marijuana, according to a police report. Drug use was common among some members of the Johnston gang.

Johnston Jr. and Robin Miller corresponded a lot and they kept their letters. In the couple's bedroom police found 67 letters addressed to Miller and 64 additional letters addressed to Johnston Jr.

Before the murder of Robin Miller, the Johnston gang was known for being involved in strong-arm robberies, tractor thefts, burglaries, drug deals, and car heists. As far as the public and police knew, the gang hadn't committed any murders.

Police had another mystery involving the Johnston gang. Johnston gang associates, recently subpoenaed to testify before a federal grand jury, were missing. Foul play was suspected in connection with their disappearances but no concrete evidence existed that any had been harmed or murdered.

The Miller murder unleashed the full force of federal, state, and local law enforcement agencies against the Johnstons. They were no longer considered small-time thieves. As former gang member Jimmy Griffin said, "After they shot Robin Miller, they knew they screwed up."

The police didn't know it at the time but Robin Miller wasn't the first person to be murdered by the Johnstons and she wouldn't be the last.

CHAPTER TWO

The Investigation Intensifies

Bruce A. Johnston Jr. was in stable condition after emergency surgery during the early morning hours of August 30, 1978. Even as Johnston Jr. recovered in Southern Chester County Medical Center police were concerned about Johnston Jr.'s safety and feared a second attempt on his life.

While Johnston Jr. was at the hospital someone tried to force open locked doors at the hospital. The locks were damaged in the failed attempt. Johnston Jr. was placed under 24-hour-a-day police protection.

AS JOHNSTON JR. struggled for his life in surgery, police sifted through the Miller grounds and farmhouse looking for clues to the killers of fifteen-year-old Robin Miller. By 5:30 AM all but Chester County Detective Anthony Massarotti and state policeman Frank Carter had departed the murder scene. Massarotti and Carter were given the duty of making sure no trespassers violated the integrity of the crime scene. Investigators would return to search for additional evidence.

A meeting was held at the Avondale barracks of the Pennsylvania State Police. After a briefing by officers in charge, the assembled law enforcement officers were given assignments. They were going to fan out across three states to locate members of the Johnston gang, family members, friends, and known associates of Johnston Jr. Johnston gang members were at the top of the suspect list since Johnston Jr. was the main witness against the gang in the grand jury investigation.

AT LEAST ONE member of the Johnston family immediately stated she believed Bruce A. Johnston Sr. was responsible for the shootings. Chester County detectives Mike Carroll and Larry Dampman tracked down Harriet Steffy, grandmother of Johnston Jr., during the early afternoon of August 30 and interviewed her, along with her daughter, Kathy Steffy.

Harriet Steffy said Johnston Sr. had contacted her several times during the days preceding the shooting trying to locate his son. Steffy confronted Johnston Sr. and told him that she had heard that Johnston Sr. was going to shoot his son. Johnston Sr. denied he intended to harm Johnston Jr. Several times Johnston Sr. stopped or drove by the Steffy home looking for Johnston Jr. Once Johnston Sr. stopped with a stranger; a man the Steffys described as six feet tall, more than 200 pounds and ugly. Steffy was convinced Johnston Sr. was responsible for the shootings.

AFTER THE STEFFY interview concluded Carroll and FBI agent Michael Melvin were among those officers dispatched to Delaware to search for James Johnston, stepbrother of Johnston Jr. James Johnston was one of the missing witnesses subpoenaed to appear before the federal grand jury. Police received information that James Johnston and three other gang members, brothers James and Wayne Sampson and Dwayne Lincoln, were staying at one of the motels along Route 40, somewhere between Wilmington, Delaware, and Elkton, Maryland. Photographs of Johnston Sr., his brothers Norman and David Johnston, and gang members Roy Myers, Richard Mitchell, Raymond Hamm, James Johnston, and James Sampson were distributed to the investigators. The officers were told Mitchell had an outstanding arrest warrant and was to be arrested if found.

The Pennsylvania police officers met with members of Troop #2 of the Delaware State Police and split into teams. Carroll was paired with Detective Charles Davis of the Delaware State Police. The all-day search for James Johnston proved to be futile and Carroll finally reported off duty at 11:00 PM, after almost 24 hours on the job.

CARROLL'S BOSS, CHIEF County Detective Charles Zagorskie, arrived at the Avondale station about 9:30 AM on August 30. A former state policeman, Zagorskie had previously been stationed at the Avondale barracks. Many of those hours at the barracks were spent investigating the Johnston gang. Zagorskie left the state police to join the Chester County Detectives on December 23, 1975.

After talking with state police Lieutenant Richard Weimer, Zagorskie and Lieutenant Mike Gavitt of the Lancaster barracks of the state police went to the crime scene. There Trooper Carter led Zagorskie to a section of the field about 100 yards south of the Miller farmhouse on the west side of Union Square Road. Tire tracks in the field led to Union Square Road. They found a piece of plastic that appeared to be recently broken from a vehicle. On the plastic were markings with the word Pontiac. The piece of plastic, later a key piece of evidence, was seized and secured as evidence. Chester County Detective Frank McGinty checked with the owner of a local car dealer, Barclay Pontiac of Kennett Square, and was told the plastic was a baffle shield from behind the front bumper of a vehicle, possibly a Pontiac Bonneville, made from 1973 to 1975.

A search of the area surrounding the farmhouse began at 7:00 AM by members of the state police and Chester County Detectives. According to Massarotti, three different areas were identified as possible hiding places used by the killers. Five Winston cigarette butts were found in a cornfield in the southeast corner of the property. Two more Winston butts and two different sets of footprints were also discovered in the southeast corner of the cornfield. The third area had tire impressions along with one set of foot impressions leading from the tire tracks to a mushroom growing house near the Miller farmhouse.

ZAGORSKIE'S INVESTIGATION WASN'T confined to the murder scene or to the Johnston gang. He checked reports that threats were made against Johnston Jr. while he was in Chester County Farms Prison. The day after the shooting, Zagorskie visited Warden Thomas Frame. Inmates told Zagorskie that news of Johnston Jr.'s cooperation with police had filtered throughout the jail. "You have to understand the paranoia that goes through a prison when the word gets out that someone is talking," one inmate said. Two inmates, neither members of the Johnston gang, had talked about killing Johnston Jr., Zagorskie was told.

THE LEADING SUSPECT in the ambush was Johnston Sr. so police checked every movement he made during the days prior to the shootings. On the day after the shooting, Detective Massarotti and state policemen Phil Perry and J. R. Campbell investigated a report that Johnston Sr. had been staying at a Howard Johnson Lodge near Newark, Delaware, on the night of the shooting. The officers seized all of the trash from the lodge, which contained two pieces of paper with the name Bruce Johnston. Massarotti, Campbell, and Martz interviewed Howard Johnson employees and checked records. Indeed, Johnston Sr. was registered in room 145 the day of the shooting.

WHILE THE SEARCH was on for Johnston Sr., members of the law enforcement team, including county detectives Carroll and Dampman and troopers Ray Solt and Gerald Maksymchock, searched for Leslie Dale, a dangerous member of the Johnston gang and another top suspect in the Miller murder. A search of Dale's known haunts, which included bars and diners, failed to locate him. The next stop was the Fox Mobile Home Motel on Route 30 in Gap, Lancaster County. Dale was renting half of a trailer at Fox for $40 a week.

Dale wasn't home when the officers arrived but they decided to stay and keep an eye on Dale's trailer in case the Johnston gang member returned. A few minutes after 7:00 PM on August 31, a Florida man who identified himself as Walter John Rought approached the police officers and asked if they were looking for Dale. Rought, an associate of Dale, said Dale had called him and stated police were going to arrest him on "murder one" charges. Dale called Rought from the nearby White Horse Inn but he wanted Rought to meet him at 8:00 PM at another bar on Route 82 outside of Coatesville, Labiak's Bar.

Rought, a truck driver, was the ex-brother-in-law of another local criminal, Richard Donnell. Rought said he didn't want to be involved in the investigation and he especially didn't want Dale to know he talked with police. Rought asked for a chance to leave the area. The officers allowed him to depart.

Police checked the White Horse Inn but Dale had already left by the time they arrived. At Labiak's Bar Dale was inside when police arrived. The officers decided against approaching Dale inside the bar and waited. Dale left the bar at 9:30 PM, got in his truck, and drove south a mile before being stopped by police. Dale didn't resist and police had a key member of the Johnston gang in custody.

Zagorskie, who had had many contacts with Dale over the years, interviewed Dale. When Zagorskie asked Dale his whereabouts during the time of Miller's murder, Dale asked for immunity. Zagorskie denied the request.

"Charlie [Zagorskie], I have to have immunity, I was pulling a job, a crime, I was stealing a tractor at the time." Dale said.

Dale showed Zagorskie his left arm, which was injured. Dale claimed he received the wound from a barbed wire, a wire he grazed while stealing the tractor on the night Miller was murdered. Zagorskie wasn't convinced. The arm wound could also have been made by a bullet. A theory developed that Dale was wounded in a crossfire by his partner during the Miller murder.

Dale also said he was at a restaurant at the other end of Chester County from the shooting scene during the time the shooting took place. After being asked to clarify if he was at a restaurant or committing a crime, Dale asked for an attorney.

At 5:30 PM on September 1, a search warrant was executed by state police and county detectives at Dale's trailer. Dale was a prime suspect in the murder and was being held on burglary, theft, and receiving stolen property charges. District Magistrate Eugene DiFilippo of Kennett Square set bail at $50,000, an amount Dale couldn't post.

ANOTHER KNOWN DANGEROUS member of the gang, Ricky Mitchell, was eluding law enforcement efforts to locate him. Police visited Mitchell's parents, Ruth and Ray Mitchell, hours after the shooting but Mitchell's parents said they hadn't seen their son in about a week.

In the early morning hours just after the shooting Mitchell called his daughter Sandy West who was nineteen years old and living in Boothwyn, Delaware County, which is between Chester County and Philadelphia. Mitchell asked his daughter if he could stay with her because he was too tired to drive home after visiting several bars. West invited Mitchell to her home and when he arrived she could tell Mitchell had been drinking. Mitchell stayed two days.

Mitchell asked West to help him get a chisel or an ice pick because he had locked his keys in his car. When she refused and asked him to leave, Mitchell grabbed his daughter around the neck, hit her a few times, and threatened to kill her. West called police and Mitchell departed. West told county detective Michael Carroll that she believed her father was hiding from the police because he wouldn't leave the apartment during the day.

Mitchell's parents called Carol Johnston, wife of Johnston Sr. and stepmother of Johnston Jr., after the police visited them. They wanted to know why the police were looking for their son.

Carol Johnston, who lived with Johnston Sr. on Blue Ball Road, Elkton, Maryland, received a visit from state policemen J. R. Campbell and Robert Martz. Carol Johnston told police that after the call from the Mitchells, Norman Johnston, Johnston Sr.'s brother, also called to say the police were visiting his apartment. After Norman Johnston's call, Carol said she called her husband at the Howard Johnson Motor Lodge in Newark, Delaware. Johnston Sr. returned home by 6:00 AM and then departed, she said. Carol Johnston told police that Johnston Sr. stayed at the hotel several nights a week but not because of marital problems. She gave no further explanation as to why Johnston Sr. spent so much time at a nearby motel.

The night of the Miller murder Carol Johnston said she was with Johnston Sr. at her mother-in-law's home in Kennett Square. During the interview with police, Carol Johnston received a phone call. Carol asked one question: "How much is the bail?" Johnston Sr. was in federal custody.

Johnston Sr. was charged with hindering the federal investigation. Assistant United States Attorney Walter Batty said Johnston Sr. was trying to stop his stepson, James Johnston, from testifying.

CHESTER COUNTY DETECTIVE Jake DeBoard and state policeman Paul Yoder were at the apartment of Norman and Susan Johnston at 5:15 AM, less than five hours after the shooting. Yoder reported both appeared to be sleeping and stated the couple said they had no knowledge of the shooting.

The next day troopers Gabe Bolla and Ed Wandishin again visited Norman Johnston. Norman Johnston told police, "My wife will tell you I don't even bother with any of those guys anymore. I heard about it and it is a big mess but I don't think I can help you. We were all down at Mom's yesterday (the day of the shooting), me, Bruce, Dave, and everyone were at Mom's. Like I said, I don't know anything about it but I will be more than willing to come down to the barracks and talk to you and answer any questions. Just give me some time to shower and I'll be there at about 12:30."

Troopers Bolla and Wandishin interviewed David Johnston, another one of Johnston Sr.'s brothers, on August 31, about noon in Kennett Square. David Johnston said, "This is kind of personal and I don't know anything about it. I do know one thing, why don't you guys get Bruce (Johnston

Sr.) off with this FBI charge and bring him up here and sit down and talk with him and an attorney and I'm sure he'll tell you what you want to know. You can get him out; this is your turf and not the FBI's. As far as little Bruce (Johnston Jr.), I hardly even know him. The one thing I do know about little Bruce is that big Bruce (Johnston Sr.) was hiding him because there were four guys after him and it had something to do with dope. I don't want to talk about it anymore."

Later, Norman and David Johnston would both be asked to appear at the state police barracks for questioning and both said on the advice of their attorney, West Chester lawyer Robert Landis, they would refuse.

Later in the day on Wednesday Yoder interviewed a Johnston associate, Roy Myers, who was a brother-in-law of Johnston Sr. Myers told police he broke off his relationship with the Johnston brothers after he discovered Johnston Sr. had made a pass at his wife. Myers did relate details of a recent conversation he had with Johnston Sr. and his two brothers, Norman and David Johnston. Johnston Sr. said little Bruce, as Johnston Jr. was known, was talking to police but the brothers weren't too worried since they had not done any burglaries with Johnston Jr.

THE JOHNSTON FAMILY gathered regularly at the home of Louise Johnston on East Birch Street in Kennett Square. At 2:45 PM Bolla and Wandishin visited Louise Johnston, the mother of Norman, David, and Bruce Johnston Sr.

"This sure is a mess," Louise Johnston told the troopers. "I really don't know what I can tell you. We were all here yesterday. It was me and Bruce, Dave and Norm, and Carol and my daughters. But Bruce, he was all upset about all this; he was sick cause deep down he loved that boy. The boy (Johnston Jr.) was in trouble cause these four guys was huntin' him

over something to do with dope. I really don't know if they
were white or black, all I know is that they were huntin' him
and Bruce, he hid him cause he was afraid. Big Bruce is really sick over this; he was here the night it happened, he was
drinkin' heavy and he was at the Anvil Inn with some of his
buddies. ... How is little Bruce? They won't tell us nothing at
the hospital and we're real worried."

David and Susan Johnston were in the room at the time
of the interview and the troopers said they wouldn't ask him
any questions because of his lawyer's instructions not to talk
to police. Without prompting David Johnston did say, "This
whole thing started in Florida and it had to deal with dope
and a lot of it. Little Bruce was involved in a dope rip-off.
The figure you are talking about is $400,000 and these four
guys were after him over it. That's why big Bruce was hiding
him. Big Bruce got a call about it and a threat that his house
would be blown up."

POLICE WERE ALSO looking for associates of Robin Miller, Johnston Jr., and the missing gang members. County detective Carroll and state policeman Paul Yoder sought out
Vicky Hanney, the fifteen-year-old former girlfriend of the
missing James Johnston. She wasn't much help as she hadn't
seen Jimmy Johnston in more than three weeks. She had
seen Robin Miller less than a week before the shooting but
Miller didn't have much to say, according to Hanney.

Carroll didn't have much better luck with Denise Evans,
who stayed at the Miller farmhouse on the Sunday night before the shooting. Evans said Miller and Johnston Jr. stayed
to themselves most of the night but Johnston Jr. was very
nervous. She said Johnston Jr. kept looking out of the win-
dows when cars would pass by the house.

In another interview Laura Wilson, who was known as

Robin Miller's best friend, told Carroll that she had not seen much of Miller in recent days because Johnston Jr. was around. Wilson did say that the couple seemed scared and Miller believed that someone had been watching her. Miller, according to Wilson, also had been receiving threats and had discussed the fears with her sister, Roxanne Miller.

ON SEPTEMBER 2 Johnston Jr. was taken from the hospital to the Douglas Woodworth Funeral home on Market Street, Oxford, for services for Robin Marie Miller. The funeral home was protected and police reported "no unusual incidents." At 2:00 PM that day United States marshals took Johnston Jr. into custody.

LAW ENFORCEMENT OFFICERS were hoping that Johnston Jr. would remember something about his assailants, but he couldn't. On September 14, county detective Frank McGinty tried a hypnosis session with Johnston Jr. State policeman Cloud and Assistant District Attorney James MacElree were in the room with McGinty, who was trained in hypnosis. FBI agent Richter, chief county detective Zagorskie and members of the United States marshals' office were in a nearby room.

The session didn't provide any information.

CHAPTER THREE

Early Investigations

During the days immediately following the murder of Robin Miller the joint investigative team of federal, state, county, and local law enforcement agents had identified a myriad of possible suspects. Clearly, the intended victim of the August 30, 1978, shooting was Bruce Alfred Johnston Jr., Miller's boyfriend, and not the fifteen-year-old girl.

Inmates at Chester County Farms Prison told police Johnston Jr. was a marked man because of his cooperation with police. Johnston Jr.'s uncles and grandmother put the finger on unnamed Florida drug dealers because of a $400,000 marijuana deal gone bad. Johnston gang member Leslie Dale, a criminal with a reputation for violence, became a suspect. When arrested Dale had a wrist wound that could have been caused by a stray bullet during the shooting of Miller and Johnston Jr. Also, on September 14, 1978, an inmate at Chester County Prison told detective Michael Carroll that Dale had confessed to the Miller murder. Another dangerous Johnston gang member, Ricky Mitchell, was doing his best to elude questioning by the law enforcement team.

The name at the top of the suspect list was Bruce A. Johnston Sr., father of one of the shooting victims and recognized
leader of the notorious Johnston gang. Johnston Sr. was trying to buy his son's silence for $12,000 as Johnston Jr. had
violated the family's golden rule; he cooperated with police.
Being Johnston Sr.'s son wouldn't save him from being a target of the Johnston gang. Hours after the shooting Johnston
Jr.'s grandmother told police she believed Johnston Sr. was
the culprit.

Police were also searching for four young members of the
Johnston gang, Dwayne Lincoln, brothers James and Wayne
Sampson, and James Johnston, Johnston Sr.'s stepson. The
four criminals disappeared after grand jury subpoenas were
issued weeks before the Miller murder. Police were convinced
the missing gang members had vital information concerning
the criminal workings of the Johnston gang.

WHILE INVESTIGATING ALL of the leads of the case, the
main focus of the law enforcement team remained centered
on Johnston Sr., his brothers Norman and David Johnston,
and other key members of the Johnston gang, including
Dale and Mitchell. Those directing the investigation had
gained many insights into the workings of the Johnston
gang during numerous investigations of the gang members
that spanned decades. In the coming months those experienced members of law enforcement would put their knowledge to good use.

TOM CLOUD WAS one of the main investigators on the
Johnston case for the Pennsylvania State Police. Cloud was
raised in the Chadds Ford area of Pennsylvania, in the center
of the area where the Johnston gang was headquartered.

"Growing up I wasn't interested in law enforcement," Cloud recalled. "I worked on a farm as a youngster and my family was in construction. I didn't even know that the Avondale barracks of the state police existed." A friend told him about life with the state police. "I thought it might be interesting," Cloud said. "In hindsight I think a career with the state police was meant to be."

State police officials usually don't assign troopers to barracks covering areas where they lived. Cloud proved to be an exception as his first barracks was in Thorndale, also located in Chester County, and then his second posting was to Avondale where he stayed the rest of his state police career.

"Avondale was a notorious station," Cloud said. "It was very busy on the criminal side as opposed to traffic patrols and accident investigations. Generally, there is less enthusiasm among troopers for postings at criminal stations because of the paperwork involved in criminal cases. In the end I thought the criminal activity made the barracks special. The people who stayed there were the workers and they stood up to all challenges. I went to Avondale and started out in patrol. In July of 1971 I was working the midnight shift over the Fourth of July weekend and a motorcycle gang murder took place in Oxford. The state was just beginning to pay overtime and the barracks had restrictions on crime guys' being called out when their shifts ended. I turned up some important witnesses over the weekend and the crime guys began to notice me. In October 1971 I went into the crime section and became a detective." He remained in the criminal investigative unit until his retirement in July 1996.

Southern Chester County was changing in the 1970s from a rural community, as when Cloud was young, to a more gentrified area with horse farms and large estates. The Unionville-Chadds Ford school system was gaining a reputation for excellence. Cloud recalled having tractors in the school's parking lot when he attended. The only tractors in the parking lot now are when the school hosts the Unionville Community Fair. The area had a mix of wealthy families, many executives from du Pont and other Wilmington, Delaware, companies settled in the area, and those who worked on the farms, especially the mushroom farms. Kennett Square is still known as the Mushroom Capital of the World. Mushroom workers at first were local Quakers and then Italian immigrants. Later Hispanic workers began filling the low-paying jobs. Second and third generation of mushroom workers eventually began owning some of the mushroom farms.

"The diversity of population caused lots of problems that had the police in the middle," Cloud said. "There were well-known criminals in the area, the Hamms and the Johnstons, and you heard about them from the day you arrived in the area."

On November 15, 1972, Cloud said, "my life changed." He was at home at 2:30 AM when he received a call informing him that his two friends, Kennett Square policemen Bill Davis and Dick Posey, had been killed during an ambush as they exited their police car in front of the Kennett Square police station. At the time three police cars, one each from the state police, Kennett Square, and Oxford had responsibility of patrolling the southern section of Chester County. "You depended on each other," Cloud said. "I would say from that moment on I did more growing up than I ever did. The reality of what this work was and what this job was really about came home. It is as simple as that."

STATE POLICEMAN J.R. Campbell was working the night of the murders of the Kennett Square policemen. Campbell and his partner George E. Duchemin found the slain officers.

"We were sitting and watching the Suburban Propane

yard, between West Grove and Avondale," Campbell said. "The yard was one of the gang's favorite places to hit. They liked to steal the copper. At that time the county had an on-the-hour check-in for police on patrol. It was early morning and George and I were sitting in the car and watching the yard. The barracks called and said the Kennett car had not checked in. We were the only car out in that southern end of the county and we joked around and said we would have to find out where they were sleeping."

Campbell and Duchemin checked on the officers. "At the police station we pulled up and saw the car," Campbell said. "I could see that the driver's door was open. We walked up and saw both of them lying there. I had only been on the job a little over a year. I had no idea what had happened. We checked and both of them were dead. The first thing in our minds was that a sniper was still out there. We called on our radio that both officers were down, shot. That started everything rolling. We thought additional officers couldn't get here fast enough."

A few days earlier Campbell had been hunting with Posey. "I knew then the Johnstons and Hamms were dangerous; before the murders I thought they were just a nuisance," Campbell said.

THE INVESTIGATION ALMOST immediately focused on Ancell Hamm. Growing up in the area Cloud knew of Hamm, Bo Darrell and the Johnstons, the central members of a loosely knit gang that committed numerous crimes. Cloud said he used to ride in the same school bus as Bo Darrell, and Darrell's sister was in his high school class. Jimmy Dotson and Jimmy and Raymond Hamm, Ancell's brothers, were also involved in criminal activity, according to Cloud.

"I was assigned to the investigation into the deaths of my friends," Cloud said. "I was part of the investigation from the morning it happened. My main part was handling a few of the witnesses and doing background checks. Charles Zagorskie had the brilliant idea of taking hundreds of policemen and firemen to search the ground leading to Hamm's house. A rifle was found and tests showed it was the weapon that was used in the murders."

Hamm was eventually arrested, tried, and convicted of the two murders and is serving life in prison. Hamm was the only one ever charged in the crime even though police believed he had plenty of help in the planning and carrying out of the assassinations.

"I was involved in the trial and this was the first time I saw the arrogance of the Johnstons," Cloud said. "David (Johnston) got on the stand, he had diamond horseshoe rings on his fingers, and he testified as a defense witness for Ancell. They never believed we were smarter, more dedicated, and tougher than they were. That was their downfall."

ZAGORSKIE, KNOWN AS the Polish Rizzo after the tough Philadelphia Police Chief Frank Rizzo, first encountered the Johnstons in the 1960s when he was working as a member of the state police. "I knew the family," Zagorskie recalled. "They were living along Route 1 in Pennsbury Township behind a chicken farm. It was near the Pennsbury Township building. I received a call one day and was told someone had stripped the new township building of its new red carpeting. It was within a stone's throw from the Johnstons' home. I went to the home and Mrs. (Louise) Johnston opened the door and it was like walking into the rising sun. There was red carpet thoughout the house, up and down the walls. She said someone had just left it on the front porch."

Many of the crimes being committed in southern Chester County in the 1960s and 1970s were linked, Zagorskie believed. "Any cop worth his salt knew that David and Bruce Johnston were committing burglaries and that Franny Matherly was a fence. We also knew that a lot of the stolen goods were being purchased by reportedly legitimate businessmen, including mushroom growers in the Kennett Square area. We knew the Johnstons and Hamms were involved in a lot of activity but we didn't know how dangerous they were until several years later."

Through criminals Gary Wayne Crouch and Kenny Howell, the Johnston gang had connections to Maryland. Gang members even managed to obtain police reports from their Maryland connections. They were brazen at times, according to Zagorskie, as a bulldozer was once found buried in Howell's yard. "It became quite evident that Ancell Hamm and David Johnston were the leaders rather than Bruce Johnston Sr. Ancell and David were the people to be afraid of."

On the night Kennett Square policemen Posey and Davis were killed, Ancell Hamm set up an alibi at his house that included David Johnston. They were playing cards before the shooting.

"I knew that night that Ancell Hamm had killed them," Zagorskie said. "I knew where he was going (after the shooting). He went across the field to his house. I had (trooper) Karl Mehn and others walk to the home to see how long it would take. It was 1,540 feet from his house to the station. We organized a search with police, firemen, Boy Scouts, and civilians and the first time we discovered something important we cleared everyone but the cops from the field. We had police from all over Chester County helping us. We found the rifle."

After the rifle was discovered state policeman Gabe Bolla thought he recognized the weapon. He believed it was one of the weapons seized from the Hamm residence and later returned. The search, seizure, and return of the rifle took place while Ancell Hamm was in prison. Hamm never knew the police had had at one point possession of the Belgium-made .308-rifle that was used to kill the two Kennett Square policemen.

Police believed the Johnstons were somehow involved in the murders of the two policemen, including driving the getaway car. Johnston Sr.'s alibi for the night was that he was watching the 1957 film *Boy on a Dauphin*, with Sophia Loren. The Johnston names did come up during the investigation, according to county detective Larry Dampman. "We never proved that Bruce (Johnston Sr.) or David was involved." Beside David Johnston, Hamm had other people give him an alibi, including one neighbor. "We nailed her ass," Zagorskie commented about one neighbor whose alibi claim deteriorated upon investigation.

The investigation of the murders of the Kennett Square policemen was intense. "I don't think I went home for four or five days," Zagorskie said. He remembers a mountain of reports needing to be typed and during Thanksgiving 1972 he took home a typewriter and typed that holiday from 8:00 AM until dinner at 4:00 PM and then typed the rest of the evening.

Zagorskie asked Tom Cloud to research the history of the Belgium rifle. "He found out more about guns than you could imagine," Zagorskie said of Cloud. "The county detectives, the FBI they were excellent during the investigation. Paul Pennypacker, Mike Cotter, Brian McDevitt, Jim Kessler, they all did a tremendous amount of work. One night they followed Ancell to the movies at Painters Crossing. Hamm saw Charles Bronson in *The Mechanic*." *The Mechanic* is about an aging paid killer who befriends a young man who wants to be a professional killer.

Hamm was arrested and tried in Harrisburg, Pennsylvania's capital, in Dauphin County court. The case was moved from Chester County because of the publicity surrounding the case. The murder investigation involving victim Robin Miller also generated intense press coverage and would have to be moved from Chester County.

A Dauphin County jury convicted Hamm of the murders of the police officers and Hamm was sentenced to life imprisonment. The Hamm case was appealed and for years arguments were made in appellate courts. Ned Hand was in charge of the appeals for the Chester County District Attorney's office and he hired attorney Dolores Troiani to help with the appeals. Troiani would prosecute the murder cases against the Johnstons along with District Attorney William H. Lamb. Lamb, who also prosecuted Hamm, later served as a member of the Pennsylvania Supreme Court.

Trooper Bolla theorized that if Hamm hadn't panicked the night of the shooting he might have avoided arrest. "If he would have gotten home with the gun he could have torched-up the weapon so fine we couldn't recognize it. He was good with the (blow) torch. We think state police cars flying down the Route 1 bypass panicked him and they didn't want to be caught with the weapon and bent the barrel of the rifle and left it in the field."

"I don't think Hamm committed the murders by himself," Bolla said.

The conviction of Hamm for murder didn't slow the Johnstons' criminal ways. "Johnston Sr. was the criminal brain, David the vicious one, and Norman the gofer," Bolla said. "And Ma Johnston, she was a piece of work." Zagorskie has a vivid memory of a photograph taken with Mrs. Johnston holding a gun in each hand along with several 100 dollar bills. "They committed burglaries, robbed, and murdered and their mother would cover up for them," Zagorskie said.

Zagorskie had a special interest in the slayings of Kennett Square policemen Posey and Davis in addition to their being fellow police officers. Dick Posey had taken the shift originally given to Kennett Square police officer Frank Zagorskie, the brother of Charles Zagorskie. "My brother was to be working that night and Posey switched," Zagorskie said. "I received a call concerning the shootings at two in the morning. There was fear throughout the town. People were scared that someone was killing cops. This was the beginning of the long-term cooperation between the state police and the FBI. The cooperation carried through the Johnstons' investigation. It was like nothing I ever saw."

THE FEDERAL BUREAU of Investigation's main special agent in the Johnston case was David Richter. His many hours of work over days, weeks and years with the state police and Chester County law enforcement members gave rise to Richter's nickname, Trooper Dave.

Unlike Cloud and Zagorskie and other investigators in the Johnston case, Richter was not a native of Pennsylvania. He was from Indiana where his father worked for General Electric. The family moved to Schenectady, New York, when his father was transferred. Richter was unsure of a profession until he talked to a neighbor who happened to be an FBI agent.

"We went to the same church and I was an usher," Richter recalled. "One day he asked me what I was going to do and I said I didn't know. He asked if I was interested in applying to the FBI as a clerical position was open in the Albany, New York, office. I thought that sounded pretty good and I ended up going to work for the FBI a little less than a year after graduating from high school. There were a number of clerks in the office going to school at night hoping to become FBI agents after graduation. I began the process and nine years later I graduated."

In April 1972 Richter was in a new agents' class in Washington, D.C. He was assigned to Charlotte, North Carolina, and was stationed there for only a few months when the FBI began seeking agents to go to Philadelphia. Richter received a transfer and was assigned to the Newtown Square office. Newtown Square is in Delaware County, just west of Philadelphia and east of Chester County. Richter would complete his FBI career working out of the Newtown Square office.

The first week on the job found Richter visiting the Avondale barracks of the state police and meeting many of the officers that would be involved in the Johnston murder investigation. He also took part in a state police golf tournament at the Kennett Square Country Club where he met his future wife, Jayne. "I didn't play any more golf from 1973 until I retired," he said.

Richter said not long after his arrival in Newtown Square fellow FBI agents and state policemen gave him information on the Johnston gang members.

A few years after transferring to Newtown Square the FBI appointed a new Special Agent in Charge of the Philadelphia office, Neil Welch. "He was a dynamic leader. He wanted quality cases and not quantity of cases," Richter said. "He also established a surveillance squad. So with these new guidelines and support of my FBI supervisors I opened a target investigation on the Johnston brothers in May 1977. For four years I had heard about all of the crimes they had done. I saw all of them with no known income, no jobs but with fancy cars, Cadillacs. Jim Dodson (a gang member) and Johnston Sr. had Corvettes and Norman had a late model Thunderbird. They had new trucks and there was no way they could have had them without working a lot. I knew they went to restaurants and lived in nice places and they would go to the tracks. I was also aware of a whole lot of farm equipment missing in southern Chester County."

Richter also knew the gang members had criminal expertise. "Some of the gang members were experts in antiques and others were excellent shoplifters. I'm not talking about nickel and dime items; I'm talking about taking a rack of fur coats. They were suspected of highjacking a tractor trailer load of goods." An Acme truck full of food was taken from the Oxford store in Chester County. Richter said they didn't learn about armed robberies until later in the investigation. "Some others were expert locksmiths and some were good at burning, that is opening safes. They were suspected of being involved in stealing cars."

Witnesses were also intimidated by the Johnstons, according to Richter. Dynamite was left in mailboxes of witnesses and in one case a barn was burned. "People were downright afraid of these guys," Richter said. "And all during this time they were driving in new cars and nobody was working. I thought if we made them a target and we did the surveillance along with the state police and others, we would work as a team and catch them in the commission of the burglaries. With police as witnesses, the intimidation factor of civilians would be eliminated." Police officers weren't immune from intimidation attempts as several received death threats during the murder investigations.

Richter began working with Terry Batty and Doug Richardson, prosecutors in the United States Attorney's office in Philadelphia. Cloud, Bob Martz, Paul Yoder and J. R. Campbell were part of the team from the state police. Richter also sought help from Zagorskie, who then was Chief Chester County Detective working out of the Chester County District Attorney's office. Richter asked for permission for assistance from Larry Dampman and Ted Schneider, two county detectives living in southern Chester County. "I thought if the Johnstons were committing a crime I could call them in case a federal violation wasn't being committed," Richter said.

Johnston Sr. was living in Maryland and any crimes involving more than one state would come under the jurisdiction of the FBI. One type of crime kept recurring, the thefts of tractors in the Pennsylvania, Maryland, and Delaware area that was prime hunting territory for the Johnston gang. "I learned more John Deere tractors were stolen in those areas than the rest of the nation combined," Richter said.

Richardson, one of the assistant United States attorneys on the case, vividly remembers the first time he heard of the tractor thefts. Richter and trooper Bob Martz were in the hallway of the federal building in Philadelphia with a four-inch printout of the tractor thefts. "Batty was on the way to lunch and forwarded the information to me as he was assigning counsel that day," Richardson said of his fellow and senior prosecutor, Batty. "I thought lawn tractors, this isn't my idea of romance. Richter came in and said the criminals were staying one step ahead of the investigation and if we could get a big hammer we could convict them. I didn't say big deal, but I had a thought along the lines that the results wouldn't be worth all of the effort. I also thought I should thank Terry (Batty) for dumping this stinker on me. Little did I know that for the next three and a half years that this case would consume most of my life and would account for the most amazing stuff I have ever done. The case is the best one I've ever done."

Richardson began listening to Richter and Martz. The tractor thefts involved millions of dollars. "Dave told me about surveillances and people crawling on their bellies. I'm sitting at Sixth and Market streets in Philadelphia and Dave is talking about Kennett Square. It could have been the moon. Criminal cases were being dismissed because of a lack of probable cause. The criminals were laughing at us. The bad guys were getting away with it."

Some of the victims had their tractors stolen multiple times. The Johnstons would steal a tractor and the victim would receive insurance money and buy another tractor. Before long, the new tractor would be missing. Also, at times someone would purchase a stolen tractor from a Johnston fence and the Johnstons would then re-steal the tractor. The victim couldn't report the second theft since it would be an admission of the crime of receiving stolen property.

Richardson was convinced the investigation warranted the force of the federal justice department. "I had the power to cause people to testify," Richardson said. "I could put the fear of God into witnesses. The first time I was with Johnston Jr. I told him his testimony was not only going to piss off his dad but that his dad would kill him." Johnston Jr.'s response: "I know."

CHAPTER FOUR

Master Plan

Besides the fancy cars and other luxurious aspects of a lifestyle that seemed beyond his legitimate financial means, Bruce Alfred Johnston Sr. had the best legal representation he could purchase. He utilized high-priced defense attorneys to gain his release from federal prison following the shooting of his son, Johnston Jr., and the murder of Robin Miller.

A federal grand jury had indicted Johnston Sr. on obstruction of justice and taking stolen goods across state lines on September 13, 1978. Nine days later Johnston Sr. was before United States Magistrate Richard A. Powers III in Philadelphia. He wanted to be allowed to post $100,000 in property as bail so he could be released. Assistant United States Attorney Douglas Richardson objected to the posting and asked to have Johnston Sr.'s bail raised to $250,000. After hearing arguments Magistrate Powers allowed Johnston Sr. to use Maryland property owned by Johnston Sr.'s sister, Mary Payne, and brother-in-law, Walter, for bail. Johnston Sr. wasn't immediately released because a necessary paper involving ownership of the land was not in possession of the Paynes.

At the federal hearing Johnston Sr. had a new attorney,

Barry H. Denken of Philadelphia, who replaced Robert Landis for the federal charges. At the hearing it was disclosed that noted defense attorney John J. Duffy was slated to handle Johnston Sr.'s trial, then scheduled for November 6. Duffy had handled many high-profile defendants, including a defendant in the Abscam case, an FBI sting investigation that involved public corruption.

Johnston Sr. was released from federal custody on September 29 but immediately rearrested by state police on five counts of burglary and eight counts each of theft, receiving stolen goods, and conspiracy. The charges were all connected to crimes in southern Chester County. Again, Johnston Sr. was released on bail, this time he was allowed to post 10 percent of the $35,000 bail set by District Justice John Catanese of Coatesville.

An avalanche of criminal charges was falling on Johnston Sr., as a second federal indictment was handed up against him in federal court on October 18. This time Johnston Sr. was charged with 12 counts involving theft in connection with John Deere and International Harvester tractors stolen from August 10, 1977, until May 4, 1978.

WHILE JOHNSTON SR. was in and out of federal and state prisons and racking up multiple criminal counts, his son, Johnston Jr., was in the protection of the U.S. Marshal Service. Father and son were to meet in a courtroom in Oxford, Pennsylvania, just blocks away from where Johnston Jr. lived, on October 24, 1978.

Security was extra tight around and inside the courtroom of District Magistrate Donald C. Brown. Heavily armed FBI agents, U.S. Marshals, state police, and county detectives provided security. They were determined a second attempt on Johnston Jr.'s life wouldn't take place. Spectators at the hearing, including members of the press, were searched before Johnston Jr. was brought into the courtroom at 3:00 PM. Johnston Jr. arrived by helicopter that landed in a cornfield near the courtroom and was ushered to the witness stand, surrounded by federal agents.

Johnston Jr. was on the witness stand for more than three hours and testified about a dozen burglaries. Johnston Sr., Leslie Dale, and George H. Smith were codefendants. Johnston Jr. spoke in low tones and didn't look directly at his father, who spent the hearing staring at his son. Johnston Jr. said he participated in the thefts with his father and the other defendants. Under questioning by Johnston Sr.'s attorney, Robert Landis, Johnston Jr. said he believed his father was responsible for the rape of Robin Miller after getting her drunk on whiskey. "She woke up the next morning naked," Johnston Jr. testified. The witness also admitted he would do anything to get back at his father for the sexual assault.

Johnston Jr. also testified about some of the burglaries. He recalled that a year earlier he was with his father and missing gang member James Sampson when they rode past the Columbia Gas Company in Oxford. A garden tractor was on the premises and Johnston Jr. said his father indicated he would like to have the $2,000 tractor. A few nights later, Johnston Jr. testified, he went with Sampson to the company, cut through a fence, broke into a shed, and stole the tractor. Johnston Sr. was notified and he came and put the tractor on his pickup truck. Johnston Jr. was paid $150 for his crime. Johnston Jr. said his usual fee was $150 for a small tractor.

During a theft committed with Dale, Johnston Jr. testified at the hearing, he was shot in the face with birdshot. Johnston Jr. said they were attempting to load a stolen tractor when the tractor's owner started firing at them. He testified he was shot in the face and neck three times. "He (the owner) was hollering and screaming. I looked right at him and he shot me in the face," Johnston Jr. said. Earlier Dana Irving testified he shot at someone in October 1977 who was stealing his International Cub Cadet. "I came within a very close distance and I fired," Irving testified. "I'm unable to describe the two people I saw. But I saw two people. They ran like hell and jumped in the truck and tried to take off. I shot again into the cab. Then the gun jammed. I took off."

Defense attorneys Landis and Michael Barranco, who represented Dale, hammered away at Johnston Jr.'s credibility with Landis delving into Johnston Jr.'s extensive drug use. Johnston Jr. said he wasn't a heavy user but he admitted smoking marijuana, at times mixed with hashish and hashish oil. He also admitted taking Quaaludes, speed, and drinking alcohol. Assistant District Attorney James MacElree objected to the testimony about the drug use but Landis's argument prevailed. "If he's a dope addict or a psychotic then the court has a right to know," Landis said.

Owners of the stolen garden tractors testified on days they wanted to mow their fields they went to their barns to find them empty. The hearing wasn't concluded that day but District Magistrate Brown held all of the defendants on some of the charges. Johnston Sr. and Smith remained free on bail while Dale was returned to Chester County Prison.

THE LAW ENFORCEMENT team was making progress on closing down the Johnston burglars but so far they hadn't made an arrest on the Miller murder. They needed a plan and they crafted one that later would be called the "master plan."

"I think the use of 'master plan' came after the fact," state policeman Thomas Cloud said. "We knew what had happened. The circumstances were so strong and obvious. Johnston Jr. was shot and Robin Miller was killed to keep them from testifying against the Johnston gang. It wasn't some passerby coming through and committing the murder. It wasn't some drive-by shooting. You have to use common sense. We could prove to anybody they were killed to shut them up."

The law enforcement team was looking for specific evidence against individuals and Cloud gives credit to Chief Chester County Detective Charles Zagorskie. Zagorskie used his knowledge to "chip away at the individuals." Cloud said the police knew the Johnston associates because they had criminal histories.

"Ricky Mitchell, he was always kind of off the wall, he would do anything and he was brazen at times," Cloud said. "We saw Mitchell as someone being used by the Johnstons, being manipulated. As for Leslie Dale, if you look up cold-blooded killer in the dictionary, you might see his picture. We thought Leslie was involved. When we checked their alibis it was easy to determine which guys were around at the critical times."

Cloud said the police were also developing charges against known Johnston associates Raymond and Jimmy Hamm, James Ray Dotson, Jimmy Griffin, and Roy Myers. "At the Avondale barracks every member understood the importance of jailing the Johnstons," Cloud said. Dotson and Myers were "inside circle guys," according to Cloud.

BEFORE THE MURDERS, according to Cloud, the hierarchy of the Pennsylvania State Police wasn't convinced the Johnstons should be a priority. "From the top, the Johnstons were viewed as a thorn in their side as we kept asking for more resources," Cloud said. "We felt the administration didn't believe us and that we were crying wolf. Our superiors felt we were exaggerating and the Johnstons weren't that bad.

We usually understated their effect on the community. If someone took a hard look at the gang members, they would try to intimidate you. They would find out where police officers lived and mention to the police officers they knew where they lived and would ask about the policeman's family."

Cloud said he was on the Johnstons' hit list. "A gang member told me," Cloud said of the threat. "Johnston Sr. had offered to pay to have me killed. (State policeman Bob) Martz told me they asked about his home. That stuff was a definite message. Leslie Dale told me to watch myself and think about getting into another line of work. Part of my thought process was that I knew there were things worse than dying and giving in to the Johnstons was one of them."

Indeed, during a preliminary hearing on March 6, 1979, gang member Richard Mitchell testified that David Johnston wanted "to assassinate Cloud because Cloud was a pain and David wanted to get him off his back." Mitchell added, "I don't mess with the state police." He said he knew of no overt acts to kill Cloud.

Cloud remembered a conversation he had with Judge Leonard Sugerman, who presided at the Johnston murder trials, and also had been threatened. "I never had many dealings with Judge Sugerman," Cloud said, "but he knew about the threats against me and asked me what I thought about being threatened. I remember telling Judge Sugerman that there are just some things you stand up to. I wasn't that fearful as I knew better than to turn my back to the Johnstons. And, I wasn't a seventeen-year-old kid. I said you couldn't back down from intimidation. Judge Sugerman said he knew that and he just wanted to see what I would say."

State policeman Ray Solt worked many of the burglary cases, especially the ones that involved Lancaster County. "The Johnstons were watching us, the police," Solt said. "I lived in a bi-level home in Lancaster County at the time and I had a dog that would not chase beyond the property line but stand and point if a problem was taking place. One night I discovered someone in the yard and saw him back in the trees. My dog took off but he stopped at the property line as he was trained. Later Roy Myers (a gang member) admitted he was out there that night."

James P. MacElree, an assistant district attorney at the time of the Johnston prosecutions and later a county judge, said at preliminary hearings the Johnstons would walk behind him as he prepared for the hearing and would say they would kill him. "Witnesses were intimidated," MacElree said. "That created an atmosphere that led to acquittals. One case fell apart the night before a trial because the victim of a burglary had a nervous breakdown," MacElree recalled. "District justices also were intimidated." MacElree said, "One district justice told me that he didn't mind finding enough evidence to hold a Johnston for trial but he would never find them guilty of even a minor charge. The district justice was afraid his house would be burned to the ground."

Cloud saw many similarities between the Johnstons and terrorists. "This group," Cloud said, "tried to remain in control by terrorizing witnesses. They set fires, used dynamite, made threats, intimidated witnesses, killed, and threatened to murder police officers. Finally, someone stood up to them. At first some police had the attitude that once enough evidence was gathered, their job was done. Well, it wasn't. It had just started. The intimidation would then begin."

The Miller murder added to the fear factor. "The deaths were sobering," MacElree said. "Witnesses were afraid of being in harm's way. We had to convince them to testify and that we could protect them."

CONVINCING WITNESSES AND gang members to turn on the Johnstons was the lynchpin of the master plan. The master plan was akin to the domino theory. Police were look-

ing for weak links and leverage to turn Johnston gang members against the gang leaders, brothers Bruce A. Johnston Sr.,
David Johnston, and Norman Johnston.

"Everybody worked together," MacElree said. The team
needed a leader and Chief County Detective Charles
Zagorskie was the person.

Dolores Troiani, one of the prosecutors in the Chester
County District Attorney's office said, "Charlie (Zagorskie)
led. He did, he led the team. The cooperation was fostered by
Charlie. It was incredible. Charlie was in charge because of
his personality and reputation. He could take charge." While
Zagorskie was the leader, everyone contributed and it didn't
matter if the investigator was a member of the FBI, state police, county detective, or local police department. All points
of view were considered and respected.

State policeman Cloud agreed. "We had the right people in the right place at the right time," he said. "Charlie
Zagorskie was the most powerful corporal in the state police.
It is a military organization, but certain people because of
personality and leadership abilities stand out and that was
Charles Zagorskie. People came to him with tough problems and that carried over when he became Chief of Chester
County Detectives. He was the glue that coordinated this
and pulled off the investigation."

"I knew all of the players," Zagorskie said. "I was never in
high management with the state police. I was the worker and
that is why I get along with Tom Cloud, Bob Martz, Karl
Mehn, and many others who never got the proper credit for
the work they did on this case."

Dave Richter was the right federal agent to be on the case,
according to Troiani, who at one time worked for the United
States Department of Justice. "The FBI wouldn't have gone
along if he hadn't been the agent," she said. "He was cooperative and he never once said 'I'm the FBI and you're the

locals.'" Zagorskie added, "Dave wanted to work. We were all guys with similar personalities and we respected each other even though we were from different agencies. That is unusual. Everyone was pretty much on the same page."

Troiani was praised for her role in the investigation. "Dolores was a tiger," Cloud said. "She was tenacious. She knew the case inside and out. To have Charlie coordinating the case, Dolores and Bill Lamb, he had the courtroom charisma, prosecuting and then Martz, Yoder, Campbell and all of the others willing to work, it was a remarkable team. It was remarkable that all of these components were in place. If not, the Johnstons wouldn't have been stopped until a lot more people had been hurt."

The core of investigators, according to Troiani, never insisted on getting credit for their part in breaking the case. "Nobody on the inside said me first," she said. "Some on the fringe wanted to point out individual accomplishments but not the close knit team."

Investigators didn't care who they teamed with for assignments. "We just worked," county detective Michael Carroll said. That isn't to say there weren't some disagreements. "Tempers flared at times," state policeman Gabe Bolla said, "but that was part of the game. Sometimes we didn't agree but we moved on and did what was best for the investigation. It is the biggest joint venture by federal, state, county, and local agencies that I ever saw. It was a tremendous job. We all worked long hours and long days."

The same attitude wasn't shared by everyone in the hierarchy of the Pennsylvania State Police, according to Bolla. He said, "Captain (Wayne) Kerr was the biggest thorn in our side. His attitude was that we were the state police and no one was going to tell us what to do." Zagorskie added, "The state police is a large bureaucracy and those in charge try to save a nickel when they can and I don't blame them for that.

They didn't fund us early in the investigation but they did come along. Sometimes they forget their mission is crime fighting."

The leadership of the FBI was skeptical at first, according to FBI agent Richter. "I received mixed support as the crimes did not fit the FBI's criteria for financial support. They were directing funds towards the mafia and political corruption in Pennsylvania at the time. The belief was that the Johnstons were a damned bunch of country bumpkins but it soon became obvious from the surveillances that we were dealing with accomplished burglars who were extremely street savvy and not going to change their way of life."

Richter also said the FBI knew they were associates of Ancell Hamm, the killer of two Kennett Square policemen. "Nobody ever turned me down for money, everyone in the FBI exposed to these guys thought this was a hell of a case," Richter said. "In fact to this day when I talk to retired agents who worked in Philadelphia, they say this was one of the most fascinating cases they ever worked on."

The investigation couldn't have been completed without funding, according to Zagorskie, and the Chester County Commissioners provided resources for the investigators. "Bob Thompson and Earl Baker gave us pretty much what we wanted, starting with the Ancell Hamm investigation and then the Johnstons. We spent a lot of money."

Thompson, a county commissioner and later a Pennsylvania senator, said, "The investigation was a perfect opportunity for a disaster and a perfect opportunity for success—it was a success." Thompson recalled that the citizens of Chester County were interested in seeing justice done in the Johnston case and he never received even one complaint about the cost to taxpayers.

Chester County Commissioner Earl Baker, who also went on to be a Pennsylvania senator, said he remembers District

Attorney William H. Lamb saying more than once that "you can't put a price tag on justice." Baker also said he didn't hear complaints from constituents concerning the cost. "Many people on the Main Line couldn't identify with the investigation," Baker said. "They felt southern Chester County was a different place than where they lived. The county was going through a transition from a more rural county with about 270,000 residents to a more populated county."

Thompson, Baker, and fellow Commissioner Patrick O'Donnell did closely watch the county's purse strings. Thompson and Baker vividly remembered complaining about charges Chester County incurred from Cambria County officials, the site of one of the Johnston gang murder trials. The trial was moved to Cambria County because of pre-trial publicity in Chester County. Cambria billed Chester County for security measures and overtime for guards. The Chester County officials believed Cambria County was taking advantage of Chester County and charging for improvements to Cambria County facilities and padding security officers from the ranks of family and friends. "The billing came to a head when Cambria wanted Chester County to pay for lights for a parking lot," Baker recalled. "They said they didn't need the lights except for the trial."

Thompson was dispatched to Ebensburg to discuss the bills with his Cambria counterparts. "We were receiving bills from Cambria County to repaint the courthouse, armor plating for the judge's bench, and the hiring of a new shift of guards," Thompson said. "We kept getting bills weekly from the county. Finally I went out to Cambria with a deputy controller to talk with them. We were met at the airport by Cambria officials and driven to the courthouse. I told them to stop spending our money and that I had to approve any expenses before the money was spent. After the meeting we had to find our own transportation back to the airport and the next time had to find transportation to the courthouse."

Thompson believed the taxpayers' money was well spent. "Bill Lamb built a professional organization with the county detectives," he said. "Judge Sugerman did an excellent job presiding as judge as did the prosecution team. All of the agencies, the feds, county detectives, state police, and local police all worked together. This type of cooperation had never been done before."

Help with paying for the investigation and trial came from then Pennsylvania senator John Stauffer. He had a $700,000 item placed in the commonwealth's budget to help cover the cost. "This was a large part of our budget in 1980," Thompson said.

Thompson was not the only member of his family involved in the Johnston investigation. His father, Joe Thompson, was the photographer for the Chester County Detectives and his wife, noted Chester County artist Nancy Thompson, drew illustrations of the crime scene that were used during the trial.

THE POLICE, ATTORNEYS, and elected officials all worked together, according to prosecutor William Lamb.

"Remember back then," Lamb said, "the relationship between the state police and the district attorney's office was much closer than it is today. The state police now tend to run their own organization. They don't consult with the district attorney's office as much as they used to do. This is not a criticism, just a fact. Charlie (Zagorskie) came to work for me from the state police in the '70s and the Johnstons were certainly on his radar screen. The federal investigation started to percolate along.

"When you talk about law enforcement organizations, you are talking about personalities. On the state side we had Zagorskie and Tom Cloud. What is not to like about those two? The same was true of the FBI with Dave Richter and Ron Bosken. We didn't look at the FBI agents as trying to take away the criminal law enforcement case. I had a good relationship with the United States Attorney's office. We did investigations together. It was a natural we were able to work together on the case. We also had on the team J. R. Campbell and Ted Schneider. They are two down to earth, basic guys trying to do a good job. And, you would never want Tom Cloud on your trail because he never gave up. That atmosphere fostered our ability to do an outstanding investigation."

Lamb needed the best team possible because the Johnstons weren't the usual Chester County criminals. "This was really rough and tumble, Elliott Ness type crime," Lamb said, "where we were riding through woods, digging up bodies, and all that kind of stuff."

CHAPTER FIVE

Criminal Roots

The taxpayers of Chester County were using their hard-earned tax dollars to investigate the Johnston gang. William H. Lamb, District Attorney of Chester County and the lead prosecutor on the case, pegged the total cost at $1.2 million. "That was a lot of money back then," he commented.

Besides the money being spent on the investigation and trials, law abiding citizens were being victimized by the Johnstons and some supposedly upstanding citizens were aiding the Johnstons by purchasing stolen goods and also acting as fences.

Who were the Johnstons?

"The whole rat pack came down here to Chester County. Most of them migrated from the Mountain City, Tennessee, area," Lamb said. "I used to call them the ridge runners because that is the way they operated, they operated at night."

LOUISE PRICE MOORE Johnston, mother of Norman, David, and Bruce Johnston Sr. and seven other children, grew up in the Price family farm in northwestern North Carolina, near Mountain City, Tennessee. She left North Carolina during the Depression, Louise Johnston told a newspaper reporter in 1979. She transported her two children from a broken marriage to Philadelphia. In the 1930s she met Passmore Johnston, a Quaker born in Swarthmore, Pennsylvania. Passmore Johnston was almost 40 years older than Louise Johnston. The couple moved to Chester County where Passmore Johnston worked on a farm and at a greenhouse.

Besides Bruce, David, and Norman, Louise Johnston is the mother of brothers Pete, Jack, and Manuel Johnston and Joe Rivera and Bill Moore. Her daughters are Mary Payne and Sandra Rivera.

Bruce A. Johnston Sr. was born in 1939; David was born in 1948; and Norman was born in 1950, according to Louise Johnston. The brothers attended schools in the Unionville district but never graduated from high school. They were expected to do chores on the family farm. "We weren't poor," she said. Her sons were brought up in the Baptist faith and church meetings were held in their farm home. She told the reporter, "Neither one of them would ever hurt anybody. They was brought up decent, brought up in the church. I know them boys. They would never pull a trigger on anyone." Louise Johnston said Bruce Sr. especially wouldn't harm Johnston Jr. "Bruce loved that boy. He bailed him out of trouble in Florida," she said.

Three months before the newspaper interview Louise Johnston had a different story to tell the investigators. On January 12, 1979, Louise Johnston told state policeman Gabe Bolla, "I'll tell you, them boys have no respect for me, no more respect than a dog. I'll have to go through this goddamn shit the rest of my life. I always stuck by them cause they was my kids. Sure, I got some money, but I spent my last dollar on them. This has to go on the rest of my life and I'm 65 now." Louise Johnston also had harsh words for her daughter-in-law, Susan Johnston, wife of Norman. Talking about Susan Johnston, she told Bolla, "She is one of the crookedest women I know. As long as Norm is with her, he will be in jail. She wants him to steal and she tells him to steal." One former gang member, Roy Myers, said Louise Johnston "knew a whole lot" and was present when at least one of the major thefts, that at Longwood Gardens, was planned.

Passmore Johnston died in 1961 and the family moved to Kennett Square. Johnston Sr. left school in the seventh grade and three years later married fifteen-year-old Jennie Steffy of Elkton, Maryland. She was pregnant with Johnston Jr. at the time. Johnston Sr. had a family to support and a fondness for cars and guns. He did some work as a groundskeeper on a du Pont estate but his professional life turned to crime. His first jail sentence was for stealing $5 worth of gasoline.

THE THEFT OF $5 worth of gas by Bruce Alfred Johnston Sr. was committed in the late 1950s, two decades before the murder of Robin Miller. He pleaded guilty and served time in the Eastern State Correctional Institution. Johnston Sr. and his loosely knit band of criminals would go on to spend two decades plundering throughout the United States. Police estimate gang members were responsible for as many as 300 thefts and burglaries, not including hundreds of stolen cars, and various assaults.

Thomas Frame, who was West Chester police chief and later in his career the warden of Chester County Prison, remembers his first meeting with Johnston Sr. "I was working at the prison during my days off from the police force," Frame recalled. "I'll never forget. I was on the third tier of prisoners and this young guy there, Johnston Sr., introduces himself. He was eighteen years old and he was bragging about what a great criminal he was. He said he did burglaries and he would go out about one or two in the morning and go to state police barracks and make sure both cars (they only had two at the time) were there at the station. If cars were at the station they would do their burglaries. I reported the conversation to the state police and from that point on one of the cars was taken home at night." Johnston Sr., Frame said, favored burglaries over stealing cars. "He believed it was easier to be caught stealing cars," Frame said.

State policeman Raymond Solt at first believed the Johnstons were just a bunch of "hillbilly burglars." Lamb called them "ridge runners" and the FBI labeled them "country bumpkins." As Solt, Lamb, the FBI, and the rest of the investigators soon discovered, the criminals were far more sophisticated than they thought. "It all changed," Solt commented.

Solt joined the state police in January 1968 and trained in Lancaster County and spent time at the Ephrata and Avondale barracks before returning to Lancaster and the state police's investigative unit in February 1973, just as the Johnston criminal spree was getting into high gear. "This was the time when many International Harvester and John Deere tractors were being stolen. Businessman Jim Mark in West Grove was fencing a lot of them and when gang member Ken Howell was caught in Cecil County, Maryland, I was assigned to the investigation. (State policeman Tom) Cloud did some of the work. The first burglary trials in Lancaster County were in 1976 and Assistant District Attorney John Kneff handled the prosecutions. There were cases in Chester and Lancaster counties. Arrest warrants for burglaries in Louisiana were lodged and dropped after convictions were gained in Lancaster County."

Cloud said when information was first received that businessman Mark was fencing stolen tractors Mark had paperwork that seemed to be legitimate. "I was thinking how could Mark do this?" Cloud said. "I was thinking that he must be changing serial numbers and changing engines. I thought about this all of the time. It turns out no one was verifying warranty records and he was putting on numbers from legitimately sold tractors."

Cloud checked with International Harvester and discovered some obviously stolen tractors were sold to big horse farms in the Chester County area. The farms were paying full price. "In 1974 they were costing about $4,000," Cloud said. "We're not talking about a lawn tractor; they were estate tractors." Cloud began checking engine numbers and finding stolen tractors. Mark was arrested and then began cooperating. The cooperation cost Mark's family as his father's barn was burned in retaliation for Mark's helping police. Cloud said one farmer in Lancaster County found dynamite under his pickup truck seat as a warning not to cooperate with the investigation.

The Johnstons didn't always steal just one tractor. At least twice, once in Adamstown, Pennsylvania, and another one in Delaware, the Johnstons stole from tractor dealerships. One time they heisted a whole truckload of tractors.

Not everyone buying stolen tractors was innocently doing so. Stolen bulldozers and backhoes were purchased by at least one mushroom grower in the Kennett Square area. State policeman Solt recalled receiving word that two farmers living outside of Manheim, Pennsylvania, were in possession of stolen tractors. "We went to the first farmer and he denied he was using a stolen tractor," Solt said. "We went to see the second farmer. He was a short guy and I'm standing on one side of the farmer and Tommy (Cloud) is on the other side. The farmer is smoking a pipe and the more we questioned him, the harder he puffed on that pipe. It looked like a train. Eventually we recovered the stolen tractors from the farmers."

The Mark investigation established a link between the

Johnstons and Roy Myers, Johnston Sr.'s brother-in-law, and stolen property. Myers's farm and homes of other gang members were used as storage for stolen goods.

MYERS FIRST MET Johnston Sr. in the early 1960s when he began dating Barbara Jordan, now his ex-wife. She is the sister of Johnston Sr.'s second wife, Carol Jordan Johnston. Myers was working for the family of John B. Hannum, an attorney, Republican political leader, and future United States District Court judge. "I never did any criminal activity until 1969 or 1970," Myers said. "Bruce (Johnston Sr.) was in charge of the gang activity and he approached me about getting involved. He was with Ancell Hamm. Bruce talked to me about how much money I could make. He knew I wasn't making much on the horse farm. I left the Hannum family and I went to Cochranville to work on another farm. He again approached me about making some extra money and I finally said yes. I was hesitant at first but the money was so darn good that I couldn't say no."

Myers's first job with the Johnstons involved dismantling stolen cars. Myers operated a chop shop out of his barn in rural Chester County. "They would bring me stolen cars," Myers said of the Johnstons. "They were usually Corvettes or trucks, but mostly Corvettes. I think I handled more than 200 Corvettes. They would go out and get cars, maybe one or two a week, and they paid me $300 a car. The cars came from all different states, Delaware, New Jersey, Maryland, and Pennsylvania. A lot of the cars came from Delaware."

Business increased and some nights Myers, along with Dave and Johnston Sr., would chop two cars. "We would thoroughly dismantle the cars. We had specialized tools for some parts. In thirty minutes we could knock a whole front end off a Corvette. It took a little longer to do the rest of the car. We would have a truck sitting out front of the barn and we would put the parts on the truck. We put some of the good parts in the back of the barn. The junk parts we would throw into the Brandywine River. There are tons of car parts lying in the Brandywine," Myers said.

Most of the parts were sold at Corvette World, according to Myers, and another gang member, Franny Matherly, was selling parts. "They sold some cars whole but not many of them. They also had other guys chopping cars, it wasn't just me. A guy in Parkesburg was doing a lot of them." Myers said a pine grove near his barn had 100 gas tanks, with 99 of them coming from stolen Corvettes. The odd gas tank was from a pickup truck. Eventually, Myers said, he went out with the Johnstons and stole lawn mowers. "I got into crime full-time," Myers said. "I did so for the money and the excitement."

Several times, Myers said, he came close to being caught. He remembers one theft at the Concordville Inn in Delaware County, Pennsylvania. "I was on the roof as a watchman," Myers said. "Norm (Johnston) was on the ground and Norm and Johnston Sr. were trying to disarm the alarm. One of the security cars came around. I saw him coming and yelled on the radio but they couldn't get out in time. I heard them hollering at the guard to get back in the car. I ran to the edge of the roof to look down, I had my gun and started to point down the gun and then gun shots were fired. I believe the guard was shot in the hand several times. We heard a helicopter and we took off running. I crawled into a drain pipe at one point when the helicopter came close. We made it to one of our cars at a diner on Route 202."

Myers said a great deal of planning went into the crimes. "We had walkie-talkies," he said. "We used to do jobs when we were down in Arkansas. One night we talked to the cops on the walkie-talkies as they were driving through a shopping center trying to find us." The gang operated all over the country, Delaware, Maryland, New Jersey, Arkansas, Virginia, New York, and mostly Pennsylvania, according to Myers. He estimates being involved in at least 150 burglaries.

To facilitate vehicle thefts the Johnstons obtained key numbers from General Motors vehicles. David Johnston had a key machine obtained from a car dealer and the Johnston gang could make their own keys. "The key machine had a lever with numbers," Myers said. "They set the numbers and put in a blank key."

Myers said the Johnstons would realize between $1,200 and $1,500 per Corvette for parts. A motor would bring $1,000. "There isn't too much thrown away on a Corvette," Myers said.

The Johnstons were also daring and resourceful, according to Myers. He said a theft took place near Chester in Delaware County, Pennsylvania, at the Macke Vending Machine Company. The business was well alarmed and utilized infrared rays and motion detectors. David Johnston entered the building from the roof and à la Tom Cruise in the movie *Mission Impossible* hung down from the roof and turned off the alarm, Myers said. "Once we were inside we had the run of the place," Myers said.

OVER THE YEARS the police arrested members of the Johnston gang, but convictions would be scarce. When convictions were obtained the Johnstons used all of their appeal opportunities. "These guys' sole aim was staying on the street," Cloud said. "They would pay lawyers, intimidate witnesses, and even pay off witnesses. "They spent their waking moments working on staying on the streets."

A major crime that caught the attention of police took place in November 1974 when a trailer loaded with food was stolen from an Acme in Oxford, Pennsylvania. Cloud said the Acme theft started out to be a safe-cracking job. When something went wrong the tractor-trailer was stolen, according to Cloud.

The stolen canned goods were stashed in the home of Benny LaCorte, a barber who was a Johnston associate. One officer said LaCorte's home looked like a grocery store. Myers said the food at first went to his farm. "Just about all of it made its way to Jim Marks," Myers said. "Bennie (LaCorte) had some of it. The majority went in a U-haul truck. I'm not sure where it was taken, I was told to Mark's place."

Another one of their more public crimes was the burglary of world-famous Longwood Gardens, a former du Pont estate. Myers said, "We knew they were going to have money in their safe over the Memorial Day holiday. Banks were closed so they would have to keep all of the money there. We started to case the place a month before Memorial Day. We would walk around the building. We would go in, not all at the same time. One guy would go one day and the others another day. Dave (Johnston) watched where they took the money. He knew exactly where it was."

The theft took place and the burglars went to Norman Johnston's apartment to split the money, according to Myers. "I knew we were supposed to have stolen just shy of $20,000. Later I heard a lot more money was taken, about $50,000. I didn't work with Bruce (Johnston Sr.) after that. He was the one that asked me to go on the job. That is all the money they brought into the house. They must have left some of the money in the car. They were in Longwood a long time. They were in there a lot longer than they should have been. They must have been counting the money."

The Johnston gang garnered millions of dollars during their decades of crime. Myers said he believes David Johnston invested some of his money while Norman spent most of his ill-gotten currency on cars and his wife, Susan. The

Johnstons regularly visited the race track. Myers said he was never sure where Johnston Sr. spent his money. Myers also said drugs, marijuana, and alcohol were used by various members of the gang.

The three Johnston brothers trusted each other but other gang members were suspect. "They always carried guns," Myers said. "David had his all of the time."

Not all of the schemes worked. The Johnstons made a trip to the western part of Virginia near the Skyline Drive where tourists visit many of the underground caves. Roy Myers said one theft didn't net much money and they returned to Pennsylvania.

Pennsylvania was the base for the Johnston gang; the place where they committed the majority of their crimes and the place where many of their customers lived. "Certain people in the community would come to Bruce (Johnston Sr.) and Dave to purchase items and some goods were stolen to fulfill an order," Myers said. "There weren't many people in the community who didn't know what we did."

CHAPTER SIX

Death of Jackie Baen

A month after the murder of Robin Miller and the shooting of Bruce A. Johnston Jr. the members of the law enforcement team were working long hours each day interviewing people who might know something about the crimes and also the whereabouts of the missing members of the gang, brothers Jimmy and Wayne Sampson, Dwayne Lincoln, and James Johnston.

State policeman J. R. Campbell questioned Sampson family members after a report was received that Jimmy Sampson was in Canada and the missing gang member had written his family a letter. Campbell was unable to verify that such a letter was sent. Police also heard stories that the young criminals were in Florida and then in the western United States. Again, their whereabouts couldn't be confirmed.

Sampson's car was found at the Philadelphia International Airport. On October 4, 1978, Campbell requested state policeman Joseph D. Reeves to process the car, a 1974 Chevrolet. Reeves photographed the vehicle and attempted to lift prints. The ones he was able to obtain from the car were of poor quality and not helpful.

A WEEK AFTER the discovery of Sampson's car, Campbell and state policeman Tom Cloud went to Chester County Farms Prison and arrested gang member Leslie Dale on tractor theft charges. Dale was transported to the Avondale barracks for processing and then taken before District Justice Eugene J. DiFilippo Jr. for arraignment. Cloud noted in his report that Dale smoked Winston cigarettes, the same brand that was found in the fields next to the Miller farmhouse where the killers waited for Miller and Johnston Jr.

An integral part of the investigator's "Master Plan" was finding a weak link in the Johnston gang and turning the gang associate against the Johnstons. Winston-smoking Leslie Dale appeared to be the most vulnerable link to the Johnstons.

CHESTER COUNTY DETECTIVE Larry Dampman was familiar with Dale and the Johnstons long before the murder of Robin Miller. As a police officer on the Downingtown, Pennsylvania, force, Dampman suspected that the Johnstons were involved in stealing cars and selling parts through a "speed shop" business operating in Thorndale, just outside of Downingtown's borough limits.

One longtime Chester County resident who grew up in Valley Township, outside of Coatesville, knew the owner of the speed shop. The man recalled being at a bar on Lincoln Highway, near the speed shop, when several of the Johnstons stopped in for drinks. The Johnstons were trying to sell an automatic weapon. To showcase the weapon the Johnstons took interested patrons into the bar's parking lot and fired rounds into a dirt bank that bordered railroad tracks.

"They were mostly into Corvettes and Chevys with big engines," Dampman said. "When I was a rookie a lot of those types of cars were being stolen and we suspected the

Johnstons were involved. I talked to the owner of the speed shop and I have no doubt he knew or suspected the criminal activity."

One night Dampman investigated what seemed to be a run-of-the-mill argument among some patrons at a Downingtown diner. Dampman charged three of the men with disorderly conduct and they were released. Within days of the charges, on August 18, 1970, one of the men, John William "Jackie" Baen of Coatesville, was found dead, floating in the west branch of the Brandywine River at McCorkle's Rock near the King Ranch. At the time the famous King Ranch of Texas was affiliated with a cattle operation in Chester County.

Police believed Baen's death was more than an accidental drowning. Baen, who was twenty-three years old, was known to have connections to a group known as the Second Avenue gang that operated in Coatesville. That group included known criminals Dale and Richard Donnell and police believe the two were in some way connected to Baen's death. Dale and Donnell were using Baen's identity card to cash stolen checks. Baen, who had a deformed hand, was identified by police as a drifter who worked at odd jobs in the Coatesville area, including sweeping out stores. Baen was questioned about the crimes but never implicated Dale or Donnell.

The doctor that did Baen's autopsy failed to find any indication of foul play and no charges were lodged at the time of the death.

The law enforcement team believed it was time to revisit the Baen death and enlisted the aid of Dr. Dominic DiMaio, a prominent pathologist and former chief medical examiner of New York City. Dr. DiMaio had more than 30 years of experience in the profession. Dr. DiMaio agreed to take another look at Baen's body and an exhumation order was secured from Common Pleas Court Judge Robert A. Wright in Delaware County. Baen was buried in the Glenwood Memorial Garden Center in Broomall, Delaware County, Pennsylvania.

"The news media picked up the coverage of the exhumation," state policeman Tom Cloud said. Actually, members of the investigative team made sure the press knew about the exhumation. Bruce Mowday, a reporter who covered the Johnstons for the *Daily Local News* of West Chester, was directed to the Delaware County courthouse in Media to look for an exhumation order. "I was told I would be interested in the document," Mowday said. The resulting news articles were a message to Dale that he was a prime murder suspect.

On Saturday, November 4, 1978, a thick morning fog covered Glenwood Memorial Garden Center as Dr. DiMaio, members of the investigative team, and reporters gathered to watch workers lift Baen's vault from its resting place of eight years. The vault was lifted from the grave. Cemetery staff used pieces of wood to loop canvas belts around the coffin and secure it to a winch. The coffin was floating in the vault and the vault had to be emptied of water.

Dr. DiMaio and Assistant District Attorney Dolores Troiani peered into the casket. Dr. DiMaio then pronounced that the skull and hands were in perfect shape for the examination. Dr. DiMaio said he was not looking for anything specific but was trying to exclude forms of possible violence. Next, District Attorney William H. Lamb informed the reporters they would have to leave as the body was too fragile to transport to a hospital. Dr. DiMaio was going to do the examination at the graveyard. At the conclusion of the examination Dr. DiMaio assured Lamb that he could prove Baen was a murder victim. A written report would follow, DiMaio told Lamb.

Leslie Eugene Dale and Richard Francis Donnell were

both charged with Baen's murder. Finding the suspects was easy as both were in prison. Dale was in Montgomery County Prison awaiting trial on state and federal charges involving stolen tractors and Donnell was in Lewisburg Federal Prison, serving time for interstate transportation of stolen goods. Both were taken to the Avondale barracks of the Pennsylvania State Police for processing. "A lot of work was put in on the case by the District Attorney's office, county detectives and ourselves. It hasn't been easy," Lieutenant Richard Weimer, commander of the Avondale barracks, said. "The personnel working the investigation have given a good account of themselves."

After processing, the defendants were arraigned before District Justice Eugene DiFillippo Jr. of Toughkenamon and returned to prison.

The preliminary hearing for Dale and Donnell was held in the then West Chester District Justice office on Gay Street. Presiding was District Justice John Catanese of Coatesville since the Baen murder took place in his jurisdiction. The small courtroom was under heavy guard and packed with spectators and the press. Donnell and Dale sat at the defense table with their attorneys, William H. Mitman Jr. for Donnell, and Public Defender John R. Merrick and Assistant Public Defender Michael S. Barranco for Dale. Dale sat smiling through most of the hearing and blew kisses at Assistant District Attorney Dolores Troiani. Dale, as was his habit, also blew kisses at some of the female reporters covering the case.

The morning session consisted of Dr. DiMaio testifying about his findings from the autopsy conducted in the Delaware County graveyard. Dr. DiMaio agreed that Baen died of drowning, the original finding in the case, but he said he found a small fracture of the skull near Baen's right ear. The fracture was inflicted near the time of Baen's death, DiMaio testified.

Catanese called for a lunch break and reporters Mowday and Gretchen Booth of the local radio station, WCOJ, headed to DeStarr's restaurant for sandwiches. On the sidewalk District Attorney Lamb stopped Mowday to caution him not to be late for the afternoon session. Lamb promised a surprise.

The surprise prosecution witness was murder defendant Richard Donnell. The prosecution had made a deal with Donnell to testify against Dale. Dale had no clue that Donnell had turned against him until Donnell was called to the witness stand. Dale immediately threatened Donnell and Donnell's young son. Donnell then began climbing the defense table to get at Dale. State policeman Gabe Bolla restrained Donnell and kept him from his codefendant, Dale. After the conclusion of his testimony, Donnell again went after Dale but was restrained by Chief County Detective Charles Zagorskie. "All I want is a couple of minutes (with Dale)," Donnell shouted as he left the hearing room.

While on the stand Donnell admitted that he and Dale murdered Baen. Donnell called Dale "a cold-blooded killer" and blamed Dale for their arrests. Donnell said he agreed to testify because he "didn't like the way Mr. Dale ran his fuck'n mouth and got us into this shit. It's his fuck'n fault we're sitting here (charged with murder). Dale was shooting his big mouth off. He was trying to be a tough guy."

Donnell said Dale had the idea to kill Baen. "I did agree to do it," Donnell testified. "I agreed because of my reputation. I didn't want that creep (Dale) to think I didn't have the balls." Donnell said Dale was afraid Baen would talk to the Coatesville police about a forgery operation. Baen had sold his driver's license to Dale and Donnell for $20 and the license was used by another criminal, Clayton Shultz of Lancaster, to open checking accounts and cash forged checks. The trio, Dale, Donnell, and Shultz, shared the money.

Coatesville police talked with Baen about his identification being used in connection with the checks. Donnell said, "Baen was half scared to death of the Coatesville police. He was scared they would lock him up for the forgery."

Donnell described the murder of Jackie Baen. On the evening of August 17, 1970, Dale and Donnell picked up Baen after the victim finished working at a steak shop on Second Avenue in Coatesville. Dale wanted to shoot Baen and Donnell had a pistol. Dale and Donnell took Baen drinking at several bars where they had whiskey and beer. The men then went to Labiak's Bar, near MacCorkle's Rock on the Brandywine, where they purchased beer and soda. Baen got sick in the parking lot. The three men then drove to the Brandywine where they ran into five men hunting raccoons. The hunters left and Dale, Donnell, and Baen continued their trip. At the Brandywine the men stayed in the car and Baen was struck several times. Baen threw up in the car.

Dale and Donnell then took Baen to the river. Baen took off his pants and shoes and was taken into the water where he was hit again with the pistol and held under water. "I think he came up a couple of times, I'm not sure," Donnell testified. When Assistant District Attorney Dolores Troiani asked how long Baen was held under water, Donnell replied, "Too damned long."

"Why is that?" Troiani then asked.

"He's dead isn't he," Donnell replied.

Donnell said he felt a sensation in Baen's body as he held him under the water and couldn't find a pulse. They left Baen in the water and threw the victim's clothes into the Brandywine. The two defendants went to Donnell's home to change clothes and then Dale went back to Coatesville. Donnell said he purchased new tires for his car the next day because he didn't want to chance tire impressions being taken from a dirt road where they committed the murder.

"Dale wasn't sorry about killing Baen," Donnell said. "Dale

said that Baen's father always wanted to know how Jackie died. After Baen's father died Dale said, 'Now he can go to hell and find out.'"

Cloud remembers Donnell was wearing reflective sunglasses. "You couldn't see his eyes, he had a demeanor that was cold and calculating," Cloud said. "He was the last person you would expect to cooperate with us. In a sense he didn't have much of a choice. There is no time limit for the prosecution of a murder. He had something to fear from Dale, if Dale did cooperate on the Baen murder."

The deal with Donnell was made the weekend before the preliminary hearing. Zagorskie and FBI agent David Richter visited Donnell in federal prison. Zagorskie knew Donnell. A deal approved by Lamb was offered to Donnell. The deal was for Donnell to serve a sentence of one-to-three years in prison to run concurrently with his federal sentence. The end result was that Donnell did no extra jail time for the murder of crippled Jackie Baen.

Also testifying against Dale and Donnell that day was Shultz. Shultz said Dale had threatened Donnell's son. "Dale said somebody had done a lot of talking and it was either him or Donnell," Shultz said. Dale also threatened his family, according to Shultz. "It is a small world. I won't be in jail forever or I will get someone to do it," Shultz quoted Dale as saying.

Shultz admitted his part in the forged check operation.

AS LAW ENFORCEMENT officers continued their search for the gunmen who shot Johnston Jr. and murdered Miller, Johnston Jr. had enough of the federal witness protection program and living in Des Moines, Iowa, where the United States Marshal Service had relocated him.

Johnston Jr. decided to return to Chester County even

though he knew his life was still in jeopardy. Since marshals weren't keeping a 24-hour-a-day watch on Johnston Jr. the young shooting victim easily eluded his protectors.

State policeman Thomas Cloud was working one Sunday morning late in October 1978 when he received a call from an informant living in Oxford. Cloud was told that Johnston Jr. was back in the area. "I called Nick Marchinisani, the United States Marshal in charge of the operation, and I told him that Johnston Jr. was back in Oxford. Marchinisani said Johnston Jr. couldn't be because he sent him far away. "I couldn't convince him my informant knew what he was talking about," Cloud said. "Since we weren't told where Bruce Jr. had been sent, I told him that the informant said he came back from Des Moines. Nick's string of expletives told me my informant was correct."

EFFORTS BY THE investigators to locate the four missing members of the Johnston gang, James Johnston, Dwayne Lincoln, and James and Wayne Sampson, continued to be unsuccessful and many within the law enforcement community believed they had been murdered. Before one court hearing, state policeman J. R. Campbell said, "Both of the Sampsons and James Johnston are presumed to be dead."

James Johnston and Lincoln were eighteen years old and Wayne Sampson was twenty at the time they disappeared. The three young men, along with Johnston Jr., were members of what was known as the "kiddie gang" branch of the Johnston theft operation. James Sampson was twenty-four years old, too old to be considered a member of the kiddie gang.

The elder members of the Johnston gang rode the rural roads of Chester County by day looking for tractors left in fields. When a likely candidate for a theft was spotted, members of the kiddie gang would be taken at night to the field and dropped off to push the tractor to the edge of a field.

The elder members of the gang would drive away in a truck. When the kiddie gang members had the tractor near the edge of the road, they would throw hay or some other object on the road. When the truck driver saw the signal on the road, he would stop, the tractor would be loaded on the truck and the gang would depart the crime scene.

The scheme worked over and over again as FBI agent Richter's long list of tractor thefts attested.

The four young men weren't the only criminals associated with the Johnston gang that couldn't be located. Gary Wayne Crouch of Elkton, Maryland, was a one-time confidant of the Johnstons. The last time the police could pinpoint Crouch's whereabouts was a year earlier. He was known to have been at the Wooden Shoe Inn in Jennersville with Johnston Sr., Leslie Dale, and James Sampson.

Police also believed Crouch had been killed. Crouch had violated a sacred law of the Johnstons, he had cooperated with police. Crouch had a habit of secretly taping conversations with the Johnstons. He admitted to 50 such recordings. One recording was made four years earlier in connection with the theft of a trailer loaded with food from the Acme Market in Oxford in November 1974.

Crouch testified at a preliminary hearing and then disappeared.

CHAPTER SEVEN

"Hit Man" Cooperates

L eslie Dale was a cocky, cold-blooded killer.
State policeman Tom Cloud said, "Leslie Dale, you know his persona, if you look up cold-blooded killer in the dictionary, you might see his picture." In a news article *Daily Local News* reporter Bruce Mowday called Dale a "hit man"—a paid assassin—for the Johnstons. Dale wrote Mowday a letter and signed it "hit man."

Dale was facing a life sentence for the murder of Jackie Baen and he didn't like the prospect of never being released from prison. Cooperating with police appeared to be his best option, especially after a meeting in prison with Ancell Hamm, the convicted murderer of two Kennett Square policemen. Hamm told Dale that the Johnstons were planning to pin all of the murders on Dale.

On Thursday, November 30, 1978, Dale made up his mind that it was time to explore a relationship with the police. While being housed at Chester County Farms Prison Dale indicated he wanted to talk to District Attorney William H. Lamb, Assistant District Attorney Dolores Troiani, and Chief County Detective Charles Zagorskie. At 3:30 PM

Zagorskie and Troiani made the 15-minute drive from the Chester County Courthouse in West Chester to Chester County Farms Prison to see Dale.

As Dale entered a secured room at the prison, he again asked to see Lamb.

"Lamb is a busy man,"Troiani said. "We're not going to interrupt his schedule for nothing. What do you want to tell him?"

Dale wanted a deal but he was not going to divulge any of the details of a murder without an agreement. Dale also asked Zagorskie to leave the room so he could talk with Troiani. Dale fancied himself a jailhouse attorney and he wanted to talk law with Troiani without the presence of the policeman Zagorskie. Dale said he learned law in prison from the best, Hamm and Richard O. J. Mayberry, who had turned a minor sentence into a lifetime in prison by committing numerous crimes while being incarcerated, including escape while in Chester County.

After Zagorskie left the room Dale told Troiani about his conversation with Hamm and the fact the Johnstons were going to blame him for all of the murders. Dale also told Troiani that David Johnston and Johnston Sr. were with Hamm on the night Hamm shot the two Kennett Square police officers. "I know Dave and Bruce were there with walkie-talkies and the getaway car," Dale said.

Dale indicated he had plenty of information that would interest the prosecution team. Dale told Troiani beside the statements the Johnstons made about being involved in the murders of the two Kennett Square policemen, he had information on Donnell and Wasyl Towber, another long-time Chester County criminal who was found dead floating in the Brandywine River. Dale claimed to know of physical evidence in connection with the murder of Robin Miller and the location of five murder victims and information about a total of seven deaths.

Dale had enough information to interrupt Lamb's busy schedule.

Zagorskie reentered the room and Dale again said he had information on murder victims, Robin Miller, Jimmy Sampson, Jimmy Johnston, Dwayne Lincoln, Wayne Sampson, and Gary Crouch.

"Is Baen the seventh victim?" Troiani asked.

Dale laughed. "I'll talk about Baen after I have my deal."

During the 75 minutes Dale talked to Troiani and Zagorskie, Dale drank coffee and smoked Zagorskie's cigarettes. Dale seemed relaxed to the two investigators, but somewhat nervous as he cracked his usual bad jokes.

"If we are going to go through all of this trouble to get you out of prison to see Lamb, you better give us at least one body tonight," Troiani told Dale. "We want to be sure you aren't lying to us and if it becomes general knowledge that you are talking, the Johnstons might go dig them up."

Dale responded by advising the two to cut off all phone calls to Ricky Mitchell for at least a day and to increase patrols in the Chadds Ford and Oxford areas. Dale believed Mitchell would telephone the Johnstons and the Johnstons would attempt to unearth bodies.

On the trip from Chester County Farms Prison to the Chester County Courthouse Dale talked generally about the murders but gave no specific details. Dale also asked to have West Chester criminal defense attorney Michael Kean represent him. Dale wanted to fire his current attorney Michael Barranco of the Chester County Public Defender's office who had represented a number of criminals connected to the Johnstons.

Dale had some additional demands while riding to the courthouse. Dale wanted a new identity, relocation to a different state, and enough money to start his own small business. Troiani and Zagorskie said they would only consider such a deal if he hadn't murdered any of the victims. Dale insisted he never pulled a trigger.

Troiani and Zagorskie had another concern about Dale. They were worried that Dale would attempt to escape. Dale assured them he wasn't going to flee. "If I'm free the Johnstons will try to track me down and kill me," Dale said.

The District Attorney's office was on the fourth floor of the new wing of the Chester County Courthouse on High Street, West Chester. At 5:05 PM Dale entered the office where Chester County Detectives Michael Cotter and Michael Carroll took custody of Dale. Troiani and Zagorskie went to see District Attorney Lamb to brief him on their conversations with Dale.

By 5:30 PM Lamb was ready to see Dale and County Detective Larry Dampman brought Dale into Lamb's office. Troiani and Zagorskie were waiting with Lamb. Dale smoked and drank coffee as he explained he could represent himself and didn't need legal counsel. He again said he would give truthful testimony in exchange for a new identity and money. Dale also didn't want any part of the federal witness protection program because of the program's lax security. "Everyone knows Bruce Jr. leaves his federal protection to return to Oxford every weekend to purchase drugs," Dale commented.

Lamb said he would make a deal on two conditions. First, Dale couldn't have been one of the murderers. Second, Dale had to show them a body that night.

Dale agreed.

Dale also reconsidered representing himself. Dale said he wanted to talk to attorney Kean. After Kean couldn't be located, Dale said he would still show them a body and talk to Kean the following morning.

A court order from Chester County Common Pleas Judge Robert S. Gawthrop III was obtained placing Dale in the custody of the police and releasing him from prison.

DETECTIVE DAMPMAN SAID Dale led them to Stotts-ville, a little village between Parkesburg and Coatesville. Rain had made the ground muddy and some of the police vehicles were getting stuck in the mud as they drove off paved roads. A detail of about 25 state policemen and county detectives were searching for police informant Gary Wayne Crouch's body. Earlier, at 6:00 PM, Chester County Detective Joseph Thompson was requested to take the county's mobile crime lab to Stottsville, meet with law enforcement officers, and then take the lab to a farm in Highland Township.

Crouch was a former Johnston associate who gave infor-mation to the Delaware State Police after his arrest on stolen car charges. Crouch had boasted that he was part of a Dela-ware theft ring that stole vehicles worth at least $200,000. Crouch had said he had once secretly taped conversations with the Johnstons and turned the tapes over to police. Crouch knew his cooperation put him in danger and one friend told him his life expectancy was that of a fly.

"We went to Stottsville and didn't go that far off the road," Dampman recalled. "There were some logs, decent size there. We started digging and there was a body."

Police knew the body of Crouch was in the grave by a dis-tinctive ring found on one of the fingers. "I remember think-ing at the time that my life was hectic and was about to get even more hectic," state policeman Cloud recalled.

By 3:00 AM Crouch's body was taken from a five-foot grave and transported to Chester County Hospital, West Ches-ter. Before the body was transported, Detective Thompson was asked to return to the scene to take photos. He report-ed snapping 14 pictures of the body and grave. Dr. Halbert Fillinger of the Philadelphia Medical Examiner's office and

Dr. Donald Harrop, Chester County Coroner, performed an autopsy on December 1 at Phoenixville Hospital. Chester County Hospital declined to allow the autopsy and the body was taken to Phoenixville. The autopsy would show that Crouch had died from a gunshot wound to the head.

THERE WAS A feeling among some of the law enforcement team that they weren't alone searching the woods off Timacola Road that night. Some believed the Johnstons were tipped off and were in the woods trying to dig up Crouch's body and rebury the remains before the police could find them.

Lamb recalled, "The night we went out to dig up the body of Crouch, we heard something in the woods and it turns out the Johnstons were shadowing us. Larry Dampman, Dolores Troiani, and I were together and I had a weapon that was issued to me when I first became District Attorney. I took it out. I don't know what the hell I would have done with it."

Troiani added, "The atmosphere that night was incredible. There was a parade of police cars. Word was out that the Johnston brothers were possibly out there and going to snipe at us." Chief County Detective Charles Zagorskie didn't believe the rumors about the Johnstons. "Who was going to shoot at 20 cops?" he questioned.

The time had come to get Dale out of the woods and Dampman took him back to the courthouse and later to a hotel.

At the courthouse Dale, Lamb, and Zagorskie received an unwelcome visitor, reporter Bruce Mowday.

Mowday was at home watching the television show *20/20* when at 10:10 PM he received a telephone call. The caller didn't identify himself and only said, "Leslie Dale is out of prison. He is cooperating. They have one body out of the ground and hope to have three more by morning. You owe me a favor." The caller then hung up. Mowday didn't say a word.

The telephone call triggered an all night futile search to find Crouch's grave. Mowday first called the paper's chief photographer, Larry McDevitt, to meet him at the newspaper on Bradford Avenue, just a little more than a mile from the courthouse. Mowday arrived first and decided to try to find out just where they should look. Chester County is an awfully big place, covering 756 square miles.

Mowday considered going to the state police station in Embreeville but decided to first visit the county courthouse. As he approached the courthouse, Mowday saw the lights were on in the fourth-floor District Attorney's office. Mowday entered the courthouse and rode the elevator to the fourth floor.

The reporter walked down the hallway and looked into the District Attorney's waiting room. There sat Leslie Dale. "Hi Leslie," Mowday said as he was surprised to see the killer sitting by himself. Mowday took a few steps down the hall and then returned to the office where a state policeman had appeared and Dale disappeared.

"What do you want?" the state policeman asked.

Mowday could hear the distinctive voice of state police Lieutenant Richard Weimer, commander of the Avondale barracks, in the background. Mowday asked to see Weimer.

Weimer didn't appear but Zagorskie did.

"What the fuck do you want?" was Zagorskie's greeting.

Mowday said he wanted to know what was going on. He already knew Dale was cooperating and that they had one body out of the ground and hoped to have three more by morning. Zagorskie told Mowday to wait in the hallway.

Next to appear was District Attorney Lamb. Lamb, always an immaculate dresser, had his necktie undone and his shoes were muddy. Mowday repeated what he was told and asked for more details. Lamb refused to give information that night but promised to talk to Mowday in the morning before his nine o'clock deadline. Lamb also refused to give the exact location of the grave, even after Mowday said he would follow the county's mobile crime lab that was parked in front of the courthouse.

"I don't care what you do," Lamb said. "I'll talk to you in the morning."

Mowday went to the building's elevator, notoriously slow moving, punched the first floor button and waited. Detective Joe Thompson, the unit's photographer and father of then Commissioner Robert Thompson, joined Mowday on the ride to the first floor.

"Muddy out there, wasn't it?" Mowday asked.

"Yes. We had a couple of cars stuck," Thompson said. "I'm going to put the mobile lab away for the night."

Mowday was trying to think of a road that might be near a burial place. Since the Johnstons were from southern Chester County, he asked about Route 1.

"No," Thompson said. "It was near the Stottsville Inn, off a dirt road in back of the inn."

Mowday and photographer McDevitt, joined by reporter Ted Torrance, were off on a night search for Crouch's grave.

DALE'S NEXT STOP was at a local hotel. Detective Dampman said Dale started to fill them in on the Crouch murder. "We already had some information," Dampman said. "We knew a stolen Caddy was used in the crime and we had a burned vehicle we thought was used." Police later discovered that the vehicle, a 1971 Cadillac belonging to Vernon Dietz of Caln Township, had been reported stolen on July 17, 1977. The car was found the next day by state police on Thouron Road in West Marlborough Township. The vehicle had been burned and contained no useful clues.

DALE SAID HE was with Johnston Sr. that night and they told Crouch that they were going to Caln Township, outside of Downingtown near the speed shop that was used to fence stolen property, to steal a car from the parking lot of Zinn's diner. Dale told the police as they were driving down a dirt road Johnston Sr. shot Crouch in the back of the head.

They buried Crouch and drove the car to a location on Kings Highway and burned the murder vehicle. A second car had been previously placed near the murder scene and was used in the getaway.

"Leslie was not one of my favorite people," Dampman said. "We were trying to decide if we believed him. We knew Leslie was telling us some of the truth. Because he was involved in the Baen murder, we thought he was involved in the Miller murder. We thought he was the shooter. He denied it. Dale told us about Jackie Baen. He said it was an accident and they didn't mean to kill him." As for Crouch, Dale said Johnston Sr. told him Crouch was a "snitch" and had to be killed.

At the same time, Ed Otter was being interviewed by Richter, Cloud, and Weiniger. Otter admitted being a fence for the Johnstons. Otter then said that Dale had told him that Dale was the one in the backseat and had shot Crouch while Johnston Sr. was driving. "You think Bruce is so tough, well he's not so tough. Bruce didn't have the guts to finish a job and I (Dale) had to finish the guy off." Dale also told Otter that Johnston Sr. wouldn't even help put Crouch in the grave. Dale claimed to have pulled Crouch out of the car and put him in the hole. Later, Dale told police that Johnston Sr. helped with the burying of Crouch.

"So, I switched seats," Dale shrugged and said as he finally admitted he fired the weapon that murdered Crouch. Dale would not receive his sought-after deal for a new identity and money for a business. He had murdered a victim, a violation of one of the conditions Lamb placed on the deal.

Dale told police that on the day before the murder he went with Johnston Sr. to a hardware store in Parkesburg and purchased two shovels and a digging bar. The two men also talked about stealing a wood chipper machine and running Crouch's body through the chipper. The two had discussed different locations for the grave, including a landfill outside of West Chester. As Johnston Sr. and Dale were digging the grave a farmer came to a nearby field and the two men had to hide until the farmer left the area.

Dale used a .38-caliber pistol to shoot Crouch. The bullet entered the rear of Crouch's head and exited from his face under his right eye. The bullet then went through the windshield of the Cadillac. The impact from the shot forced Crouch to fall forward in his seat and then he rocked backward and slumped to his right. Crouch's lifeless body came to a rest against the window of the right front door of the car. Crouch's blood ran down the window and door and into the window well. Johnston Sr. took Crouch's wallet, containing $80 and handed the money to Dale, who pocketed the bills.

Crouch was taken to the grave and buried. Johnston and Dale then took the car to Springdell Road and set it on fire. Dale obtained the fuel for the fire from an all-night gas station located near the Avondale barracks of the state police. The two murderers then returned to the grave and completed burying the body. After disposing of the digging implements in the Brandywine River near Modena, Johnston and Dale went to Elkton, Maryland, to change clothes. Dale was paid $2,500 that night by Johnston Sr. The amount was to have been $3,000 but Dale owed Johnston Sr. $500.

About a month after the murder, Dale and Johnston Sr. used two bicycles to go back to the grave and make sure it hadn't been disturbed. It wasn't. Later, Johnston Sr. remarked to gang associate Jimmy Griffin that he (Johnston Sr.) had given Crouch a new job. "He said that Gary wasn't snitching anymore, but was pushing up daisies," Griffin quoted Johnston Sr. as saying.

DALE'S COOPERATION WAS one of the major turning points of the investigation.

"It was a huge break for us," Cloud said. "It was the first time I knew in my heart that the Johnstons' house of cards was about to fall. I figured when we dug up Gary Crouch, these guys didn't know it but it was over. This is not going to end until they are in jail. We were not going away. There is no intimidation that they could do that would make us go away. It was too intense. The group made the same mistake, murder, twice."

Because of Dale's propensity for not telling the truth, the police knew they would have to prove everything Dale said. "It was difficult in pinpointing the facts," Cloud said. "If there is anything I know about police work, it is that everything will be scrutinized. You have to get everything accurate. Leslie didn't use credit cards so we made a time line and we put on that time line things he was 100 percent sure about."

While Dale had lost his sweetheart deal, he hadn't lost his bizarre sense of humor. Troiani recalls one meeting in the Chester County District Attorney's office with members of the state police. "Someone had commented that Crouch was a pain and he could have killed him," Troiani recalled. "Leslie pulled down the paper he was reading and said 'I did' and then went back to reading the paper."

"Dale's cooperation was the beginning of the end. Baen's case was important but this was the beginning," Troiani said.

EARLY IN THE morning of Friday, December 1, 1978,

Lamb called reporter Mowday as promised. Mowday hadn't slept and was completing his first draft of the story when Lamb phoned. Lamb wouldn't confirm Dale was cooperating but he did confirm that Crouch's body had been found in a grave near the border of Highland and East Fallowfield townships.

The story in the Friday edition of the *Daily Local News* ran on the front page above the fold and the headline read, "Missing burglary informant found dead." The story also detailed Mowday's observation of Dale in the District Attorney's office.

As the law enforcement team continued its investigation into the last days of Crouch, county Detective Ted Schneider and state policeman J. R. Campbell interviewed John Pugh of Nottingham. Pugh said he saw Crouch late in the evening of July 16, 1977, at an Oxford area business. Pugh said Crouch told him that he had just left Johnston Sr. at the Wooden Shoe Inn in Kennett Square and he was to meet Johnston Sr. at his home.

"Crouch said he would be back, but he didn't return," Pugh said.

ON DECEMBER 1, 1978, Dr. Halbert Fillinger, an assistant Philadelphia medical examiner, performed an autopsy on Crouch. Fillinger reported that the body was fully clothed. Crouch's pack of Marlboro cigarettes and a multicolored lighter remained in his shirt pocket.

The final positive identification that the murder victim was Gary Wayne Crouch came on January 8, 1979, when the Pennsylvania State Police crime laboratory reported that the fingerprints from the body matched a fingerprint card for Crouch.

DALE MAINTAINED HE had not participated in the murder of Robin Miller but he told Pennsylvania State Policeman Tom Cloud on December 6, 1978, that Norman Johnston admitted taking part in the ambush killing. Dale also told Cloud that one of the guns used in the murder was one he stole and later sold to Johnston Sr.

"Norm said that it was he and Dave who had done it and that he said that it was impossible for little Bruce to be alive. He said that every time little Bruce got hit, he was shaking and he said that when he reached for Robin, that she got hit from a bullet that went through Bruce Jr. He said the gun that was used was the gun that I had sold to Bruce. This was a .38 that I had gotten, that was on a .357 frame. I got the gun from a truck stolen in Sadsburyville. I stole the truck and the gun was in the glove compartment. I sold the gun to Bruce a short time after I stole it. I think it was some time about the beginning of August."

The stolen weapon had belonged to Walter Davis of Sadsburyville. He had purchased the gun in Downingtown and it was in his truck when the vehicle was stolen. When police recovered the truck, the tires, his sunglasses, and his pistol were missing.

To prove that the weapon, last known to be in the possession of Johnston Sr., was one of the pistols used to murder Miller and wound Johnston Jr., spent bullets that Davis had fired were needed to be matched against the bullets found at the murder scene. Davis said he only fired the weapon one time. He remembered taking the weapon to a hunting cabin in Potter County, Pennsylvania, to do some target shooting.

On December 7, the day after Dale made his statement, state policeman J. R. Campbell and Davis went to the Chester County Airport outside of Coatesville and flew in a state police helicopter to Potter County. A state policeman then drove Campbell and David to the hunting cabin. Davis pointed to an area where he used a soda can for a target. He said he believed he fired 12 rounds. A tree was directly in back of the can. Campbell searched the tree and the ground in front of the tree and found 10 projectiles.

Campbell turned over the recovered spent bullets to the state police crime lab to determine if they matched the ones recovered at the Miller murder scene. They did.

AS LESLIE DALE'S cooperation amounted to the turning point in the murder investigation, the testimony of two of Johnstons' fences led to the unraveling of the Johnstons' burglary ring. Boyertown residents Edward Henry Otter and David "Buffalo" Schonely, were cooperating with police.

On November 29, 1978, FBI agent David Richter and state policeman Tom Cloud interrogated Otter while Schonely was interviewed by state policemen Walt Weinger and Barry Pease.

Otter and Schonely told the investigators that Bruce Johnston Sr. had visited Otter's home in early November and had a pointed message for them. Both men believed the Johnstons would kill them if they snitched. The Johnstons showed them a newspaper with a story about the death of Glenda Sampson Chamberlain, the sister of two missing members of the Johnston gang, James and Wayne Sampson. The story indicated that Chamberlain and her boyfriend were found dead in a car in Lancaster County in November. Schonely said he believed the message was that he too could die if he cooperated.

Otter said he was having dinner with his son Todd when the three Johnston brothers entered, Johnston Sr., Norman and David, along with James Dotson.

"How's the heat up here?" Johnston Sr. asked, wanting to

know if the police were applying pressure. "Is anybody talking?" Johnston Sr. showed Otter a newspaper with Dale's photograph and told Otter to not worry about Dale's talking. "He is tough as nails," Johnston Sr. said.

The Johnstons wanted to talk to both Otter and Schonely and Schonely joined them. Johnston Sr. wanted to make sure Otter and Schonely had good lawyers and suggested they hire either Robert Landis or John Talerico. Johnston Sr. offered to help pay the legal fees. At the time the men were represented by attorney John Murphy.

"You know that you and Dave could really hurt us up here," Johnston Sr. said. Johnston Sr. told them that if they were offered immunity that they should blame the tractor thefts on Bruce Johnston Jr. and Jimmy Sampson. Otter told Richter and Cloud that the three Johnstons and Dotson were the ones who delivered the tractors.

THE DAY AFTER the interviews, Richter went to see United States Assistant Attorney Douglas B. Richardson in Philadelphia and three federal complaints were filed against Johnston Sr., David, and Norman Johnston charging the brothers with obstruction of justice for attempting to intimidate Otter and Schonely.

After the criminal charges were lodged against the Johnston brothers, FBI agent Robert T. Daull and Cloud reinterviewed Otter. Otter said he first met Johnston Sr. at a Stowe, Pennsylvania, auto body shop and Johnston asked if he knew anyone who wanted to buy tractors. Otter admitted he began fencing stolen tractors for the Johnstons, first on a small scale and later on a much larger scale.

Otter then told the investigators about a typical deal. Otter recalled in the spring of 1977 he received a call from Johnston Sr. asking if he would like three tractors. Otter said he consulted with Schonely and decided they would have no trouble selling the stolen items. Johnston Sr. even offered to knock off $100 from the price if they would come to his home in Elkton, Maryland, to get the John Deere tractors. Before, Otter said Johnston Sr. would deliver the tractors to them. Otter told police he would pay $1,000 for a John Deere Model 400 and about $400 for a John Deere eight horsepower model.

In a separate interview with FBI agent Dennis Dempsey and state trooper Robert Martz at the Holiday Inn in Pottstown, Schonely confirmed Otter's story. Schonely added that between April 1977 and November 1978 he had received between 20 and 40 tractors from the Johnstons.

Police recovered approximately 200 John Deere tractors during the investigation and other pieces of heavy equipment. One year after the gang was off the streets, Pennsylvania dropped out of the top ten states in the country for thefts of farm and heavy equipment.

CHAPTER EIGHT

Three Murder Victims

A s December 1978 began the three Johnston brothers were free but their days of freedom were dwindling. David, Norman, and Bruce Johnston Sr. all posted bail in October on theft charges involving interstate transportation of stolen tractors and cigarettes.

Johnston Sr. was on the streets after he offered his property as security for his $100,000 bail. David Johnston was free after posting 10 percent of his $50,000 bail. Norman Johnston also posted enough cash to be released. One of the persons who helped Norman Johnston secure bail was his mother-in-law, Estelle Ricketts. In December Ricketts called police asking for her son-in-law's location. She said Norman and her daughter, Susan, owed her $2,000 for the money she loaned them to get Norman out of jail.

Norman Johnston and his brothers had more than Estelle Ricketts on their trail as the FBI began seeking the brothers on obstruction of justice charges involving the intimidation of the Pottstown fences.

On Friday, December 1, 1978, Johnston Sr. was scheduled to be at the pre-release program office in the federal courthouse in Philadelphia. Johnston Sr.'s appearance was part of his bail requirements. FBI agents were at the federal courthouse that day to look for Johnston Sr. They also visited the office of his attorney, John J. Duffy. Duffy cited attorney-client privilege and refused to talk with the agents. The agents failed to locate Johnston Sr. and he remained on the loose, along with his brothers.

FBI agent David Richter received a number of reports as to Johnston Sr.'s whereabouts, including one that placed the wanted man in Canada. Efforts to locate the Johnstons by contacting the Johnstons' family, friends, and gang associates failed. Two of the gang members personally contacted by Richter were James Dotson and James "Disco" Griffin. Before departing Richter gave both men a bit of advice; they should consider obtaining legal council and make the best deal they could.

The first Johnston to lose his freedom was David Johnston, who surrendered to federal officials on December 12, 1978, in the company of his federal parole officer, Paul Michner. United States Magistrate Tullio Gene Leomporra set bail at $15,000. Leomporra warned Johnston that he would revoke bail if any of the witnesses in the case received any communications from him or his associates. Johnston was fingerprinted and additional information was obtained. He told officers that he was born on December 14, 1947, in Chester County and stood five feet, eight inches tall and weighed 180 pounds. He had a mustache and reported he was unemployed.

Investigators continued to search for Johnston Sr. and Norman Johnston and were told that Norman had been calling Frank "Deuce" Reinert, a garage mechanic from Gilbertsville, near Boyertown. Reinert told police that Norman had called him on December 1, wanting to know if he had heard from Otter or Schonely, the fences now cooperating with police. Norman Johnston also asked Reinert to work on his car. Reinert said he received a second call on December 11 and again was asked about Otter and Schonely.

Another Johnston brother, Passmore, was stopped on December 12 after police believed he was his brother, Johnston Sr. Passmore Johnston said he was aware of the arrest warrants for his brothers but did not know their location. Passmore, known as Pete, Johnston had been prosecuted by Lamb's law partner, James McErlane, in the 1970s on receiving stolen property charges and then Passmore went straight, according to McErlane.

A neighbor of Norman and Susan Johnston, Denise Hamilton, told police she had been receiving death threats after FBI agents contacted her on December 11. Hamilton told FBI agent Michael Melvin that an unknown caller told her, "I know you talked and you'll be next." She received another call and the person said, "If you talk, we will get you."

On December 13, 1978, Johnston Sr. and Norman Johnston were both in custody, along with their wives, Carol and Susan Johnston. The four were arrested in Berks County on shoplifting charges at a Boscov's store just north of Reading. Carol and Susan Johnston were charged with concealing a person from arrest. The four were charged with attempting to steal eight dollar, eight-track stereo tapes. One policeman reportedly quipped Johnston Sr. had an eight-track stereo and a one-track mind.

Boscov's security officer Richard Hommas told FBI agent Alan Reighley that about 20 minutes before closing he saw the Johnstons in the store near the record and tape area. Hommas observed Norman Johnston put a tape inside his jacket. The security officer saw two more tapes go into the same jacket. Then Johnston Sr. put a tape into his jacket. Hommas and other security officers followed the Johnstons as they walked through the store.

When Norman and Susan Johnston left the store without paying, they were confronted by security officers. Norman Johnston denied the allegation but pushed away the security officers and fled by running through the parking lot and over a fence and through the Reading Fairgrounds. Susan Johnston was taken into custody and later released because she had not taken tapes.

In a few minutes Carol Johnston and Johnston Sr. left the store and they were confronted. Johnston Sr. attempted to escape but was subdued by three store staff members. Carol Johnston fled but was apprehended in the parking lot and later released.

Muhlenberg Township police officers hunted for Norman Johnston. The officers were successful as they apprehended Norman Johnston, along with Carol and Susan Johnston, at a Holiday Inn.

AT THE FEDERAL bail hearing on December 14, Leomporra set Norman Johnston's bail at $100,000 while the wives' bail was $7,500 each. As for Johnston Sr., his bail was set at $150,000. Federal prosecutor Douglas Richardson wanted a bail of $500,000 because Johnston Sr. was an obvious flight risk. Richardson also wanted $50,000 bail for Carol and Susan Johnston. Defense attorney John J. Duffy said Richardson's half million dollar bail request amounted to ransom. Norman and Susan Johnston told Leomporra that they couldn't afford an attorney. The husband and wife received court-appointed attorneys.

During the bail hearing Duffy said state police Lieutenant Richard Weimer had previously told him that he was going to give Johnston Sr. "a Christmas present, murder one charges." Weimer said Duffy must have misunderstood him. "The conversation was precisely as I stated," Duffy responded.

While Johnston Sr. was being fingerprinted, FBI agent Richter asked the defendant if he wanted to talk. In response, Johnston Sr. shook Richter's hands and said the government had won and had beaten him. Johnston Sr. said he would talk about the burglaries and to contact his attorney. Johnston Sr. also told Richter that he was aware of the FBI's surveillance airplanes. Johnston Sr. went on to give details of the FBI's operation. Johnston Sr. said the planes had been kept at the Atlantic Aviation Company at the Philadelphia Airport and that the agents had stayed at the Tally Ho Motel before moving to the Treadway Inn in West Chester. Johnston Sr. also said he had photographs of some of the FBI vehicles and agents.

The Johnston gang had tailed the FBI.

Another bail hearing was held in Philadelphia on December 19, 1978, this time before Magistrate Richard A. Powers III. Powers found probable cause against Johnston Sr. and bail stayed at $150,000 but he found no evidence concerning obstruction of justice against Norman Johnston and ordered his release. No evidence of harboring a federal fugitive was found against Carol Johnston and she too was released. Susan Johnston was held on the harboring charge and bail continued at $7,500.

As for David Johnston, he had previously posted his $15,000 bail but was immediately arrested on theft charges from Lehigh County. He was imprisoned after failing to post another $50,000.

"After building up these guys as big-time hoodlums they then get caught shoplifting in Reading," Richter said. "It was kind of embarrassing because it didn't look like major crimes to federal prosecutors. But in reality the Johnstons were excellent shoplifters and they didn't pay for anything."

WITH TWO OF the three Johnston brothers in custody, legal maneuvering began that would last more than a year before trials would take place. In late December Johnston Sr.'s attorney, Robert Landis, asked to have all of the cases transferred out of the Philadelphia area because of the vast amount of coverage newspapers were giving to the theft and murder cases. The petition said the articles have "poisoned the minds of prospective jurors in Philadelphia and all of its surrounding communities to the degree that Johnston Sr. could not receive a fair trial in any such jurisdiction." The petition also charged law enforcement officials with deliberately leaking information to the press.

Within days newspapers would have more fodder for their columns.

WITH ONE ADMITTED killer cooperating, Leslie Dale, the investigating team needed another inside source with information on the Robin Miller murder. At this point the investigative team was also convinced that the missing gang members—James and Wayne Sampson, Dwayne Lincoln and Jimmy Johnston—were also dead. The next weakest link was Ricky Mitchell. Working with Mitchell, an epileptic with a multitude of physical ills, would prove to be frustrating for the investigators.

"Ricky was such an obnoxious s.o.b. It was difficult for the cops to be in a position so close to him," said Chester County Detective Mike Carroll. "He was not only obnoxious but also demanding. He wanted bananas and peanut butter delivered to him daily. When Ricky was testifying it was difficult to keep him on track as he had the attention span of a two-year old. There was one instance where Dolores (Troiani) asked him on the witness stand the color of a car and he didn't answer. About five minutes later and several other questions later he finally says, 'red.' 'And this is our witness,' we asked ourselves."

State policeman Gabe Bolla remembers Mitchell asking for steaks and lobsters for his meals that were being paid by Chester County taxpayers. Mitchell also wanted a supply of Pepsi and a popcorn machine for his hotel room when he was being readied for trial, according to Bolla.

Another state policeman, Tom Cloud, was a little kinder in his description of Mitchell. He said, "Ricky is the most unusual person I've been around in my life. I once arrested Ricky for having a stolen car and his parents brought him a strawberry milkshake to the barracks. He wasn't a young guy. His parents were unusual too. Charlie (Zagorskie) used to say Ricky was in a bad car accident that caused his medical problems, but I don't believe it because his parents acted just like him and they weren't in the car. The Johnstons didn't believe Ricky was capable of laying out the details of the crime. Also, he had been caught many times and he had gone to jail many times without talking."

In December 1978 Mitchell was being held in Delaware County Prison and giving the prison officials a difficult time. Mitchell believed he wasn't getting his proper medication and had filed a lawsuit against the prison. When Chester County Assistant District Attorney Dolores Troiani and Chief County Detective Charles Zagorskie went to talk to Mitchell at first Mitchell refused to see them. Mitchell wanted his medicine before seeing the investigators and Troiani and Zagorskie went to the warden to settle the medicine dispute.

"We were telling Mitchell that he was in trouble with the Johnstons and he better cooperate," Zagorskie said. "A visit from Susan Johnston (Norman Johnston's wife) at the prison helped convince Ricky that he was in danger. We had information that a contract was out on Ricky and that is why he cooperated."

On the day before New Year's Eve Troiani and Zagorskie picked up Mitchell from the prison hospital. Mitchell was in his pajamas and Troiani gave him her sister's jacket to wear. "That was the night he took us to the bodies," Troiani said. Zagorskie added, "Ricky rolled and we dug for bodies." That night the police, with the help of Mitchell, found the grave that contained Wayne Sampson, Lincoln, and Jimmy Johnston.

Mitchell was taken to the Ramada Inn in Delaware County where he worked out a deal with the police through his attorney, Frank Bove. County detective Mike Carroll said, "Mitchell was given a sweetheart of a deal but everyone knew he was going to lie. He went from a sentence of 10 years in prison to life in prison but that change in sentence was on Mitchell. Everyone expected him to lie."

At 11:00 AM on December 30, 1978, a plea agreement was signed by Bove, Troiani, and Mitchell. The agreement said Mitchell had to give truthful testimony and unqualified disclosure of information concerning the deaths of Robin Miller, James Johnston, James Sampson, Wayne Sampson and Dwayne Lincoln. In exchange for his testimony Mitchell was to be charged with the murder of one of the victims and plead guilty. The sentence would be 10 to 50 years in prison. Mitchell would also plead guilty to the outstanding charges against him in both state and federal courts. The sentences for those charges would be served concurrently with the murder charge.

Troiani said, "We had to make sure we had the truth. Ricky lost his deal."

"Mitchell lied when he told us he didn't shoot anyone," Zagorskie said. "He lost his deal. When we pressed him on evidence that showed he might have killed one of them, Mitchell said, "All right. I shot him." The sentence was changed to life in prison and he was fine with life." Mitchell would prove to be a constant irritant to Zagorskie. "He used to call me once a week and drive me crazy," Zagorskie said. "He said he could see the Atlantic Ocean from his California jail cell or the Specific Ocean."

Cloud said, "Once Ricky agreed to cooperate he provided the information that really gave us the framework to prove the case. He was present at the triple murder. When we dug at the spot he pointed to, we found the bodies. He was also present at Jimmy Sampson's murder and he was aware of the planning of the shootings of Robin Miller and Bruce Johnston Jr. He was part of Johnston Sr.'s alibi."

DURING THE LATE afternoon of Saturday, December 30, 1978, Mitchell took investigators to a field in Pennsbury Township, Chester County. The land was owned by former Wilmington, Delaware, Mayor Harry G. Haskell Jr. It was two and a half miles from the Delaware line and just south of Chadds Ford.

Mitchell led Cloud and county Detective Larry Dampman down a tractor path and through several cornfields to the grave site.

"It was still daylight," Cloud recalled. "When we got to there, it was decided I would take Ricky and we went walking up through that field. Ricky looked around the fields and came to a spot that was a half mile from the road. He walked to a small triangular patch of woods and he looks up. I had never seen anything like it before. He looks up in the trees. He looks down and there was a small tree with leaves and he says, "Dig here.""

"Are you sure?" Cloud asked Mitchell.

"No, I'm not sure, I'm positive," Mitchell responded.

Cloud said, "He had a way that would make a nonviolent person want to strangle him. It was pure Ricky. We kept him nearby until we were sure it was a grave site."

State policeman Bob Martz reported that a "mounding of dirt" indicated the site of the grave measuring nine feet and six inches in length and five feet, two inches wide. The mounding was about six inches and a large tree limb had been covering the site. "The grave was camouflaged," District Attorney William H. Lamb added.

Cloud and Dampman began digging with spoons so as not to disturb the grave. The time was 6:50 PM. At 7:05 PM Dampman found denim material from a piece of clothing. At 8:10 PM the officers determined the four-foot grave had three bodies. The first victim was removed from the grave at 10:30 PM, and fifteen minutes later the second victim was carefully lifted from the grave followed by the third young man. The bodies were carried down the hill to a waiting ambulance from Avondale Fire Company. The remains were taken to Phoenixville Hospital to await autopsies that were performed by Philadelphia Medical Examiner Halbert Fillinger.

"It was getting dark and Philadelphia Electric Company came with high-powered lights," Cloud said. "We slowly dug up the three bodies. It was not pleasant smell-wise. We were out there a long time. I think we were out there the next day to make sure we recovered all of the evidence. It was cold."

Daily Local News reporter Bruce Mowday received another phone message that evening. As he returned from watching a Woody Allen triple feature at the Warner Theater in West Chester, he was told of the discovery and immediately headed to the scene but didn't arrive in time to ask questions of the lead investigators.

Some of the reporters covering the case assumed Dale, and not Mitchell, was the person who led police to the bodies. On New Year's Day Mowday received another phone call, this time from one of the investigators. "Mowday, you don't know anything," he was told. "You don't even know who is talking. It's not Dale; it's Mitchell." The next day the *Daily Local News* was the first newspaper to have the stories of the three victims, their identifications, and the fact Mitchell was cooperating.

ON NEW YEAR'S Eve Zagorskie received phone calls from Ruth Mitchell, Ricky's mother. Mrs. Mitchell told Zagorskie that Bob Landis, who was one of the attorneys representing the Johnstons, was representing her son.

Landis tried to contact Mitchell at Sacred Heart Hospital in Delaware County. Mitchell had been taken to the hospital after suffering an epileptic seizure. After prison officials refused to allow Landis access to Mitchell, Landis called Zagorskie. Zagorskie had a few sharp words for Landis, "I'm going to tell you something; you aren't going to represent Mitchell. You can't represent the Johnstons and Mitchell." At that point the Johnstons knew for sure that the prosecutors were working with Mitchell.

Even though the investigative team had direct information on the Johnstons' connection to the murder, Lamb wasn't ready to bring homicide charges against the brothers. Lamb said at the time, "We want to put all of the pieces of the puzzle together before making any decisions. We have to decide if charges should be brought and who should be charged."

AS THE INVESTIGATIVE team continued to put together the pieces of the puzzle another unsolved murder was being reviewed, that of Wasyl Towber of Coatesville, who was found floating in the east branch of the Brandywine River in July 1975. State policeman George March said the murders of Baen and Towber were similar and the two victims had criminal friends in common. Towber had been described by police as a "one-man crime wave." Towber had served time in prison on a number of theft and burglary charges and he lost his right arm in 1973 from a shotgun blast as he tried to enter illegally a Coatesville-area home. In 1959 Towber had escaped from Chester County Farms Prison. Towber, like Baen, had been struck on the side of the head before being dumped in the Brandywine. No connection was found with the Johnstons.

DR. HALBERT FILLINGER of the Philadelphia Medical Examiner's office completed the autopsies on the bodies of the three young victims found in the grave. Their identities were confirmed by the Chester County District Attorney's office. They were Johnston gang associates James Johnston, eighteen years old; Dwayne Lincoln, seventeen years old; and Wayne Sampson, nineteen years old. District Attorney William Lamb said dental and medical records and some physical characteristics were used to confirm the identifications.

The three teenagers had been in the grave since August, the month the victims were subpoenaed to testify before the federal grand jury. Dr. Fillinger reported each had been shot in the head.

The victims had a lot in common, according to family members. They were all from broken homes and had dropped out of high school. None of the victims held a steady job and each had a history of being involved in petty crimes and marijuana use. Marie Sampson, mother of Wayne and James Sampson, told a newspaper reporter, "Why Wayne and Jimmy took up stealing, I don't know. They just wouldn't listen."

The investigative team was still looking for James Sampson.

Ancell Hamm was convicted of murdering two Kennett Square policemen, Richard Posey and William Davis. He is serving two life terms in a Pennsylvania prison.

Bruce A. Johnston Sr. was the leader of the Johnston gang and was convicted of murdering six persons. He ordered the execution of his son and raped his son's girlfriend. Carol Johnston was married to Johnston at the time of his murder trial.

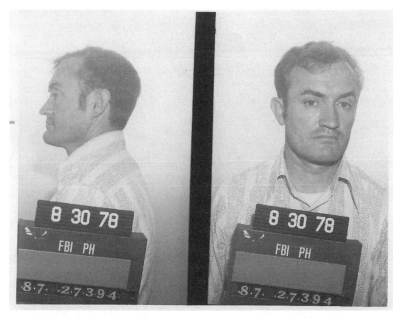

Bruce Johnston was convicted of murdering six people but he has been linked to at least 10 deaths. He personally fired the fatal shots that killed his stepson, Jimmy Johnston.

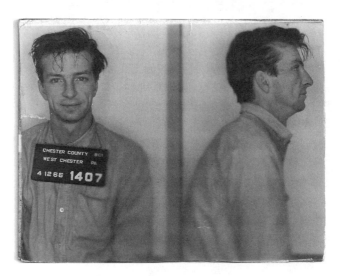

Leslie Dale was a hired killer who referred to himself as the "Hit Man." He was convicted of murdering police informant Gary Wayne Crouch. He was a key witness against the Johnston brothers.

David Johnston was convicted for four murders and is serving a life imprisonment term. He was recognized as being the most ruthless of the three Johnston brothers.

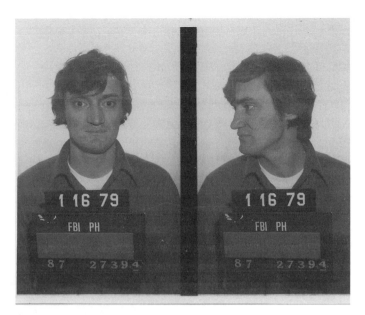

Norman Johnston, the youngest of the three Johnston brothers, escaped from state prison in 1999 and was the subject of a massive search by law enforcement. He was re-captured after more than two weeks of freedom and is serving life imprisonment terms for four murders.

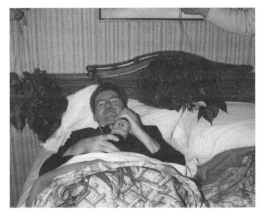

Ricky Mitchell took part in the digging of the grave that was used to bury three of the murder victims. After he began cooperating with police he led officers to the grave. He also shot one of the young men in the grave. Photo shows Mitchell in bed after having collapsed from one of his sessions on the witness stand.

Pennsylvania State Police trooper J. R. Campbell discovered the bodies of slain Kennett Square policemen Richard Posey and William Davis. He conducted many of the interviews in the Johnston brothers investigation.

Gabe Bolla provided a key identification of a weapon used in the murder of two Kennett Square policemen by Ancell Hamm. He also was one of the main Pennsylvania State Police troopers investigating the Johnstons.

Tom Cloud was the lead Pennsylvania State Police investigator on the case. He worked tirelessly to gather information on the Johnstons. The Johnstons put out a contract on his life.

Chester County Detective Michael Carroll said of the cooperation among law enforcement members, "It didn't matter who you were working with, you just worked." Carroll was instrumental in the preparations for the murder trials of the Johnston brothers.

Chester County Detective Charles Zagorskie is credited with coordinating the investigation of the Johnston brothers. As a member of the Pennsylvania State Police he was a key member of the team that convicted Ancell Hamm of murdering two policemen.

Some of the law enforcement officers involved in the investigation of the Johnston brothers gathered for a photograph in 2008. They are from left: Tom Cloud, Ray Solt, David Richter, Charles Zagorskie, Mike Carroll, Gabe Bolla, Larry Dampman, and J. R. Campbell.

Chester County Detective Larry Dampman was one of the investigators who used
a spoon to carefully remove dirt from the
suspected grave of three murder victims.
Dampman found denim material from a
piece of clothing of one of the victims, thus
establishing the grave was where informant Ricky Mitchell stated.

William H. Lamb was the District Attorney of Chester County and successfully
prosecuted the three Johnston brothers. He
later served as a Justice of the Supreme
Court of Pennsylvania.

State policeman Ray Solt worked many of the burglary cases, especially the ones that involved Lancaster County. "The Johnstons were watching us, the police," he said. A Johnston gang member admitted going to Solt's home to spy on him.

David Richter was the lead FBI agent in the investigation of the Johnston brothers. He was instrumental in obtaining a federal grand jury investigation of the gang. Because of his cooperation and work with the Pennsylvania State Police, he was known as "Trooper Dave."

CHAPTER NINE

Pieces of the Puzzle

Gathering evidence and verifying every statement by the prosecution's two key witnesses—admitted murderers Leslie Dale and Ricky Mitchell—would be crucial for the prosecution case. The investigative team knew defense attorneys would challenge the credibility of Dale and Mitchell. The prosecuting team couldn't rely on just the word of the witnesses to gain convictions. The prosecutors needed corroborating evidence.

The verification of the stories of Dale and Mitchell, and putting the pieces of the puzzle together as District Attorney William H. Lamb said, was an all-consuming process during the year of 1979. Law enforcement members would painstakingly track down every lead and investigate every statement made by the two police informants.

One of the first steps involved the search of records of the Peter Lumber Company in Kennett Square. On January 2, 1979, the day of the autopsy, state policemen Paul Yoder and J. R. Campbell checked the company's invoices for August 1978. They were specifically looking for records dated in mid-August, the time the three murder victims had disappeared

and were killed. They were looking to see if digging implements and a bag of lime had been purchased. The lime was
used to help decompose the bodies of the murder victims.

Invoice GW18186 indicated the sale of two shovels and a
bag of lime. Cash was used for the $15.57 purchase. The iden-
tity of the purchaser was not known by the employees of the
lumberyard. The date of the invoice was August 16, 1978.

RICKY MITCHELL WAS about to supply a major piece of
the puzzle, that is if he was telling the truth. During the afternoon of January 2, Mitchell was released from Sacred Heart
Hospital in Chester into the custody of the Pennsylvania State
Police. Mitchell was taken to the Treadway Inn in West Chester where he gave a statement to Assistant District Attorney
Dolores Troiani, Chief County Detective Charles Zagorskie,
and state policemen Tom Cloud and Bob Martz.

"One morning we were at Louise's house (the Kennett
Square residence of Louise Johnston, mother of Norman,
David, and Bruce Johnston Sr.), and Bruce asked me to dig
a hole. He said he'd make it worth my while, he'd fix my car.
He didn't tell me what the hole was for, and I didn't ask any
questions. When you work with those guys, you don't ask
questions. I told him I wanted to go home and eat first and
I left. When I got home, I got my father's .32 caliber pistol
and came back. I didn't trust them and I didn't want to go out
digging any holes without some protection," Mitchell said.

"When I got back to Louise's they said they'd take me to
the place to dig. I think we went in Norman Johnston's car,
the Thunderbird, the car had an electric trunk lock, cinder-
blocks, that kind of stuff. They sent me in and told me to
buy two shovels and a bag of lime. I didn't ask any questions.
They told me what to buy and I did it. Then we all went back
to Louise's.

"Norm, Dave, and I then drove out to the grave. Norm drove. When we got to the gate, Norm and I got out and started walking through the fields and Dave drove around. Dave dropped the lime getting it out of the car and the bag broke. We walked into the woods and Norman showed me where to dig. We both started digging and after a little, Norm left to get a six-pack of beer. I kept digging. I just about had a seizure, I had to stop and rest. Norman came back with his beer, already drinking one. He stayed there for a while and then left again. It took quite a while to dig the hole. I got it about five and a half feet deep and figured it was deep enough. To tell you the truth, I suspected the hole was for Bruce Johnston Jr. Nobody said anything, but they had been talking about how Junior was talking and I figured that was what was going in the hole.

"I finished before Norm got back, so I walked down to the edge of the woods and watched for him. He came up the dirt road and walked up to the hole. I waited till he passed me and walked up behind him. I wanted to make sure there wasn't anyone with him and that he didn't have a gun. I didn't want to end up being the one in that hole. When I was sure everything was okay, I went up to him and said, 'Let's go.' We walked down to the road to wait for David. We left the shovels at the grave. We waited about a half hour for David to get there. I think he was driving Mrs. Johnston's car. I'm not sure. We went back to Louise's and I got my car and left."

As Mitchell was departing he was told to return to Mrs. Johnston's home that night. Mitchell did as he was told and he made sure he remembered to bring along his father's gun.

"When I got to Louise's, Jim Johnston was there and Louise was there. Bruce, Norman, and David were not. I just went in and watched TV. Shortly after I got there, Bruce, Norman, and David and the first kid in the hole arrived. I don't know his name. I only saw him maybe once before.

While there, I walked into the kitchen and one of the Johnston brothers—I can't remember which one—told me what
was coming down. He said, 'We are going to take him up to
the hole.' I heard Bruce telling the kid that we had a tractor
hid in the woods and we needed help to get it out. Bruce told
him that it would take at least three guys to push it out in
case it got stuck in the mud. We were at Louise's for about
twenty minutes and then we left.

"Bruce drove, Dave sat up front, Norman, the kid and I sat
in the back. I always sat in the back. I wasn't going to have
any of those guys behind me. I'm not sure whose car we used.
As we were leaving, I saw Bruce with a .22 caliber revolver.
It had a long barrel, maybe six inches. When we got into the
gate, Bruce got out; Dave went up—the kid—then me. Norman took the car and drove around. Bruce led the way and
I was last. Bruce had a big six-volt flashlight. When we got
about 10 feet from the hole, Bruce turned around and shined
the flashlight in the kid's eyes and then fired. I pulled my gun
and jumped to the side. Bruce fired three rapid shots. He was
at least ten feet away. Dave and Bruce drug him to the hole
and threw him in. Before that, they went through his pockets
and took his shoes off. I stayed back, like I said, I didn't feel
all too safe. They didn't cover him up or nothing. We left
right away and walked back to the road. Norman came by
right away and stopped. We all got in and Bruce said 'I got
to go pick up the other two.' That is the first I knew there
was going to be more. Bruce said something like he wanted
to put Leslie Dale in the hole, too, but he was afraid to bring
Leslie along because Leslie would screw it up."

Mitchell said they drove back to Kennett Square and
threw away the victim's shoes in a dumpster. Mitchell told
police he stayed with Mrs. Johnston while the three brothers
departed. The brothers returned with two other young men.
Johnston said he didn't know them. The Johnstons told the

two teenagers the story about the stuck tractor.

"Bruce gave Dave the gun and Dave said, 'This one is mine.' He had something to settle with the one kid, the second one in the grave. When we got to the gate, Bruce led the way again. The kid was second, then David, then me. Norman and the other kid drove around. When we got up to the hole, Bruce flashed the light several times and Dave pulled the gun and shot the kid in the back of the head, but he didn't fall. He started to turn around, holding his head, and David shot again, twice more. They went though his pockets and took his shoes off, and then threw him in the hole. One of them reloaded the gun and Dave handed it to me. He said, 'You take care of the next one.' I said that 'I don't have nothing in this' and he said, 'You got to,' to make sure we're all involved. I said I didn't want to be involved, but he said that I had to and I knew what he meant.

"I walked down to the road. I'm not sure about Dave; I think he waited at the hole. Bruce didn't stay at the hole. When the car came up, I told Norman and the third kid that we got the tractor stuck and we needed help to get it out. The kid was a little reluctant to come along. I told him that they sent me down to get him—they need help. We walked up, right to the hole and as I pulled out the gun, he turned around facing me. He must have heard me pulling the gun out. He looked at me and said, 'Is that a real gun?' I fired two shots at his face. I was real close. He fell right on the edge of the grave. Dave and Bruce went through his pockets and pushed him into the grave. They didn't take his shoes. I don't know why. They started covering him up with dirt and they said that I should help. I said that I dug the hole and they could fill it. They covered the kids up. They scatted some leaves over the grave, but that big limb, that was over the grave when I showed you guys, that was still attached to the tree. They told me later that they went back about two or thee days after the shooting and did that. I was not along when they put the limb over the grave.

"We went back to the car and took the shovels, the pick and the one kid's shoes. We went a short distance and stopped on a bridge. They shut the car off and jumped out, and got the two shovels out of the trunk. One of the Johnstons threw the two shovels off of the bridge into the creek. They didn't throw the pick. The shoes, they stopped at the same dumpster and threw them there. Then we went back to Louise's and I got my car and went home."

Mitchell said Johnston Sr. admitted the three teenagers were murdered to keep them from testifying before the grand jury. Mitchell also said Johnston Sr. kept his word and paid for repairs of his white Mercury car. Mitchell estimated the cost was $1,500. The car was repaired by Frank Reinert Jr., of Gilbertsville. Later, Mitchell told police that the gun used to kill the three teenagers was melted down and destroyed.

Law enforcement officers showed Mitchell a series of photographs and Mitchell selected the one of Jimmy Johnston as the victim shot by his stepfather, Bruce A. Johnston Sr. He believed he shot Wayne Sampson and he couldn't identify Dwayne Lincoln.

On January 9, 1978, Mitchell again talked to police about the triple murder and he added details that weren't contained in his first statement. Mitchell said he went with Norman Johnston to scout out the location for the grave. A site was chosen where David Johnston had shot a "white buck." Mitchell also said gang associate Jimmy Griffin was involved in the purchasing of the shovels and lime. Griffin, according to Mitchell, "was bitching that he didn't want to get involved in the killings. Norman and I were in the backseat and I told Norman that I didn't want him with us if that's the way he felt. When we got to Louise's, we took the stuff out of Griff's car and he left. He was too scared to go along."

Mitchell again described the murders and added to his first statement that he had fired and missed on his first shot. "The kid turned around and said 'Is that a real gun?' I put my arm up to my eyes to shield the light and I fired twice more."

THE NEXT DAY state policeman J. R. Campbell and county Detective Larry Dampman questioned the prosecution's other admitted murderer, Leslie Dale, regarding what he knew about the triple murder. Dale first admitted he had watched after Jimmy Johnston at the Oh Shaw Motel on Route 30 in Lancaster County on August 15 and 16. On August 17, the day after the murders, Dale said he went to Louise Johnston's home to find out what happened to the teenagers. Norman and David Johnston were there when he arrived. Norman Johnston then told him about the shootings, Dale said.

"Norman said that Jimmy Johnston was shot in the head and that Jimmy grabbed the back of his head and went down on his knees. Norman then said that Jimmy was a hard son of a bitch to kill and that when Jimmy went down we shot him again and he was still gurgling." Norman Johnston told Dale that Jimmy Johnston was probably alive when they filled the grave.

THE REVELATIONS BY Mitchell and Dale concerning the deaths of Jimmy Johnston, Dwayne Lincoln, and Wayne Sampson allowed the law enforcement team to reconstruct the events that led to the mid-August murders of the three young men, two weeks before the murder of Robin Miller and the shooting of Bruce A. Johnston Jr.

State policeman Tom Cloud remembers he became aware of Johnston Jr.'s willingness to cooperate at the end of July 1978 when he received a call from the Chester County District Attorney's office. "Bruce Jr. is a classic introvert," Cloud said. "Both his mother and father were introverts. He was mad because of his girlfriend. He fixated upon her while he was in jail. What pushed Johnston Jr. over the edge was when his father gave Robin alcohol, took her to a motel, and raped her. He then told us about what he knew about the thefts and it was essentially that they had been stealing tractors and turning them over to Dad. He was also aware where some of the tractors had gone, including to Otter in Pottstown."

Cloud said the police began to call the young thieves the kiddie gang. "They would steal a truck, steal a tractor, and steal gas to drive the stolen truck to steal a tractor," Cloud said. "There would be four police reports for one stolen tractor. The boys were tough on the paperwork. We thought it would strengthen the case by talking to the other boys. We saw Jimmy, Wayne, and Dwayne to get their cooperation. I clearly remember the day we had them all in the state police barrack, it was within 24 hours of when they died. We had them at the barracks and Bob Martz, Paul Yoder, and I literally put our change together so we went to the Penn Supreme store to buy lunchmeat and bread to make sandwiches for them. Another guy was there, older criminal, repeat criminal from a different group. He overheard us and did a scared straight routine for the kiddie gang members. He was telling them what would happen to them in prison."

The events that led to the death of the kiddie gang members, and especially Dwayne Lincoln, cause Cloud emotional distress even today.

Cloud said during the investigation of the tractor thefts the police discovered that a vocational technical teacher from Delaware County, Tom Rebert, was selling stolen tractors. Rebert's connection with the Johnstons, Cloud believed, was through the Hamm family. Raymond Hamm, brother of convicted police killer Ancell Hamm, was one of his students. In early August 1978 a John Deere tractor dealership in Bloomsburg, Pennsylvania, had a number of tractors stolen. Through phone records, police knew Rebert was talking with Johnston associates. The officers then paid a call at Rebert's home.

"We saw the garage door open and a John Deere tractor crate," Cloud said. "We believed it came from the Bloomsburg robbery. We went to Lieutenant Dick Weimer (chief of the Avondale barracks of the state police) and asked for authorization to watch Rebert's house. Weimer told us we could go but he had a concern about paying us overtime. He said if we made an arrest he would pay us half of the overtime we were due and if we didn't make an arrest we wouldn't get paid anything. We were going no matter what. We worked all night and we saw Dave Johnston's truck pull into Rebert's driveway and it was loaded.

"We asked Upper Chichester police to stop the truck and I went back to the Upper Chichester police department to type a search warrant. While I was there a report came in that a man with a gun was behind the Conchester Bowling Alley. I called Dave Richter and we made sure the police officer at Rebert's house wouldn't respond to the call. Another police car went to the bowling alley and the call turned out to be false. The Johnstons were trying to get police away from the Rebert home so they could move the truck.

"I typed the search warrant. Earlier I had talked to Dwayne Lincoln and he had told me about another tractor theft with one of the other kids and that David paid them for the job. I added that fact to the probable cause warrant. Later on, when Ricky Mitchell told me that when Dwayne Lincoln was taken to the field to be killed David Johnston said this one is mine. I know that David Johnston said so because of my quoting Dwayne Lincoln in that search warrant. The fact that Dwayne Lincoln would have been killed anyway is of little consolation to me. I'm not a person who blames Bill Clinton or George Bush for people flying into towers, I blame the people who planned and carried it out. I try not to blame myself but there is a lot involved. I was trying to do what was right."

Cloud said he doesn't remember if Weimer paid them overtime for the night's work. "I do know we were paid some for the trials and I made the most money in my life the year (1980) of the trials, $28,000."

DAVE RICHTER AND other FBI agents joined the state police, county detectives, and other law enforcement officers in spending numerous hours investigating the Johnstons.

Richter recalled, "One morning we were doing surveillance in Chester County and about 8:00 or 9:00 in the morning two of the Johnstons' trucks pulled into the Radio Shack store on Route 41 in Chatham. They bought some supplies and we followed that day from Avondale to Harrisburg and Williamsport and then to New York to Troy and Elmira. I don't know how many miles we went. We watched them steal some vehicles. Their plan was to park their trucks on a mountaintop and take the stolen trucks to steal the John Deere equipment. While police were looking for the stolen trucks that would be used in the burglary, the Johnstons would return to the mountaintop and transfer the stolen tractors to their trucks and return home. We followed them for 30 hours and the burglary didn't happen. It was a loss. We knew then what we were dealing with."

Not all surveillances ran smoothly, some were dangerous and some had a less serious side. Richter recalled one that involved police in Elmira, New York. The FBI was using an airplane for surveillance work and handheld radios were used for communication. Because of the long hours the batteries in the radios needed to be changed and one FBI car had a trunk full of radios. The FBI enlisted the aid of a county sheriff's office to take radios to an airport but one sheriff refused to believe an FBI agent on the plane was authentic because of his long hair and beard. "The agent, Mike Sandell, was working undercover. The sheriff made him go back to the plane to get his identification."

There were few amusing moments during the summer of 1978. As the investigation continued, the FBI used the Treadway Inn, West Chester, as a base of operations. "Some of the agents were staying at the inn and we had cars in the parking lot," Richter said. "We had an agent in the parking lot because we knew the Johnstons were trying to identify the agents' vehicles. One night David, Norman, and Bruce Johnston Sr. and gang associate Jimmy Griffin were in the parking lot and approached one of the cars. The agent in the parking lot notified the agents inside the inn. They came out with guns drawn and shotguns. The Johnstons retreated to Griffin's car and they tried to escape by driving up a hill and into a garden where Griffin's car became stuck. Some tickets were given but that incident made everyone more aware how aggressive these people were."

Law enforcement agents certainly knew on August 9, 1978, that the Johnstons were after their identification. That evening at 10:00 PM FBI agents Judith Brown, Michael Zizzo and Albert Bodnar were checking Norman Johnston's Kennett Square apartment. While approaching Kennett Square Bodnar spotted a car driven by Susan Johnston, Norman's wife. In the car was Susan Johnston, another woman, and a child. Bodnar was in one car while Zizzo and Brown were in a second FBI vehicle. At one point the Johnston vehicle pulled along Bodnar's car and the woman in the car with Susan Johnston took three photographs of Bodnar. When Brown and Zizzo passed the Johnston vehicle, they also had their photographs taken.

Despite the intimidation tactics the law enforcement team continued to apply pressure to the gang associates to get them to cooperate. "The cat was out of the bag that we were searching for evidence," Richter said. "We were turning up the pressure all over the place. We went to Phoenixville and got a bunch of tractors back. We didn't have a vehicle that could transport the first load so we borrowed a truck from a mushroom grower. We ran into one guy who was cutting his lawn with a big John Deere tractor. The guy was sick. He said his wife was going to kill him. She didn't want him to buy the tractor in the first place. He then asked to be allowed to finish cutting his grass before we took the tractor.

"We flipped Otter and Schonely and they began cooperating. Schonely was a workaholic, a decent man. We put pressure on these guys. We were applying pressure everywhere we could. Everyone was scared. That is the point I went to see Doug Richardson in the United States Attorney's office. We were dealing with three brothers and members of their gang that didn't fit into the traditional organized crime element. But they were organized."

Richter recalls giving Jimmy Johnston a subpoena at the state police barracks in Avondale. Johnston was to appear before the grand jury the next day and police told him not to tell anyone about the subpoena. "Jimmy admitted what Johnston Jr. was telling us about the thefts was true. He was agreeable to testify before the grand jury. The next day I went back to the barracks to get Jimmy and he didn't appear. The Oxford carnival was going on at the time and we had information that Johnston Sr. had seen Jimmy the night before at the carnival. We weren't concerned that the witnesses were dead; we figured the Johnstons were hiding them in various motels. We didn't believe we were looking at homicides at that point. They were bad guys though, absolutely. Then came August 30 and the murder of Robin Miller."

LESLIE DALE, A murderer himself, almost tipped off the police about the murderous plans of the Johnstons. Richter said in mid-August 1978 he received a call from Dale. Dale wanted to meet Richter at the Wayside Bar on Route 322 outside of Downingtown. They were to meet at 2:00 PM. Richter and FBI agent Bill Whalen were at the bar but Dale didn't show. Later, Richter said, Dale told him that he was going to tell Richter that he was offered the contract to kill Johnston Jr. "That was a week to 10 days before the shootings at the Miller farmhouse."

MITCHELL POSSESSED THE key information on the one missing gang member, James Sampson, and during the afternoon of January 4, 1979, he was ready to talk to state policemen Tom Cloud and Bob Martz. Mitchell was taken to the Longwood Inn where the interview was conducted. He told police:

"Norm and David Johnston and I met at Louise's and Jimmy Sampson and Bruce came up to the house, it was in the evening sometime after the triple murder happened. Prior to this Bruce had said in a conversation I overheard with Jimmy Dotson that (Dotson owed Johnston Sr. $4,000). I remember Bruce saying someone has to go, and he was meaning someone else other than Bruce, Norm, Dave, and I. Dotson and Bruce walked around the side of the building. Anyhow, this night that I'm talking about when Bruce and Jimmy Sampson came up to Louise's and met Dave, Norm, and I. We went to Norm's T-bird and drove to a dump. We had walkie-talkies and everything like we were going to do a burglary. Dave kept a walkie-talkie and he drove the car back and forth. Bruce had a walkie-talkie. We were walking out into the dump and I said that his place smells like a dump and Sampson started to say something like the same thing and that is when I heard a shot and I started to pull my gun because I did not know what was going on at that time. There was only one shot. I looked and saw Norman."

The price for the murder was $10,000 to be split among them, Mitchell quoted Johnston Sr. as saying. Mitchell said the murder weapon was his father's gun and Mitchell had sold the weapon to Johnston Sr. for $75. Later Mitchell's father, Ray, confirmed that one of his .22-caliber pistols was missing.

Four days later Mitchell divulged additional details of the murder. As to the planning, Mitchell said he told the Johnston brothers he wasn't going to dig any more graves because the last one nearly killed him. "Bruce said we could put him in a landfill, like so-and-so. I don't remember the guy's name that he mentioned, but he said someone else was in the landfill. It was finally agreed to take Sampson to the landfill on the pretense that we were going to do a burglary. It was said that everyone would get a full share of $10,000....It was also said by David that Norman would do this killing, it was his turn."

As for the night of the murder, Mitchell said, "We all went in Norm's T-bird to the landfill and we went in like it was planned, Norm told me to stay by a bulldozer that was parked in there. They brought Sampson in, I did not stay by the bulldozer, I went to another location, Norm and Sampson were walking towards the bulldozer and Bruce was over on the side on a hill to make sure no one was coming. I walked up behind Norm and Sampson and I told them I was okay but that I lost my glasses near the bulldozer. They went over like they were looking for the glasses and Norm shot Sampson on the right side of the head and he went right down. Bruce came down and he and Norman kicked out a hole in the garbage and then Bruce grabbed his hands and Norm and I each took a leg. Bruce went though his pockets before we put him in the hole. Bruce took a wallet from him. He had no money on him that I knew about. They threw stuff on top of him. We then went and hooked up with Dave. Bruce told Dave that Sampson was dead before he hit the ground."

Mitchell said they took Sampson's car to the Philadelphia International Airport and left it in the parking lot. The next day, Mitchell said, Johnston Sr. dropped off $2,500, his share of the murder payment.

CHAPTER TEN

Murder Charges Lodged

With the revelations by Ricky Mitchell and Leslie Dale concerning the multiple murders, the law enforcement team wanted Norman Johnston back in custody. Norman Johnston had been free since December 19, 1978, when he was released from federal custody. The Johnston brother had been keeping out of sight.

State policemen Tom Cloud and J. R. Campbell at one point stopped the car of Susie Johnston, Norman's wife, along Route 1 looking for Norman Johnston. A search of the car, including the trunk, didn't yield the wanted man.

"We received a call from Kennett Square police," Campbell said. "They had stopped a cousin of the Johnston brothers who was driving Norman's car. In the car was a key for the Red Coach Motor Inn in Aberdeen, Maryland. The relative was held by Kennett Square police and wasn't allowed to make any phone calls. We didn't want him alerting the Johnstons."

Campbell and state policeman Paul Yoder went to Maryland and contacted the Maryland State Police. Maryland troopers joined them at the hotel and a front desk person was shown a photo of Norman Johnston. The wanted man was registered at the hotel but under an assumed name. Norman Johnston wasn't there when the police first checked. A search warrant was obtained to make sure it was Norman Johnston's room.

"We knew he would be back," Campbell said. "I called the Avondale barracks to see if I was authorized to spend $50 to rent a room next to Johnston's room. These are some of the things we had to put up with during the investigation. My request for the authorization was passed along to Lancaster troop headquarters. We were asked if we couldn't just wait outside the hotel. We wanted to be in the room next to him. It would make for an easier arrest. We were part of a major homicide investigation and they wouldn't authorize the spending of $50. I said forget it and paid for the room myself."

Yoder recalls staying at the motel more than 12 hours before Norman Johnston drove up to the hotel in a car that had been stolen in Philadelphia. "The Maryland trooper asked if he was Johnston and he said no," Yoder said. "I stuck my head in the room and said 'the hell you ain't.'" Norman Johnston, according to Yoder, said, "Yoder, you aren't allowed to be in Maryland." Yoder added, "I'll never forget that."

Norman Johnston was arrested on burglary warrants. He had black clothing and a ski mask in the room along with a police monitor. "It was state-of-the-art," Yoder said. "You could hear all of the police monitors. The trooper made a bet that Johnston didn't have the confidential state police channel. He called for a test and Johnston had it programmed on the monitor."

On January 13, 1979, at 5:00 PM, Assistant District Attorney Dolores Troiani, Chester County Chief County Detective Charles Zagorskie, and state policemen Tom Cloud and Bob Martz interviewed Norman Johnston at the Maryland State Police barracks in Bel Air. After being advised of his constitutional rights, Johnston said he wanted to make a deal. Johnston told the police they were receiving incorrect information and for a deal on the burglary charges he would cooperate. Troiani and Zagorskie told Johnston they didn't travel to Maryland to talk about burglaries; they wanted information on the five murders. Norman Johnston denied killing anyone.

The fifteen minute conversation was terminated after Johnston said he wanted to return to Pennsylvania to obtain an attorney to work out a deal for him. On January 16 Norman Johnston changed his mind about returning to Pennsylvania and refused to waive his extradition rights. He was held in Harford County Detention Center, Bel Air, after failing to post $215,000 bail.

Federal agents took custody of Johnston on federal charges on January 16 and brought him back to Philadelphia, ending Johnston's attempt to fight extradition and stay in Maryland.

THE DAY BEFORE Norman Johnston's hearing in Maryland, Bruce Johnston Sr.'s attorney, John J. Duffy, was in Chester County court asking Common Pleas Judge Leonard Sugerman to order the prosecution to stop talking about the Johnstons. "I feel devastated sitting in Philadelphia, picking up the paper and seeing my client described as a crumb-bum." Duffy wanted the "adverse hostile publicity" stopped. District Attorney William H. Lamb said the investigators "have been extremely careful to release only the relevant facts."

Lamb also noted no one had been charged with the murders and that Duffy's request was premature. Judge Sugerman didn't rule on the motion and took the matter under advisement. When reporters later asked Duffy about the hearing, Duffy said it would be illogical to make the request to stem publicity and then discuss it with the media.

On January 26, 1979, Judge Sugerman did issue an order that limited information that was to be given to reporters.

POLICE WERE ALSO receiving information concerning the whereabouts of Jimmy Sampson, murder victim Wayne Sampson's older brother. Statements from Mitchell indicated Norman Johnston shot Jimmy Sampson at the Lanchester landfill, which is on the border of Chester and Lancaster counties near Honey Brook. The Johnstons were afraid Jimmy Sampson would cause trouble over the disappearance of his brother.

State police contacted Francis Fair of the Pennsylvania Department of Environmental Resources about conducting a search of the landfill. On January 22, 1979, Fair told police that the landfill encompassed an area of approximately ten acres and was 70 feet deep. He said about 800 to 1,000 tons of refuse was dumped in the landfill each day.

Fair told police that any attempt to find a body would take weeks or months and would involve numerous environmental problems, including odor and birds. A large number of birds would descend on the landfill if a dig took place.

The information on James Sampson's death came from Ricky Mitchell. Mitchell told police that the Johnstons were worried that Sampson would make good on his promise of going to the police if they had harmed his younger brother, Wayne. At that time Wayne was already dead. Mitchell said the Johnstons recruited James Sampson to go with them to the landfill on August 21, 1978, to commit a theft. The real reason for the trip was to kill Sampson and Norman Johnston shot Sampson, according to Mitchell.

Sampson's body was buried in the landfill and never found.

IN LATE JANUARY the police were also reinterviewing
David "Buffalo" Schonely and Ed Otter, the two fences from
the Pottstown area. On January 23, Schonely told police that
he had purchased two tractors from Johnston Sr. in April
1977. On November 8, 1978, he said he was summoned to
Ed Otter's home to talk to the Johnstons. "We were all in
the kitchen. I remember Bruce had a newspaper and when
he put it on the table, the headlines were about digging up a
body. The discussion went on about changing lawyers. I was
also told that if I was called before the grand jury to blame
Jimmy Johnston and Jimmy Sampson for the crimes. I said
that I wouldn't because it would be an out and out lie. They
said you can use Jimmy Johnston's name because nobody will
ever see him again. They said that Ed and I were the only
two guys that could put the finger on them. We talked about
Bruce Jr. cooperating with police and Bruce Sr. stated, 'It's a
shame he didn't die.'"

Schonely also told police that on the day after the Miller
murder he was at the home of Louise Johnston. He said he
went with Johnston Sr. to buy a newspaper. At the store,
Schonely said, Johnston Sr. tried to conceal his identity from
a man who got into a car that said Longwood Gardens on
the door. "We robbed that place and I guess he might know
it is me," Johnston Sr. commented, according to Schonely.

On the same day Zagorskie and state policeman Gabe
Bolla also interviewed Otter. Otter also talked about the
November 8 meeting with the three Johnston brothers,
Schonely and gang associate James Dotson. Otter said it was
the first time Schonely had met David Johnston. "They said
Dave could stare someone in the eye and tell if he was okay
or not and we were sitting there in the kitchen, Dave sure
was staring at Buffalo," Otter said.

Otter also disclosed statements made by the Johnstons
during the months between the August killings and the end

of 1979. When discussing the missing kiddie gang members, Norman Johnston said, "Let's put it this way, you'll never see them again." Johnston Sr. also talked about killing a police informant, Kenny Howell, and state policeman Tom Cloud. "He (Johnston Sr.) said Cloud was a gung-ho cop and Bruce talked very badly of him. One other time Bruce mentioned to me that he didn't care about anyone, he didn't care who they killed and he was only worried about himself." Howell, a police informant, was not murdered.

POLICE ALSO WANTED to question another gang associate, James "Disco" Griffin. The police had warrants charging Griffin with robbery, burglary, and conspiracy. His girlfriend, Jean Masciantonio, told police that Griffin was in Florida. On January 25 Griffin contacted state policeman Paul Yoder asking if any warrants were outstanding against him. He said he was working at a restaurant in Miami Beach and he would voluntarily surrender to police. Chief County Detective Zagorskie told Griffin he would pay for Griffin's airline ticket to Philadelphia and arrangements were made for Griffin to return on January 25. Griffin was not on the flight but later told police that he was advised by a Florida attorney to not to return to Philadelphia.

Law enforcement officials finally charged Griffin with being a conspirator in the deaths of the three members of the kiddie gang. At the time Griffin was being held in the Dade County jail in Miami. Griffin finally made a deal with the prosecuting team to testify against the Johnstons and returned to Pennsylvania.

JIMMY GRIFFIN HAD reason to fear the Johnstons. He recalled driving a car with the Johnston brothers and Johnston Sr. put a shotgun to the back of his head. Griffin told Johnston Sr. to remove the gun or he would wreck the car and kill all of them. During another crime, a home invasion, Griffin was acting as a lookout. The Johnstons had sawed-off shotguns and took jewelry and cash. I could hear them screaming. That scared me. All it took was one idiot to pull the trigger. It was scary. They were desperate."

The Johnstons, especially Norman, weren't always polished professionals. Griffin said one time they were casing a home to rob near Exton, Pennsylvania. The owner reportedly had lots of money. "We were outside waiting for the man to go to bed and Norman accidentally shot off his gun," Griffin said. "Another time Norman was being chased by police and Norman ran the car off the road. David was real upset."

Griffin said he first met the Hamm brothers, associates of the Johnstons, when he was in 10th grade in Kennett Square High School and became friendly with Raymond Hamm. "We would steal tires and shit like that and cars. They didn't bring me in on too many jobs. One time I ran away from home and stayed with Raymond and Ancell Hamm and their mother. I then went to western Pennsylvania with my mother. They would come out and we would do a burglary. I was arrested and spent two years in prison for burglary and stealing a car."

When he was released Griffin returned to Kennett Square where he began stealing John Deere tractors and robbing gas stations. Griffin said Rebert, the vocational-technical teacher, would buy any type of stolen items they had, including a number of tractors. Also, Griffin said they took stolen items to a large flea market in New Jersey where the Cow Town rodeo is held. Another favorite target was drugstores where they would steal amphetamines.

Griffin said he never understood why the Johnstons resorted to murder. "A good attorney and they might have done a year or two. They didn't do anything that bad to commit murder. As they say, once you commit one crime you have to keep on going. They were unusual people. Money and power were their motivations. They thought they were invincible. They were arrogant. They had attorneys from West Chester and believed no one could touch them. After they shot Robin Miller, they knew they screwed up."

Griffin said he was offered $2,000 to dig the graves for the three members of the kiddie gang. "If I was greedy, I would have taken that money and I would have been in the grave with them. I got along with them but I was an outsider to them." Griffin also recalled a conversation between David and Johnston Sr. when David asked about being paid for shooting Johnston Jr. Johnston Sr., according to Griffin, said, "Why should I pay you? The motherfucker is still alive and he is going to testify against me. David then said, 'don't say anything in front of Disco.' They stopped talking."

On Christmas Day 1978 Griffin and his girlfriend were in Miami Beach. The Johnstons contacted him, wanting to tell him what to say to police.

ON JANUARY 26, 1979, police went to District Magistrate Eugene J. DiFillippo, Jr. in Kennett Square to lodge homicide charges against Ricky Mitchell. Mitchell's co-defendants would be charged in a matter of days.

THE MURDER CHARGES against the Johnston brothers came on Monday, January 29, 1979. State policemen Bob Martz and Paul Yoder went to the Philadelphia Detention Center in Philadelphia and transported Johnston Sr. and Norman Johnston to the state police barracks in Avondale. At 10:15 AM Johnston Sr. was advised of his rights and charged with six counts of homicide in connection with the deaths of Robin Marie Miller, James Alex Simpson, Gary Wayne Crouch, James David Johnston, Dwayne Howell Lincoln, and Wayne David Sampson.

At 9:30 AM Chester County Detective Larry Dampman and state policeman Tom Cloud picked up David Johnston at the Chester County Farms Prison and took him to Avondale where he was charged with five counts of murder. He was not charged with Crouch's death. After arraignment David Johnston was taken to Lehigh County jail by Constable Wilson Fox.

Yoder returned Norman Johnston to Philadelphia Detention Center after his arraignment on five murder charges. He also wasn't charged with Crouch's murder. During his ride to Philadelphia Norman Johnston commented on a radio report that the three Johnston brothers were being charged with murder. He said Jimmy Johnston was not Johnston Sr.'s son. He then asked about the deals for gang associates Ricky Mitchell and Roy Myers. Norman Johnston said he would strangle Myers if he had the chance.

The news of the murder charges was given during a press conference held in the Chester County Courthouse. Sitting before television cameras and print reporters were District Attorney William Lamb, Assistant District Attorney Dolores Troiani, Assistant United States Attorney Douglas Richardson, state police Lieutenant Richard Weimer, and Assistant District Attorney James P. MacElree II.

Besides the murder charges against the Johnston brothers, reporters were told of the five murder counts against Ricky Mitchell and the one against Leslie Dale. Lamb told reporters that the murders were committed to eliminate witnesses who could give police information concerning criminal activity of the gang.

Jenny Johnston, the mother of Johnston Jr. and the slain

Jimmy Johnston, was contacted by a reporter on the day the murder charges were filed. "I just hate them," Jenny Johnston said of her former husband, Johnston Sr., and his brothers, Norman and David Johnston. Jenny Johnston said since the previous August when Jimmy disappeared and Johnston Jr. was shot, her life was miserable. Jenny and Johnston Sr. divorced in 1972, six years before the murders. She told the reporter that she suspected the Johnstons were involved but she really didn't know who committed the shootings.

"I hope they get what they deserve," Jenny Johnston said. "I hope they give to them what they gave to those kids."

CHAPTER ELEVEN

A Year of Investigations

Lieutenant Richard Weimer of the Pennsylvania State Police made one of the biggest understatements of the case when he told reporters during a news conference on January 29, 1979, that some investigative leads needed to be followed before cases were ready for trial.

The investigative leads and legal maneuvering by the attorneys involved in the case would take the law enforcement team across Pennsylvania for the next twelve months. In the process hundreds of leads were investigated and a multitude of witnesses and potential witnesses were questioned by police. Many had little or nothing to add to the investigation but all leads were checked.

The lengthy process to prepare for the murder trials was taking a toll on the defense, especially the defense's ability to pay for legal representation. In January attorney Robert Landis asked to be relieved from representing Johnston Sr. During an arraignment before District Justice Eugene Di-Fillippo at the end of January all three of the Johnston brothers said they were without legal counsel.

THE JOHNSTONS MIGHT have been without legal representation but they had their defense strategy set. The Johnstons were placing the blame for the murders squarely on former associates Ricky Mitchell and Leslie Dale.

On February 1, 1979, Pennsylvania State Policeman Bernard Dickerson and a member of the United States Marshal Service transported Johnston Sr. from the Philadelphia Detention Center to the district justice court in Coatesville. Johnston Sr. told Dickerson, "Ricky Mitchell is crazy and I don't know why you are listening to him, Mitchell is a killer and insane." Dickerson reported to the investigative team that Johnston Sr. was quite emphatic about Mitchell being a killer and that Mitchell was insane.

TRANSPORTATION OF PRISONERS and lodging and protection of witnesses posed logistical problems for the law enforcement team for more than a year. Protecting Mitchell and Dale from harm was a major concern and the law enforcement team enlisted the aid of business and civic leaders. The Burroughs Corporation complex in eastern Chester County was used to house Mitchell at one time early in 1979.

Norman Johnston was certainly interested in Mitchell's location and tried to extract information from state policeman Joseph Blackburn during a February 11, 1979, transport from the Philadelphia Detention Center to a preliminary hearing. As for Mitchell, Norman Johnston said, "That man is a basket case. I mean he already admitted to killing six people. I can't believe you guys are listening to him. You better watch out, if you keep talking to him he might admit to killing more people." Norman Johnston at one point was direct, asking, "Where are you keeping Mitchell?" When Blackburn said he didn't know, Norman Johnston said, "Bullshit, you know, you're keeping him at his mother and father's."

Norman Johnston also said he was glad he wasn't being housed with Dale at Chester County Prison. "Well, I'm glad I'm not over there," Norman Johnston said, "This way if he gets killed, you can't blame it on me."

Another piece of information being sought by the Johnstons involved former gang associate Jimmy Griffin. "Did those guys get back from Florida with that Griffin guy?" Norman Johnston asked. Blackburn didn't reply.

In fact, Griffin wasn't brought from Florida to Chester County until February 17, 1979. State policeman Gabe Bolla and Chester County Detective Larry Dampman went to Dade County, Florida, for a hearing before Judge Arthur Winton where Griffin voluntarily agreed to be extradited to Pennsylvania. Griffin was then charged with conspiracy to commit murder. Upon his arrival in Pennsylvania, Griffin was taken before District Justice John Catanese, sitting in West Chester, arraigned and released on $1 bail into the custody of the Chester County District Attorney's office.

Griffin told police the reason for his fleeing Pennsylvania to Florida, "The Johnstons don't value human life before and I know they won't have any value on mine, and I would be on their list, that's why I left."

Griffin was taken to the Treadway Inn and on February 18 he met with his attorney, Michael Kean. Kean had told Griffin he wouldn't represent him if Griffin had committed any of the murders. Also at the inn was Griffin's protective detail, state policemen Robert Martz and Tom Cloud, Chief Chester County Detective Charles Zagorskie, and Assistant District Attorney Dolores Troiani.

At 11:00 AM Kean told the law enforcement team that Griffin would cooperate totally and would answer all questions concerning his knowledge of the homicide.

"The first time I knew anything about any murders being

planned was the day we bought the shovels and lime," Griffin told the members of the prosecution team. "I was in Lake George, New York, the first week in August and it was maybe a week or so after that. I think this thing with the shovels was maybe a Tuesday or Wednesday. I was in New York again, when Robin Miller was killed, and this was before that.

"Bruce, Norm, and Dave Johnston and Ricky Mitchell came to my apartment early one morning. They may have called first, I'm not sure. When they got there, they got me out of bed. I was busy washing up and brushing my teeth, and they were sitting in the living room talking. I didn't hear anything that was being said and I don't remember all of the exact conversation, but I do remember Bruce saying something about one of those kids getting a subpoena to testify before the grand jury and Norman saying that Dwayne Lincoln and Wayne Sampson would talk too. 'All of those kids are friends and they'll stick together,' he said. Norman or Dave also said to Bruce, 'You know, those kids sold you a lot of stuff, tractors and tailgates; they can really hurt you.'

"When I came out of the bathroom, Bruce was ready to leave. At this point, I didn't know anyone planned to kill anyone. They must have come in the same car because Bruce said that he was going to leave and Dave said, 'All right, we'll get Griff to drop us off.' Then Dave said, 'We'll take care of our end, you just take care of yours.' Bruce told them he'd meet them back at Mrs. Johnston's at 7:00 or 7:30, and Norm or Dave said, 'Just be there!' Like I said, the exact conversation is vague.

"Bruce left and the rest of us went in my car. I drove and Dave sat up front. Mitchell sat behind Dave and Norman sat behind me. We left my apartment and Dave told me to go to Gawthrop's. I pulled in and Dave told Mitchell to go in and get two shovels. Mitchell asked if he should get an axe or something because they might have to cut some roots.

Honestly man, I didn't know what was going on but I started getting the picture. I said to Dave, 'Hey what are you guys up to?' Dave answered that they were going to bury somebody, the exact words I don't remember. He made some smart remark about a new mailman for someone, a groundhog, or something. Then Norm said they were going to bury some snitches, plural.

"Norman asked me if I wanted part of the action. I told him that I'd rather not and then Mitchell came out. Dave reached over and hit the automatic trunk release and Mitchell put the shovels in my trunk. Dave asked him something about the lime and they argued. Mitchell walked back inside and came walking out with a bag of lime. I asked Dave what the lime was for and he told me that it makes the bodies rot. Then, he started getting on me about not having the heart to kill, the guts. Mitchell came back and got in the car. He was saying something about wanting to kill a guy named Steve from Chester. This Steve dimed Mitchell out about having a gun to the cops and they hit his place with a search warrant. At this point, I wasn't sure who they were going to kill. I thought they might be digging a grave for this Steve.

"We started heading toward Manuel's (Johnston) and they all started riding me, calling me a pussy, and telling me I had no heart. They were really downing me and I said, "Hey man, I'm a burglar, not a murderer.' Someone said, 'You mean you couldn't kill someone that's putting you in jail?' I said that I was in jail before and I'd just pull my time. Dave then asked me if I didn't want to make some good money. Mitchell called me a pussy and Dave said that all I'd have to do is drop them off to dig the hole. I said that I'd rather not. He said it again, that all I'd have to do is drop them off and pick them up, and I said, 'What about the FBI? What if they're following us or something?' Norman said, 'Fuck the FBI.'

"Norman said, 'Fuck it, we'll take care of it ourselves, take us to my car.' It was down at Manuel's. Dave said something about wanting to use his truck but they didn't. I don't think, because when we go to Manuel's, they took the stuff out of my car and put it in Norman's Thunderbird. As they were putting the stuff, two shovels and lime, into Norman's car, they agreed that Mitchell and Norm would do the digging. They were also looking for something to put dirt on so nobody could see any signs of digging, a tarp or tar paper or roofing paper. They put something like that in Norman's car. Norman wanted some water and Mitchell wanted some booze, it was really hot that day.

"They really started getting on me again. It was around 11 AM or so, I think, and I believe I had a date with my girl for lunch because Dave kept saying, 'Oh, go play with your pussy,' and 'go stick your head up her ass,' and stuff like that. Norman and Mitchell kept saying that I just didn't have any heart. Then Dave said to me, 'I'm disappointed in you man.' I told him that I just didn't want to get involved and he said, 'You are already involved.' I left."

Griffin continued his statement to police and discussed later conversations with the Johnstons. Griffin said during October and November of 1979 they would drive to Delaware and the Johnstons would have him go down Tea House Road, also known as Cossart Road, near the site of the grave. "They would always get me to slow down at the same spot," Griffin said. "They were just too worried about the spot. I figured that's where they dug the grave."

The Johnstons were upset that Dale was cooperating and were worried about Mitchell also talking, according to Griffin. Griffin recalled a conversation at Mrs. Johnston's home where Dave told Norman, 'You should have shot Mitchell and left him in the hole with the other three.' Norman said that he would have but Mitchell had a gun and he wouldn't give it up. I heard Dave say that to Norm at lease twice."

Griffin's interview concluded at 2:50 PM that day but Griffin wasn't through giving statements. On February 20, 1979, he was again questioned and told trooper Robert Martz that he had had numerous conversations with the Johnston brothers concerning the killings. The Johnstons said "the groundhog is their new mailman" and David Johnston told his mother that she'd see a hand coming out of her garden when she picked tomatoes, according to Griffin. Griffin also said he was threatened. David Johnston told Griffin, "The shovels are still out in the shed, if I didn't act right, I'd join Sampson," Griffin told police. Johnston Sr. said the FBI search for the missing kids should include a visit to a groundhog. "Why didn't the FBI go and see the groundhog? He can tell them where to find them." The Johnstons made hundreds of remarks, Griffin said. "So much was said during that three-month period that I knew Bruce, Norm, and Dave and Mitchell were the ones."

The next day, February 21, Griffin was asked about hearing any threats against Leslie Dale. He had. "At Mrs. Johnston's just after Dave received a letter from Dick Donnell saying that Dale had snitched on him (Donnell). Dave was saying to Bruce, 'You should have went ahead with Dale.' Bruce said to Dave that he would have, but he couldn't find him. Bruce said something like 'things just weren't right that night.' Dave just said, 'You fuckin guys!' One other time Dave told me that Mitchell was going to kill Dale one night. Dave told me that Mitchell was riding with Bruce looking for Dale, but they couldn't find him."

State policemen J. R. Campbell and Robert Martz also asked about the killing of informant Gary Wayne Crouch. Griffin said the Johnstons discussed digging up Crouch's body and taking the remains to a quarry and destroying the remains. Once Johnston Sr. made the comment that he had given Crouch a new job. "He said that Gary wasn't snitching anymore, but was pushing up daisies," Griffin told police.

During the same interview Griffin said the Johnston brothers also talked about "assassinating Kenny Howell." Howell met the Johnstons through Francis Matherly, a Johnston associate who used to own a speed shop in Kennett Square. Howell had an interest in cars, especially Corvettes. Howell admitted being involved in stolen cars with the Johnston brothers and taking part in other crimes. After being arrested Howell cooperated with police.

WHILE GRIFFIN PROVIDED inside information on the workings of the Johnstons and statements that indicated the Johnstons were guilty of murder, Griffin also had his issues as a witness. When county Detective Dampman and trooper Gabe Bolla picked up Griffin in Florida, a cellmate of Griffin said Griffin had admitted to the murder of Robin Miller and an FBI agent.

Dampman, Bolla and two Dade County, Florida, law enforcement officials interviewed inmate Leslie Monroe at 3:00 PM on February 15, 1979. Monroe, who lived in Miami, said Griffin admitted shooting a girl two times and an FBI man four times. Monroe said the issue of *Time* magazine that reported on the Johnston case was circulated in the prison. Monroe told the officers that Griffin "said he was the one who shot the girl two times in the mouth with a .45 caliber automatic pistol, and some guy named Richie shot the boy with her eight times. They were driving a yellow Volkswagen." Monroe also said Griffin admitted killing an FBI agent in March 1977. Monroe also said he had information on the other murders and he would gladly volunteer to go to Pennsylvania to testify.

One of the Dade County officers cautioned Dampman and Bolla that "Monroe didn't always tell the truth" and that

Monroe had a mental problem. On the surface Monroe's story had problems. Miller was shot once with a different caliber weapon.

Louise Johnston, mother of the Johnston brothers, told police on March 19, 1979, that Griffin was "the biggest liar of all." Mrs. Johnston also called Mitchell a "liar." She then gave her sons David and Norman an alibi for the night of the Miller murder. She said the two brothers and other members of her family were at her home watching Elvis Presley on television and that David stayed the night at her home because of an upset stomach.

AFTER GRIFFIN BEGAN cooperating, the prosecution looked for opportunities to have him relocated while he waited to testify. Griffin and his girlfriend Jeannie were in Florida where Griffin was working for a survey company and Jeannie as a hairdresser. Somebody from Kennett Square visited the establishment where Jeannie worked, so the couple believed the Johnstons would find them.

The couple drove back to Pennsylvania and Detective Larry Dampman met them halfway and accompanied them back to Chester County. Meanwhile Zagorskie and Troiani were trying to get Griffin into the Federal Witness Protection Program. The marshals wouldn't take them unless they were married so a wedding was arranged.

"Blood tests were done and I approached (Judge) Rob Gawthrop while he was on the bench during a trial," Troiani said. "I said I need an emergency order to allow a wedding and I need him to do the wedding. Gawthrop turned to the jury and said I need to set a wedding with this young woman."

Troiani went into Judge Gawthrop's chambers and told him the story. "I went home and got a dress for her and Larry (Dampman) got her a ring," Troiani said. "The FBI

brought the champagne. Mike Kean had the flowers. At 7:00
PM Rob (Judge Gawthrop) sang and married them. Charlie
(Zagorskie) stood for the bride and Judge Marrone was in
the wedding. She later died of cancer."

BEFORE THE FIRST preliminary hearing on murder
charges on March 5, 1979, the Johnstons had new court-
appointed attorneys from Chester County. Anthony Picciotti represented Johnston Sr., John Lachall represented
David Johnston, and Larry Goldberg represented Norman
Johnston.

The preliminary hearing was held in the Chester County
Courthouse in West Chester amid tight security. Law enforcement officials were worried not only about the safety of
prosecution witnesses but also that an escape attempt might
be in the offing. All persons entering the courtroom were
searched and photos of known gang members were distributed to police officers guarding the courtroom. The guards
were also told females associated with the Johnston brothers
were considered dangerous.

Armed officers from the West Chester police force were
posted throughout the area, including the roof of the F &
M building, the tallest building in West Chester. The struc-
ture, known as the first skyscraper built in the suburbs of
Philadelphia, is located directly south of the courthouse at
the intersection of High and Market streets. Also, state policemen, county detectives, FBI agents, and sheriff's deputies
patrolled the hallways of the courthouse and especially the
corridor outside of Courtroom Number Four on the second
floor of the building.

Before the hearing began the defense attorneys argued
they didn't have time to properly prepare for the hearing and
each defendant should have separate hearings. Also, the de-

fense objected to the hearing being videotaped. District Attorney William Lamb wanted the testimony memorialized and available for trial because of his concern for the safety of his witnesses. All of the defense motions, including one to have DiFillippo removed from the case, were denied.

The first major witness for the prosecution was Ricky Mitchell. During six hours of testimony Mitchell repeated the statements he made to police concerning the murders of the three young gang members. The defense attorneys, especially Goldberg, closely cross-examined Mitchell. Mitchell answered many of the questions by saying "I can't remember," or, "I could have." At one point Mitchell told Goldberg, "I'm just a dumb country boy."

Goldberg asked DiFillippo to declare Mitchell an incompetent witness. DiFillippo called Mitchell evasive but allowed him to continue even though later DiFillippo said he was losing his patience with Mitchell. "He's your witness. Straighten him out or he'll be disqualified," DiFillippo told Assistant District Attorney Troiani.

James Griffin made his first appearance as a prosecution witness during the hearing. He related a conversation between Norman Johnston and Johnston Sr. "This isn't the 30s anymore. You can't go around shooting federal witnesses and young girls," Griffin said Norman told his brother. Griffin also said Johnston Sr. told him that police informant Gary Crouch, another murder victim, "had a new job, pushing up daisies."

Leslie Eugene Dale appeared for the prosecution and gave a reason why he turned police informant. Dale said on the day he talked with Zagorskie and Troiani he had just received a letter from his son's mother saying his son was getting straight A's in school and was good at playing ball. Dale's son was the same age as the murdered Robin Miller and the young girl's murder bothered him. Dale also testified

that he believed the Johnstons wanted him dead. "I'm no
goddamn dummy," Dale said. "I'm aware of why they wanted
me at that hole."

The preliminary hearing turned out to be one of the lon-
gest in Chester County's history. After eight days and three
nights of testimony, all three Johnston brothers were ordered
held for trial on the murder charges by DiFillippo on March
14, 1979.

THE WEEK AFTER the preliminary hearing Roy Myers,
brother-in-law of Johnston Sr., was sentenced to a ten-year
sentence in federal court after admitting to charges of interstate transportation of stolen property. Myers admitted
to taking part in the April 2, 1978, burglary of the Macke
Vending Company in Delaware County, Pennsylvania. In
the theft more than $5,000 worth of cigarettes were stolen
and transported to Elkton, Maryland. Also charged in the
theft were the three Johnston brothers and Ricky Mitchell.
At the federal sentencing session, Assistant United States
Attorney Douglas Richardson announced Myers was cooperating with authorities.

Myers's attorney, David Wood of West Chester, said his
client would serve his time in a federal prison away from
any of the other Johnston gang. The obvious reason for the
court directive, according to Wood, was Myers's safety. Myers had reason to worry because he knew a lot about the
criminal operation of the Johnstons. Richardson told United
State District Court Judge Louis H. Pollak that Myers had
admitted to taking part in armed robberies, thefts, and other
crimes with the Johnstons. Myers was either skillful or lucky
to escape criminal prosecution before the Macke charges, according to Richardson.

As part of Myers's cooperation he gave a statement on

March 15, 1979, to state policeman Paul Yoder concerning a rip-off of Pottstown drug dealers. Myers said he and Johnston Jr. drove back an empty truck from Tucson, Arizona, to Chester County in December 1977 that was used to transport the stolen drugs to Arizona. Johnston Sr., according to Myers, gave him an account of the crime. Johnston Sr., Ed Otter, Jimmy Sampson, and "a man named Richie from Pottstown" were involved. Later, Otter verified most of Myers's account of the crime.

Information on the transportation of more than 1,000 pounds of marijuana from Florida to Pennsylvania by a Pottstown drug dealer was obtained by a man by the name of Richie from a woman who was seeing the drug dealer. Johnston Sr. was contacted to see if he wanted to steal the drugs from the drug dealer and a plan was formulated.

Johnston Sr. and others waited for the drug dealer to stop at a restaurant along Interstate 95 in Virginia and while the man was getting a cup of tea, they stole his truck. They transferred the drugs to Johnston Sr.'s truck and that truck was driven to Johnston Sr.'s home in Elkton. Johnston Sr. said he sold the drugs for $300,000 and personally cleared $100,000, according to Myers. Myers said Johnston Sr. came to his home one day with a suitcase full of money, $78,000, that Johnston Sr. said came from the drug rip-off.

Myers said the Pottstown drug dealers were after both Johnston Sr. and Johnston Jr. The drug rip-off was the foundation for the Johnston brothers' claiming that drug dealers were responsible for the ambush of Johnston Jr. and the murder of Robin Miller.

IN STATE COURT the prosecutors were preparing for the murder trials. The attorneys for the Johnston brothers wanted the trial moved from Chester County because of all of the publicity the case was generating. Almost daily stories were printed in the local newspapers, including the Philadelphia *Inquirer*, Philadelphia *Bulletin*, West Chester's *Daily Local News*, the Pottstown *Mercury*, Coatesville *Record*, and the Wilmington *News Journal*. WCOJ radio, with studios in West Chester and Coatesville, reported daily on the progress of the cases as did Philadelphia stations. The coverage wasn't limited to the regional press as the *New York Times* assigned a reporter to cover the case as did national news magazines, including *Time* and *Esquire*.

On March 23, 1979, Chester County Common Pleas Judge Leonard Sugerman ordered a change of venue in eight theft-related cases against Johnston Sr. "It can't be disputed," Judge Sugerman said, "that a vast amount of publicity has appeared in the local and Philadelphia print media. The case has been more thoroughly covered than any other in the county in my memory." Johnston Sr.'s attorney, Anthony Picciotti had subpoenaed copies of the stories and the file of stories was estimated to have weighed 30 pounds.

Judge Sugerman also made a unique request. He asked the Pennsylvania Supreme Court to have a jury picked in another county and brought to Chester County where the trial would be held. The reason was to save money. Three weeks later the state Supreme Court ordered Johnston Sr. to be tried on burglary charges in Westmoreland County in western Pennsylvania. The change of venue wouldn't be the last as the prosecution and defense teams were about to crisscross the Commonwealth of Pennsylvania.

Later in the spring Chester County Common Pleas President Judge D. T. Marrone ordered the murder cases to also be tried outside of Chester County because of the publicity. The Supreme Court decided the murder trials would be held in Schuylkill County in Pennsylvania.

AS THE INVESTIGATION continued, Lieutenant Richard Weimer, commander of the state police barracks in Avondale, retired in April 1979. Weimer, then fifty-three years old and a 30-year law enforcement veteran, left to take a job in private industry. Weimer said he agonized over his decision to retire before the Johnston cases were completed.

INFORMANTS LESLIE DALE and Ricky Mitchell received the maximum sentences on interstate burglary charges when they appeared before federal Judge Pollak in May 1979. The pair had worked out plea agreements and Dale received 10 years in federal prison and Mitchell 15 years.

CAROL JOHNSTON, WIFE of Johnston Sr., was having her own problems with the law as she was arrested for having 21.7 grams of marijuana in her purse when she attempted to enter a courtroom to witness a hearing for her husband on May 31. Carol Johnston was stopped and searched by Chester County Detective Debbie Houpt and the drug was found.

In June Carol Johnston was in court in Berks County along with her sister-in-law, Susan. The women were on trial on charges of hindering the apprehension or prosecution of a fugitive and conspiracy. Susan Johnston, wife of Norman, and Carol Johnston, wife of Johnston Sr., were both convicted after a five-day trial. The charges stemmed from the arrest of the Johnston brothers after the shoplifting attempt in Reading.

IN JULY, A federal grand jury sitting in Philadelphia indicted Norman, David and Johnston Sr., along with gang associates James Dotson, James Hamm, Thomas Rebert and businessman Anthony Fragale, on theft and interstate transportation of stolen property charges. The Johnston brothers and Dotson were charged with taking more than $5,000 in jewelry from a Wilmington, Delaware, home on October 30, 1978, and driving a stolen car into Pennsylvania.

Hamm and Dotson were charged with taking $5,000 from a store in Grantsville, Maryland, and taking the property back to Pennsylvania. Rebert was charged with a tractor theft from the North Star Elementary School in Wilmington, Delaware, on February 2, 1978, and Fragale, a mushroom grower, was charged with conspiring with the Johnston brothers to steal farm equipment.

Rebert, a Delaware County schoolteacher, maintained his innocence when arrested, saying his connection with Johnston associates was from his work as a teacher. Rebert told reporters that Jimmy Hamm brought a car to be repaired to his home, where he operated a shop. He said Hamm and his friends, including Roy Myers and James Dotson, brought him cars to repair. He also said he repaired lawn tractors for the Johnstons.

Later in the year a federal jury didn't believe Rebert and found him guilty of selling stolen goods obtained from the Johnstons. United States District Court Judge Clarence Newcomer sentenced Rebert to three years on charges of conspiracy, perjury, and receiving stolen goods.

AS THE FIRST anniversary of the murders of the three young gang members approached, one of the relatives of Jimmy Johnston decided to talk publicly of the murders and the Johnston brothers.

"I think at night he will come around and say, 'Mom, I'm home," said Sarah Martin, who raised Jimmy Johnston from the time he was two weeks old. Jimmy Johnston was Martin's step-nephew. Jimmy's mother, Jennie Johnston, is the daughter of Harriet Steffy, Martin's sister. Martin expressed fear that the murder charges would be dismissed because of a violation of the defendants' rights to a speedy trial. "They are smart," Martin said of the Johnstons. "I hope I never come face-to-face with Bruce. I just couldn't stand to look at him," Martin said.

Martin kept numerous photos of Jimmy Johnston in her home. In one corner a pair of Jimmy Johnston's sneakers sat on a red stool. They had been untouched for about a year. "It seems like I can't let go. I feel he is going to come home. I think at night he will come around and say, 'Mom, I'm home.' I really know he won't. People say take the pictures and sneakers away. I can't. I dust them off and put them back. I've always had his school pictures out. His clothes are still in the closet. Things are just like they were when he was here."

Martin also recalled the last time she saw Jimmy Johnston. She said it was August 14, 1978, and he was in front of their trailer. "It seems he is still standing there," she said.

Johnston Sr. was responsible for getting Jimmy Johnston into trouble, according to Martin. "I know Jimmy did a wrong, but he was still my boy and I loved him. They did wrong and should be punished, but not that way. It was just an awful, awful thing. How can people do these things? To me, they are animals, how can anybody do that. It wasn't their place to do it."

Martin had kind words for the investigators. "I'll always have a place in my heart for those men. They worked day and night. The FBI and state police risked their lives," she said. "I'm not afraid. I say things because I mean it. It is the truth and I'm not afraid. I'd give my life if I could have Jimmy or any of those kids back. Jimmy can't be hurt now. I can go now at least to where his body is. We go every week."

NOT EVERYONE WANTED to talk to the investigators. The law enforcement team tried to interview members of the Johnston family and some cooperated and some didn't. State policeman Bernard Dickerson tried several times to interview Mary Payne, the Johnston brothers' sister, on March 8, 1979, while they were at the Chester County Courthouse for a hearing.

When first asked, Payne said "no" and entered the courtroom, according to Dickerson. "At 11:34 hours, this officer again attempted to interview Mrs. Payne in the corridor outside of Courtroom Four. At this time, Mrs. Payne refused to speak to the officer and entered the ladies' room. This officer waited in the hallway again and at approximately 11:55 hours, this officer again attempted to interview Mrs. Mary Payne at which time she removed her high-heeled shoes and ran down the corridor on the second floor of the courthouse and then out of the building refusing to be interviewed by this officer," Dickerson's report said.

BY EARLY NOVEMBER two of the Johnston associates, James Hamm and James Dotson, were sentenced in both federal and state courts for their part in a number of burglaries.

In state court, Hamm received a sentence of 1½-to-3 years for burglarizing a Ben Franklin store in Parkesburg during March 1978. Taken were $9,000 in coins and jewelry. The sentence ran concurrently with the three-year federal sentence he received from the robbery at a Grantsville, Maryland, store.

Dotson's state sentence was 2½-to-5 years for the Parkesburg store as well as a robbery at a West Fallowfield home in March 1978. Dotson's federal sentence was nine years for the Grantsville robbery and robbing a Wilmington, Delaware, couple at gunpoint on October 30, 1978.

Gang member Jimmy Griffin supplied information against Hamm and Dotson. He told police that Dotson hid inside the Ben Franklin store and after it closed he let in Hamm and himself. Griffin also said the three Johnston brothers were involved with Dotson in connection with the robbery of the Wilmington couple.

DURING THE FIRST week of December of 1979 an incident at Delaware County Prison led Johnston Sr. to be treated for a possible concussion and four cracked ribs. For more than a month Johnston had been held in the state prison at Camp Hill but his defense attorney, Anthony Picciotti, asked to have Johnston Sr. moved closer to Chester County so he could prepare his client's defense.

According to Delaware County Prison Warden Thomas Rapone, Johnston Sr. tried to set fire to his cell and he resisted the correctional officers responding to the fire. Rapone reported that Johnston Sr. swung at the officers, broke a cell window, and threw lighted paper at the officers. Correctional officers put out the fire and the only damage was to sheets, clothing, a pillowcase, and some commissary items.

Johnston Sr. was taken to Sacred Heart Hospital in Chester and treated for injuries. After being taken back to Delaware County Prison he was transferred to Chester County Prison to appear in court on December 10 in connection with his murder case. While at Chester County Prison, Johnston was taken to Chester County Hospital, West Chester, for treatment of his injuries.

Newspaper reporters had been seeking interviews with Johnston Sr. concerning the case and until his injuries in Delaware County Prison he had declined. After appearing in Chester County Court in connection with his murder case, *Daily Local News* reporter Bruce Mowday was told which exit the police were using to take Johnston Sr. to waiting police cars for transportation to Chester County Prison. To prevent any possible escape attempts law enforcement officials used different courthouse exits to take Johnston Sr. to waiting police cars to transport him back to prison.

Daily Local News reporter Mowday ran down the stairs from Judge Leonard Sugerman's second-floor courtroom and to the waiting state police car on High Street in West Chester before Johnston Sr., in handcuffs, made it to the car.

"Do you want to talk now?" Mowday asked Johnston Sr. as he was being placed in the police car.

"Yes, but just about being beaten by the guards," Johnston Sr. replied.

Mowday told Johnston Sr. he would contact him. The reporter went back to the newspaper's office and called Warden Thomas Frame of Chester County Prison. Frame told Mowday that Johnston Sr. was just going to be housed at his facility that night. Johnston Sr. was going to be transferred to a state prison the next day. Frame said if Johnston wanted to give an interview, he would arrange that meeting.

During the early evening hours Mowday went to Chester County Prison where he was searched and led to a holding room. Johnston Sr. was brought into the room. He was still walking gingerly because of his rib injuries, and sat down for a two-hour interview. Mowday took notes and recorded the session. For the first hour Johnston Sr. talked about what he considered being mistreatment at the hands of the Delaware County Prison guards and other law enforcement officers. Then, Mowday turned the interview to the murders and for the next hour Johnston gave his alibi.

What Johnston Sr. told Mowday and what Johnston Sr. testified to at trial concerning a crucial point of the alibi were different. That difference did not escape District Attorney William H. Lamb.

CHAPTER TWELVE

Trial Preparations

The prosecution team faced a major problem three weeks before the murder trial of David and Norman Johnston was to begin in Ebensburg, Cambria County. District Attorney William H. Lamb's term concluded on January 1, 1980, as one of Lamb's assistants, James Freeman, was elected to succeed Lamb.

"I wanted to do the prosecutions," Lamb said. "Jim Freeman and the commissioners realized I should be the guy since I had been the one handling the case. It made sense." An agreement was made that kept Lamb as special prosecutor at the rate of $50 an hour. "I wanted to stay on the team but a risk was involved. I had received the benefits of solving the case. I was the DA who called the press conference. To the extent I was looking for any political juice, I had gotten a big bang and I could have stepped out of the case. I could have said it was someone else's job. When asked if I would continue, I said yes."

Lamb was the last of Chester County's part-time district attorneys; Freeman was the first one to have the job full-time. "As district attorney I had my nights and weekends free to practice law," Lamb said, "and I had a lot of municipal work. I was coming off eight years of public service. When the change of venue to Ebensburg was ordered, I thought, 'What did I get myself into?' I was going to Ebensburg and the trial took twelve weeks. Johnston Sr.'s trial took about a week and a half less. The time commitment was great but I had decided to do the job, so I did the job."

NORMAN JOHNSTON WASN'T so sure the police could do the job. While being transported to Allentown for an appearance in Lehigh County Court on June 4, 1979, Norman Johnston told state policeman Robert Martz and Chester County Detective Ted Schneider, "They could offer me ten years for everything and I'd turn it down. I'm going to take you guys all the way on every charge. You always fuck up. You just got too much going. You guys always try to do too much and don't do anything right. You have to make mistakes and we'll beat you. Oh, you may convict me on a couple of charges, but I'll beat the rest."

Martz then asked about the murders. Norman Johnston responded, "You've already fucked up. You don't tell us when these murders happened, so how are we supposed to properly prepare our defense. And I'll tell you, I don't know how you can believe those guys. Dale is a fucking murderer, Mitchell is a crazy man. He's nuts, you'll see. I don't know how you guys can believe that bullshit they're telling you."

THE SUPREME COURT of Pennsylvania had assigned the murder cases to the court system in Schuylkill County because of the pre-trial publicity in Chester County. The transfer was short-lived. Assistant District Attorney Dolores Troiani remembers having the distinct feeling Schuylkill

County officials didn't want anything to do with the case and would have dismissed charges under the Commonwealth of Pennsylvania's speedy trial rule if they had a chance.

Members of the press were excluded from the first pretrial hearing held in Schuylkill County under the guise that too much publicity had caused the case to be moved from Chester County. At the hearing *Daily Local News* reporter Bruce Mowday complained to the court but was not allowed in the courtroom. Attorneys representing newspapers were contacted and a legal battle over open courtrooms in Schuylkill County was pending.

At a break in the hearing Mowday went up to Norman and David Johnston to ask what was taking place behind the closed doors. A Schuylkill County court guard asked for the reporter's identification and David Johnston responded, "That's Bruce Mowday of the *Local*, everyone knows Bruce." Indeed, those at the trial knew Big Bruce (Johnston Sr.), Little Bruce (Johnston Jr.) and Local Bruce (Mowday). The guard backed away without asking any other questions and Mowday talked with the brothers about the court proceeding.

The case was eventually moved from Schuylkill County to Cambria County and Chester County Common Pleas Judge Leonard Sugerman was assigned as trial judge. William Lamb was special prosecutor and Assistant District Attorney Dolores Troiani was a prosecutor. The trial of Johnston Sr. was separated from his brothers, since Johnston Sr. was the only Johnston brother charged with the death of Gary Crouch. Handling the defense were attorneys Lawrence Goldberg and John Lachall, both experienced lawyers from West Chester, Pennsylvania.

WITNESS PREPARATION AND planning for the logistics involved in transporting witnesses to testify in Ebensburg were major undertakings for the prosecution team. The traveling distance between the two Pennsylvania county seats is 225 miles. The number of potential prosecution witnesses approached 100.

Also, a challenge was getting witnesses such as Ricky Mitchell and Leslie Dale ready for the witness stand. The two admitted murderers and other informants wrote numerous letters during the months leading up to the trial, mostly to Assistant District Attorney Dolores Troiani or Chief County Detective Charles Zagorskie. Most of the letters involved a mixture of complaints, threats and requests.

During the summer Mitchell wrote to Zagorskie, "I have been here in this joint two weeks now. They are keeping me in the hole (solitary confinement). I am getting a little tired of being in the hole everyplace I go. They lost my suit at New York. I was not allowed to bring anything at all with me. That means legal papers and all. I have been here two weeks with no money, if I am to be here long I want to know how long. And I desire to have me some money by 7-18-79 so I can order me some things I need to keep my body and denture plate clean. What's the case on my watch? And if you can not send me my watch, I do not want to get burnt on that. ... I am not getting ½ the medication that I was in New York, and New York would not even give me what I needed. So, I want to get the hell out of here before I start bringing legal action on a great number of people."

In another letter Mitchell again complained about being identified to other prisoners as a snitch, still not having money, and being transported by state policemen Tom Cloud and J. R. Campbell whom he believes didn't treat him properly. Mitchell also threatened to disclose information during trials that would be detrimental to the prosecution's case. "I don't think you will like what I am going to say in the courtroom. And everything I say is true, so I think you better plug up some leaks if you get my hint on that one." Mitchell demanded to have answers to his many questions within 15 days.

Campbell admits having problems with Mitchell before the Miller murder. "He was a thorn in our side," Campbell said. "We would investigate a crime scene and it had Ricky Mitchell written all over it. One time Weimer sent me down to check out a car near Mitchell's home. Ricky came out and he was going to go after me. His mom came out and stopped it. He was a sleaze; I wanted to get him on assault on an officer." Mitchell, according to Campbell, was the only witness who caused a problem. "He was a loose cannon. I'm surprised Dolores didn't strangle him."

State policeman Tom Cloud recalled prepping sessions with fellow trooper Bob Martz and Mitchell. "We would go to prepare Ricky," Cloud said, "and Bob, who was a great guy and always up to date on the status of the case, and Ricky would start. Bob would lie down on the bed and rub his temples and listen to me to try to prepare Ricky. Later he would try to help but Ricky would give him a headache in three minutes."

FBI agent Richter recalled one day Mitchell fell asleep on his bed while still dressed in his blue suit. "All of the marshals and everybody that was there went to Mitchell's room," Richter said. "We gathered some flowers from the hotel and we put them around Ricky and he looked like he was in a coffin. The marshals took the photo."

Richter also told a story about Dale ordering breakfast. "One day Leslie wanted to order breakfast and we said he could. So he called 7:00 or 8:00 AM and asked for room service. He said he wanted two eggs, the white part really burnt and the yolk real runny, and the toast black and the bacon done so when you touch it, it breaks up. The waitress said she wasn't sure if we could prepare the order as Dale ordered. Leslie said, 'Why not? You did it yesterday.'"

One day Judge Sugerman received a subscription to *Playboy* delivered to his office. Dale was the person who ordered the magazine unbeknownst to Judge Sugerman. Dale also submitted an application to a mail-order company in the name of reporter Mowday. Mowday was issued a card that made him a minister with full power to marry people.

Martin Knecht, another criminal that was testifying for the prosecution, wasn't in a joking mood. He complained to Troiani that he wasn't admitted to Norristown State Hospital as promised. He was sent to Camp Hill state prison where he was housed in the "hole" over a cell containing Johnston Sr.

From his jail cell in Terre Haute, Indiana, in November 1979 Dale sent a series of letters complaining about his scheduled court appearances and not being in Chester County so he could talk with his attorney, Mike Kean. "Hell, he is the best lawyer in the county, besides me," Dale wrote. He continued, "If you don't bring me back this week you are going to have a lot of trouble out of me in court, don't say I didn't tell you." In the same letter he talked about the murders of Kennett Square policemen Davis and Posey. Dale wrote, "Dolores (Troiani) did you know that Dave (Johnston) was home with a toothache when the cops got killed. And when the killing happened in Oxford guess what, Dave was at Mrs. Johnston's with a toothache again. I know right were he was at when those cops got it and also big Bruce was sitting right on the main st. with a radio two-way when the cops went by on the way to the police st (station)."

TO TRANSPORT WITNESSES to Cambria County, the prosecuting team ran what they called "Chester County Airlines." State policeman Tom Cloud called the moving of witnesses from Chester County to Cambria County "a big logistical nightmare." A car trip would take five hours. Also, snow fell during most days the trial was held in Ebensburg. One snowy day with Cloud at the wheel of a car and trooper Bob Martz and witnesses in the car, the vehicle slid on the slick road in Ebensburg and went across railroad tracks, just missing sliding into a train. Another time a car blew a tire while making the trip to the courthouse.

Assistant District Attorney Joseph Carroll had a frightening ride, but in an airplane. "Detective Ted Schneider ran the Chester County airline service," Joseph Carroll said. "One day I came back with attorney Mike Kean and two witnesses. It was foggy and we were diverted to Wilmington. During the landing we just missed some power lines. From that point on I drove."

At first the prosecution team made an older motel in Ebensburg its headquarters but a decision was made to stay in a Sheraton hotel in Indiana County, 20 miles away through a mountain pass. "The motel in Ebensburg would never have worked," Cloud said. "It wasn't large enough. We had a lot of witnesses and many of them needed guards around the clock. The state police made a tremendous effort during the trial. We were there almost eight weeks."

Chester County Detective Sergeant Mike Carroll recalled the weather as being bitterly cold most of the time. Ebensburg sits on the edge of the Allegheny Mountains and can receive 100 inches of snow a year. During evenings the team didn't venture far from the hotel and ate at local restaurants. "The diner across the street was making a mint," Carroll said. One restaurant even put up a plaque commemorating the fact the prosecution ate so many meals at the place. Troiani recalled most of the time was spent in preparing witnesses for the next day's trial. "There was not much else to do," she said.

"We had a corporate jet that we flew back and forth from the Chester County Airport, just outside of Coatesville in Valley Township," Cloud said. "We were constantly bringing in and taking back witnesses. Mitchell and Dale were there the whole time and being guarded around the clock. I didn't go out much; I'm not a drinker, so I was locked in with those guys during much of that time period."

Chester County Detective Jeff Gordon handled the schedule of witnesses and transportation, according to Lamb. The weather and other factors sometimes threw off the timing. "Judge Sugerman wanted to keep the trial moving," Lamb said. "When we didn't have a witness readily available we put Charlie (Zagorskie) on the stand."

Detective Carroll said, "Logistics in Ebensburg will never be matched. We were there six or seven weeks and we rotated guards during the trial. After each day we had a meeting to check what we had to do to prepare for the next day. We had people in Chester County waiting by the phone to help. It was quite an effort."

Detective Carroll said the prosecution team was constantly worried about security and rumors about escape schemes were rampant. "There was a lot of surveillance. Every day we had security for Judge Sugerman. State police guarded the grounds outside the courthouse. The atmosphere was tense. Carroll recalled that one day a juror threw a firecracker out a window and everyone thought it was gunshots. Another time *Daily Local News* reporter Bruce Mowday was taking photographs to illustrate one of his articles and a state policeman leveled a rifle at Mowday and ordered him to surrender the camera. Police were afraid photos were being used to help plan an escape. Mowday surrendered the camera but later Judge Sugerman ordered it returned to the reporter.

JOSEPH CARROLL, THE young assistant district attorney, became involved in the case to do legal research. He reacted to issues Judge Sugerman deemed important and provided

legal background for Lamb and Troiani. "I became involved
in the case two or three months before the trial of David
and Norman Johnston," Carroll said. "I was hired in October
1979 in the District Attorney's office to handle appeals. I
had previously interned in the office. I was the third wheel
of the prosecution. I did legal research and later helped with
the prep of the witnesses.

"The first week I had to familiarize myself with the case.
There were a number of pre-trial issues. I had known some
of the officers but not many of them. The relationships I
made during the trial have helped me as District Attorney.
(Carroll was elected District Attorney of Chester County in
2003.) I would do briefs on legal issues and at Ebensburg I
did witness preps, including Ricky Mitchell. Ricky called us
Mr. Cloud and his associates. I also interviewed potential
witnesses with a detective. I really reacted to whatever Judge
Sugerman thought was important. We all worked together
under Bill Lamb's leadership, it was spectacular. We would
find new information to check as it proceeded. It was like a
mosaic and as we went we looked for the missing tiles. It was
exciting for me."

Carroll also was impressed with the work of Judge Sugerman. "He was great on the law. He would listen to arguments
even if you didn't have case precedents. He would play devil's
advocate if something was new. We were fortunate to have
someone like him on the case. He protected the record. He
made sure the rights of the defendants were also protected.
He was demanding as he wanted all of the information before
him before he would make a decision. He was a brilliant guy."

During interview sessions, Lamb and Troiani included
Carroll. "They gave me opportunities," Carroll said. "I remember Bill would cross-examine defense witnesses and I
would think there was nothing to be gained for the prosecution and he would find things. I would never even have

thought of asking the question. He was using his experience
and also going fishing for information in a safe way."

THE SETTING FOR the trial was the county seat of Cambria County, Ebensburg. The county was founded in 1804
and at the time of the trial Ebensburg had a population of
about 4,500, about a third of the size of West Chester, the
county seat of Chester County. Cambria County's population was about 200,000.

The early settlers of Cambria County included Ger-
man settlers and emigrants from Wales. The Welsh founded
Ebensburg. The Welsh were especially important as coal
mining was a main occupation in Cambria County as it was
in Wales.

During January 1980, the prosecution and defense teams
descended on Ebensburg along with regional reporters and
photographers from Philadelphia, West Chester, Pottstown,
Coatesville, and Wilmington, and national organizations
including the Associated Press, United Press International,
Time magazine, *Esquire* magazine, the *New York Times*, and
People magazine to name a few.

Some of the Chester County and wire service reporters
stayed in the same small motel on the western side of Ebensburg. Reporter Nancy Pinkerton of the Pottstown *Mercury*,
upon registering, called out to Mowday of the *Daily Local
News*, "I have the hooker's room!" Indeed, Pinkerton's room
was done all in pink.

The residents of Ebensburg, outside of those who worked
at the courthouse and regularly attended trials, seemed to
pay little attention to the murder trial from suburban Philadelphia. As the trial opened Philadelphia *Inquirer* reporter
Julia Cass wrote an article that noted the local weekly paper
contained items about a nine-year-old girl winning a pup-

pet contest and the Moose's monthly meeting but nothing on the trial. The article did rile some local citizens as they believed it pictured them as a hick community.

The Johnston brothers were housed in Cambria County's jail in Ebensburg. A tier was reserved for the defendants, security measures were undertaken and extra guards were hired and those already employed were given overtime. A fear of the prosecution team was that the Johnstons would escape and that gang associates were constantly plotting to make any escape attempt a reality.

ONE JOHNSTON GANG member, James R. Dotson, had broken out of Chester County Farms Prison on November 10, 1979. Dotson and inmate George R. Smith escaped from their second-tier cell by cutting a 12-by-14-inch hole in a window and jumping to the ground. They used their blankets and socks as a grappling hook to climb an eight-foot fence and disappear into the Chester County countryside.

Dotson was recaptured in the first week of January 1980 just as the trials of David and Norman Johnston were set to begin. FBI agents and Chester County detectives worked to apprehend Dotson in Chattanooga, Tennessee, on January 6 in a motel room.

A convicted murderer, Martin Knecht, testified in January 1980 in Chester County Common Pleas Court that Johnston Sr. took part in another escape attempt. William Maxwell, who resided in Avondale, was tried on charges he attempted to escape from Chester County Farms Prison in April 1979 with a number of other inmates, including Johnston Sr. Knecht told a jury he helped Johnston Sr. smuggle hacksaw blades into the prison.

Knecht said the planned escape was cancelled twice. Once, the escape was called off after David Johnston hadn't received the $40,000 in bail money he had posted for his release and then due him since he was incarcerated. The second attempt, according to Knecht, was cancelled because security at the prison was too tight. Knecht said the Johnstons had made arrangements for automatic weapons to be available and that prison guards were to be shot if they resisted. Two getaway cars were to be positioned near the prison grounds.

Maxwell testified during his trial that he indeed used a smuggled hacksaw blade to saw part of his prison window, but he denied intending to escape. Maxwell, who grew up with Johnston Sr., told the jury he had no intentions of escaping with Johnston Sr. because he was afraid Johnston Sr. would kill him because of a "prior" run-in he had with Johnston Sr. Maxwell didn't give details of the prior incident.

The Chester County jury convicted Maxwell on charges of attempted escape, possessing implements of crime and conspiracy on January 16, 1980.

THE TRIAL IN the Cambria County's 135-year-old French Provincial-style courthouse took place in courtroom one, an expansive theater with marble pillars. Carl Harrison, head of the courtroom personnel and also unofficial courthouse historian, told reporters that Indians gave the county ground for the courthouse. The dome was made of imported French glass, Harrison said. He also mentioned Ebensburg got its name from Reverend Rees Lloyd's son, Eben. Lloyd was an early settler.

For courtroom security, a bulletproof steel plate was added behind the juror's bench. Also, a metal detector was borrowed from Trans World Airlines to screen those wishing to enter the courthouse. For those wishing to enter the Johnston courtroom, a second screening, with a handheld scanner, took place. About 90 percent of those entering the courthouse set off the scanner and most had to make two or three passes before being allowed into the building. In 1980, metal detectors were rare, not the common security measure that they are today.

The bill for all of the extra security precautions given to the Chester County taxpayers prompted a visit from Chester County Commissioner Robert Thompson to caution the Cambria County officials that they didn't have an open checkbook. Chester County Controller Lawrence Wood, an attorney and future judge, commented that the case was costing Chester County taxpayers an "arm and a leg."

Also, the winter weather was a concern and officials had a four-wheel drive vehicle and snow plow at the ready to transport Judge Sugerman and the jurors to the courthouse each day, if needed.

HAVING JUDGE SUGERMAN at the helm of the trail was vital; he was a no-nonsense jurist with a strong hand and sense of fairness. Besides preserving the rights of the defendants and protecting the record, Judge Sugerman could keep the trial from becoming a circus, which was a concern.

At the top of the witness list for defendant David Johnston was Watergate burglar and former FBI agent G. Gordon Liddy. David Johnston's attorney, John Lachall, listed Liddy as a possible alibi witness. Lachall said Liddy and Johnston spoke to each other while both were prisoners in the federal institution at Danbury, Connecticut, in July 1977, the time Gary Crouch was murdered. "Liddy places David somewhere else at the time," Lachall said.

Liddy would not appear at the trial as special prosecutor Lamb decided not to pursue the Crouch murder case against Norman and David Johnston. The defendants would face only five murder charges involving the deaths of Robin

Miller, James and Wayne Sampson, Dwayne Lincoln, and Jimmy Johnston during the Ebensburg trial.

A major legal issue was still to be decided by Judge Suger-man. Lamb and the prosecution team were pushing to have the defendants face the death penalty if convicted. Lachall and Lawrence Goldberg, representing Norman Johnston, objected, contending the death penalty wasn't valid because state law didn't call for the sentence when the victims died. The attorneys gathered in West Chester on January 10, 1980, to argue the issue before Judge Sugerman.

Lamb contended the death penalty law was in effect when the murders of the five victims took place even though a jury couldn't have imposed the penalty. A Pennsylvania Supreme Court ruling said the death penalty law at the time was de-fective since it didn't include mitigating circumstances. Lamb argued the law wasn't totally voided by the Supreme Court, and the Legislature cured the problem by adding mitigating circumstances in September 1978. The change was made by the lawmakers just weeks after five of the murders.

Lachall countered by saying the change in the law was substantive and the amendments couldn't be retroactively applied. Judge Sugerman promised to have a prompt ruling, before jury selection was slated to begin in Ebensburg on January 18.

At the January 10 hearing the defense team did win a concession from Lamb. Lachall and Goldberg had peti-tioned the court to be allowed to review FBI surveillance reports to see if information in the reports would help their clients' defense. Lamb contended no such information was in the reports and he wanted them sealed and given to Judge Sugerman to review for exculpatory evidence. Lamb finally allowed the defense attorneys to review the reports.

At the same time legal maneuvering was continuing in Johnston Sr.'s case. Johnston Sr. was scheduled to go on trial in Ebensburg at the conclusion of his brothers' cases. Johnston Sr. wasn't happy with his attorney, Anthony L.V. Picciotti, and he wanted new counsel. Picciotti told Judge Sugerman that he and Johnston Sr. didn't agree on the defense strategy and that Johnston Sr. wouldn't communicate with him. Lamb contended that Johnston Sr. was just trying to delay his case and might continue to ask for new attorneys so he wouldn't have to face trial.

"This conduct can continue forever," Sugerman noted. Sugerman didn't rule immediately but mentioned he might order the Cambria County Public Defender's office to supply the next attorney for Johnston Sr.

While Johnston Sr. was trying to shed his attorney, defense attorneys Lachall and Golderg were trying to have Lamb taken off the prosecution's team. Days before jury selection was scheduled to begin the defense attorneys filed a petition to have Lamb removed because he was to be a possible witness in the case and that he was barred from prosecuting since he was no longer District Attorney. Goldberg also alleged that the prosecution had an "ongoing vendetta" against the Johnstons. The month before Johnston Sr. told a reporter that the police were out to get him because they believed he was involved in the murders of the two Kennett Square policemen, Richard Posey and William Davis.

The defense attorneys were also upset that Lamb was being paid more per hour than they were. Lamb was receiving $50 an hour while the defense received $15 an hour for office time and $25 per hour for court time. The defense petition contended the unequal pay was "demeaning and detrimental" to the defense.

Lachall also asked to have the Ebensburg murder trial delayed because he wasn't prepared. Lachall said since David Johnston, his client, was housed outside of Chester County communications were difficult. Lamb pointed out the defense had a year to prepare for trial and David Johnston was moved from Chester County Prison because of his "shenanigans." The shenanigans, according to Lamb, included David Johnston's participation in a prison disturbance.

As jury selections neared, Judge Sugerman issued his rulings on pending motions. The unequal pay for prosecutors and defense would remain but the allowance for a defense investigator was increased. Also, the trial would begin as scheduled in Ebensburg, Lamb would remain as prosecutor and the Johnstons would not face the death penalty.

TWO WEEKS BEFORE the public spotlight turned on the murder trial of brothers Norman and David Johnston in Ebensburg, Johnston Sr. received press on his story. Three stories were printed in the *Daily Local News* as a result of the prison interview given to reporter Bruce Mowday in late 1979. The stories gave a preview of the defense to be used during the trial.

Johnston Sr., of course, denied any involvement in the murders, the sexual assault of Robin Miller, and the shooting of his son, Johnston Jr. "I thought the world of that kid and he knows it," Johnston Sr. said. "I didn't have anything to do with it." Johnston wouldn't name those he believed committed the murders but he did have a theory on each murder.

Miller was killed and Johnston Jr. shot because drug dealers were out to get Johnston Jr., according to Johnston Sr. The other theories of Johnston Sr. centered on the main prosecution witnesses against him, Leslie Dale and Ricky Mitchell. Johnston Sr. claimed that Dale hated his son. Johnston Sr. recalled a meeting with Dale, who had been heavily drinking, at the Oxford Diner where Dale threatened Johnston Jr. Dale was upset about a tractor theft and a farmer taking a shot at Dale, according to Johnston Sr. "Now, Dale, he was really raisin' the devil about that. I never really talked to Dale after that. I never used to fool with Dale. I wasn't really friends with him because he always drank too much, and I didn't really like Leslie Dale," Johnston Sr. said.

Johnston Sr. claimed Dale was giving false testimony against him to escape a life in prison term for the murders Dale had admitted committing, those of Gary Crouch and Jackie Baen. Johnston Sr. said he saw Crouch and Dale at the Wooden Shoe Inn the night Crouch was murdered but he was not present at the killing.

The murders of the three young gang members and Jimmy Sampson were probably done by Mitchell, according to Johnston Sr. "Mitchell was capable of doing these things, more capable than people thought," Johnston Sr. said, "but I never really thought that Mitchell was dangerous. Mitchell was always strange."

Another key prosecution witness, Jimmy Griffin, was also lying, according to Johnston Sr. "I don't know where he ever came up with that (testimony)," Johnston Sr. said. "I was never close to Jimmy Griffin and he can't really say anything about me. You see, Griffin never liked me. He never has and me and him was never what we call friends. And he had threatened me before, not to my face."

Before his brothers' trial began, Johnston Sr. received his wish and defense attorney Anthony L.V. Picciotti was taken off the case. Picciotti said he was frustrated by the experience and lost a law partner and business over his representation of Johnston Sr. "Very frustrating," Picciotti said. "From the legal point of view, the case is extremely interesting. There are all sorts of issues. It is just fascinating. Especially interesting are the issues dealing with the subject of the death penalty, the conspiracy issue and the issue of what can and can't be admissible at trial from the admission of the so called co-conspirators."

Picciotti said he was a little apprehensive when Chester County Common Pleas president Judge D. T. Marrone appointed him in February 1979 and asked Bob Landis, Johnston's former attorney, to accompany him to Chester County Prison to meet Johnston. "Frankly I was surprised. Bruce Johnston is a very mild-mannered, soft-spoken guy. He has never called me anything but Mr. Picciotti. As a matter of fact, he is very respectful. So far as a person, he is difficult to communicate with because of his own limitations."

After Picciotti was relieved of Johnston Sr.'s defense, Judge Sugerman called Downingtown attorney John Talierco, who was vacationing in Rome, Italy, to ask him to represent Johnston Sr. Talierco accepted but had second thoughts about the case and when he returned to the United States he traveled to Ebensburg and asked to be taken off the case. Judge Sugerman agreed to the request.

As his brothers' case proceeded to trial, Johnston Sr. was unrepresented by counsel.

CHAPTER THIRTEEN

The Ebensburg Murder Trial

On the last Saturday of January 1980 Cambria County Jail Warden Ray Gittings received his celebrity prisoners, thirthy-one-year-old David Johnston and his younger brother, twenty-nine-year-old Norman Johnston. Gittings was concerned about providing proper security to prevent an escape by the Johnston brothers and also taking care of the more than 100 other prisoners unconnected to the Johnston case that were being housed in his jail.

The small town of Ebensburg was preparing for the small army of people taking part in the trial: Judge Leonard Sugerman, the attorneys, law enforcement officers, defense investigators, trial spectators, members of the Pennsylvania and national media, and an estimated 150 prosecution and defense witnesses.

Meetings usually held at the courthouse at night had to be rescheduled. One notice said, "The Cambria County Young Democrats have changed their meeting from the courthouse to the VFW because of the Johnston brothers' trial."

On January 29, 1980, the jury selection began. The process of selecting the 16 jurors, including four alternate jurors, took until February 7. Eleven men and one woman made up the first 12 jurors with most of the jurors being either workers in the steel mills or coal mines. Before the jury was seated the original 200-member jury pool was exhausted. Cambria County officials hand-delivered juror notices to 30 additional persons selected for the new jury pool.

Not all of the Cambria County residents called as prospective jurors were happy to be considered and more than one tried to escape jury duty. After one woman said she had a fixed opinion of the Johnston brothers' guilt, Judge Sugerman gave her a lecture. Another lecture followed when a man said he believed the Johnstons were guilty because they were caught and should face the death penalty.

Few citizens took the opportunity to watch the trial as it began. One exception was June Fether, a former newspaper reporter who often visited courtrooms. Her husband had given Fether a blouse with "veteran courthouse observer" printed on the front. Another visitor to the courtroom commented after seeing Dolores Troiani work that she had "never seen a lady attorney."

Residents not attending the trial had few opportunities to see the Johnston brothers. Each day they were transported from the county jail, two blocks from the courthouse, to the basement of the courthouse. Guards with shotguns stood in the hallway as the passageway was cleared of people and the brothers quickly taken to the courtroom. Guards made sure Norman and David Johnston didn't spend a second more than needed in the hallways of justice.

THE CAMBRIA COUNTY jury didn't wait long before being told the prosecution's story of the Johnstons, a crime family that plotted to kill each other and hired murderers to assist with the murderous deeds. On February 8, 1980, the prosecution's opening statement was delivered in 90 minutes. District Attorney William Lamb first explained to the jurors why they were deciding a case that involved crimes committed across the Commonwealth of Pennsylvania in Chester County.

"There is no room in this courtroom for emotion," Lamb told the jurors. "We will appeal to your sense of reason, logic and understanding." Lamb also warned the jurors, who would be sequestered in a local hotel for the duration of the trial, that proceedings would be long and at times tedious with more than a hundred witnesses to be called. Lamb also told the jurors the reason for the murders, to silence witnesses.

Assistant District Attorney Dolores Troiani then outlined the murder cases against Norman and David Johnston. Troiani told the jurors that the case hinged on the testimony of Richard Mitchell, Leslie Dale, and James Griffin. She called Griffin's story the crux of the prosecution's case.

The crux of the prosecution's case, defense attorney Lawrence Goldberg told the jury in his opening, was defective. Goldberg wasted no time in attacking the credibility of Mitchell, Dale, and Griffin. The defense of the Johnston brothers was based on destroying the credibility of the key prosecution witnesses. Goldberg told the jurors they shouldn't believe witnesses that don't seem to be telling the truth.

"They are murderers, liars, connivers, and snitches," Goldberg said of Mitchell and Dale. "They are the most dangerous type of murderers. They are paid assassins. When the heat got too close to them, they pointed their fingers at David and Norman Johnston. Not one word of truth came out of their mouths."

Goldberg contended that Norman and David Johnston never committed a crime with the murder victims and did not have a motive to kill them. Goldberg also took a swipe at the police, saying they didn't uncover fingerprints, bullets, blood samples, guns, or any other piece of evidence directly linking the Johnston brothers to the murders.

Dale and Mitchell had the opportunity to conspire to place the blame on the Johnston brothers, according to Goldberg. "These are criminals who made deals in return for leniency, in return for agreements to put the blame on David and Norman." Goldberg also attacked Griffin. "When James Griffin gets on the witness stand," Goldberg told the jury, "he will testify like a scared puppy. He will whimper and he will tell you how he was afraid of the Johnstons, yet he slept in their living room. He was with David regularly. Where David went, there was Griffin behind. He has a deal. The whole District Attorney's case is tainted with deals."

The jurors were ready to hear from the witnesses and first one to be called to the witness stand was a young, slender man with blond curls falling over his white ski sweater— Bruce Alfred Johnston Jr.

THE MEMBERS OF the Cambria County jury heard first-hand from Johnston Jr. about the death of fifteen-year-old Robin Miller on August 30, 1978, after the couple had returned to Miller's home from an outing at Hersheypark. After turning on an inside car light to locate a pocketbook Johnston Jr. had purchased for Miller, the shooting began, Johnston Jr. said.

"I started getting shot. It stunned me, it dazed me. I staggered around a bit, and I fell into the car. Robin was still in there. My head was between the seats. I was looking up at Robin. She screamed. I still heard shots being fired. I thought I saw a little red mark on her jaw.

"She ran into the house. I ran in and Robin was lying on the bed. I tried to help her breathe because it didn't look like she was breathing. I called the police and started looking for a gun. I was afraid the people who shot me would come in and finish me off."

Johnston Jr. told the jury he couldn't identify his assailants but he did stand in the witness box and pointed to areas of his body where he was hit. He pointed to his ear, to the back of his head, to his neck, to his shoulder, to his chest, to his shoulder blade, to his stomach, to his arm, and to his elbow.

The jury also heard the reason why Johnston Jr. began testifying against his father and other family members. "I was mad," Johnston Jr. said. "I was mad about Jimmy Sampson and my father. They raped my girlfriend. I first learned about it in jail. Robin wrote me a letter. Robin said she was at a friend's house and my old man and Sampson picked her up on a pretense. They wanted to know what happened to me. They bet her $100 she couldn't drink so much of a bottle of whiskey. She woke up in a motel room without any clothes on."

Johnston Jr. testified he did not see his father much as a youngster, maybe only three or four times before 1978. He said he did live with his father for several months in 1975 but mostly lived with his grandmother in Homeville, outside of Oxford. Then the father and son started stealing. Jimmy Johnston was also involved in the family business of crime. Johnston Jr. said his father once gave him a message for Jimmy Johnston. The message: "If he (Jimmy) ever said anything to the police he (Johnston Sr.) would hate to have to hurt him."

The defense zeroed in on Johnston Jr.'s drug use and his involvement in the drug theft from Pottstown. Johnston Jr. admitted selling 100 pounds of the stolen marijuana in southern Chester County. He also admitted taking hallucinogens, marijuana, Quaaludes, alcohol, and angel dust on parsley flakes. "It deranges your mind," Johnston Jr. commented.

Johnston Jr. also said he never committed any crimes with his uncles, Norman and David Johnston. Johnston Jr. had bolstered the defense of his uncles as his attorneys portended the drug dealers had reason to ambush Johnston Jr. and Norman and David Johnston didn't have a reason to kill him.

Robin Miller's mother, Linda Jean Miller, was another early prosecution witness who testified about her daughter's relationship with Johnston Jr. Miller, who was a nurse's aide at Chester County Hospital, West Chester, told the jury that at the time of the murder she lived in the farmhouse with her three children, Roxanne, John, and Robin. Linda Miller said the first time she met Johnston Jr. was at Easter dinner in 1978 and the next time she saw Johnston Jr. was several days later. "I got up and got ready for work and Bruce was in Robin's bedroom, and I told him to get dressed and come down, I want to talk with them." The couple didn't come down the stairs but fled the house through Robin's bedroom window and stayed away for several days. "She (Robin) called me one evening and asked me for permission to marry Bruce, and I said this is something that we should talk about," Linda Miller testified.

The young couple eventually returned to Miller's home and in August, after Johnston Jr. was released from Lancaster County Prison, Johnston Jr. and Robin Miller stayed together in the house. Miller was not asked about the last time she saw her daughter alive.

Harriet Steffy, grandmother of Jimmy Johnston and Johnston Jr., did remember the last time she saw Jimmy Johnston. Steffy cried as she told the jury the last time was on August 15, 1978. She told the jury she was worried about the safety of both of her grandsons and told Johnston Jr. to be "awful careful. You're going to be killed."

Jimmy Johnston's aunt, Sarah Martin, was also worried about him. Martin had raised Jimmy Johnston since the time he was two weeks old. Martin recalled two unsettling encounters with Johnston Sr. Martin said she asked Johnston

Sr. to make sure Jimmy Johnston had enough to eat. Johnston Sr. replied, "Jimmy has friends and where he is he won't
be hungry." A few weeks later Martin said she saw Johnston
Sr. in a local diner. Johnston Sr. didn't say anything but went
to the jukebox, put in his money, and played the song: "Only
the Good Die Young."

AS THE JURY waited for the three key prosecution witnesses—Ricky Mitchell, Leslie Dale, and Jimmy Griffin—to
testify, the prosecution called a series of witnesses, including
most of the case invesitagors, local police, county detectives,
state policemen, and those from the United States Attorney's office and the FBI. The prosecution was recounting
almost every step taken during the investigation. Besides
family members, the jury also heard testimony from Miller
neighbors and friends of the murder victims.

ON FEBRUARY 12, 1980, the Cambria County jury heard
from the silver-haired Ricky Mitchell, the twenty-third witness for the prosecution. Before Mitchell took the stand
Judge Sugerman gave a lengthy explanation to the jury on
credibility of witnesses, especially accomplices to crimes.

Judge Sugerman told the jurors that such witnesses should
be "looked upon by you with disfavor, because such testimony comes from a corrupt and polluted source, that source
being the accomplice witness. Secondly, you should examine
the testimony of the Commonwealth's accomplice witnesses
closely and accept such testimony, if you do accept it—and
that matter is for you to determine—only with caution and
care. Thirdly, you should consider whether the testimony of
the accomplice witnesses that one or the other of the defendants committed the crime is supported or corroborated in

whole or in part by evidence other than the testimony of the Commonwealth accomplice witness alone, for if it is so supported or corroborated by independent evidence, then it is more dependable, of course."

After the jury instruction the jurors went to lunch but the attorneys stayed in the courtroom for a defense motion—to exclude Mitchell's testimony from the trial. Defense attorney John Lachall subpoenaed a representative of the United States Social Security Department to testify about Mitchell's medical records. The defense alleged Mitchell was incompetent to testify.

"Those medical records will indicate by Mr. Mitchell's own admission at times, and I think in his own handwriting, in some instances, that he has an extremely bad memory. There are diagnoses of traumatic epilepsy, bilateral optic atrophy, and bilateral motor disorganization. He again claims that he cannot remember," Lachall said.

Lachall added, "The records indicate he shows diminished judgment and ability to interpret proverbs, and that his mental status would prevent successful employment."

"Proverbs?" Judge Sugerman questioned.

Goldberg responded, "That is a testing device which they use to evaluate him for Social Security purposes, Your Honor."

"Astonishing. The Social Security Administration uses proverbs," Judge Sugerman replied.

The defense attorneys wanted Mitchell examined to make sure he was competent to testify. The prosecution pointed out that a doctor had previously observed Mitchell at the defense's request. Judge Sugerman denied the request for an examination.

Assistant District Attorney Dolores Troiani handled the questioning of Mitchell and she quickly elicited information from the witness about his deal with the prosecution and the murders. One of Troiani's first questions dealt with Mitchell's plea bargain. Mitchell told the jury his sentence was life imprisonment and he had agreed to give truthful testimony. Mitchell was first asked about the triple murder and he identified photographs of the victims, saying Johnston Sr. killed Jimmy Johnston, David Johnston killed Dwayne Lincoln, and that he "was forced" to shoot Wayne Sampson.

Quickly, the questions changed to the murder of Jimmy Sampson in the landfill in Honey Brook. Mitchell said, "Norman Johnston shot him in the head." Then, Troiani directed Mitchell to information on the murder of Robin Miller and the shooting of Johnston Jr. Mitchell said Johnston Sr. showed him a photo of Johnston Jr. and offered him $15,000 to murder Johnston Jr. Mitchell said the offer to pay for Johnston Jr.'s murder was not the first time that summer that Johnston Sr. mentioned he wanted his son dead.

"Bruce Johnston Sr. preferred to have Bruce Johnston Jr. kidnapped, brought directly to him so he could murder him himself; if not, he would like to have him murdered, and if possible the body disposed of so that it would look like he jumped bail, because he had just got out of Chester County Farms Prison and Lancaster County Prison," Mitchell testified.

After Johnston Jr. was released from prison, Mitchell said Johnston Sr. drove him and David and Norman Johnston to the Miller home. Johnston Sr. wanted them to kidnap or murder Johnston Jr. Mitchell also testified about stealing a car and going to the Miller home with Norman and David Johnston where they put the stolen car in a field and watched the home for signs of Johnston Jr. Johnston Jr. was in the home and the three men discussed ways to deal with Johnston Jr. Mitchell said David Johnston wanted to go through the front door and shoot Johnston Jr. The trio couldn't agree on a plan and left the area.

Mitchell and Norman and David Johnston returned to the Miller home on a number of occasions, some with Johnston

Sr. but they never made an attempt on Johnston Jr., Mitchell testified.

The day Robin Miller was murdered Johnston Sr. told Mitchell he needed to be seen by a number of people that night because Johnston Jr. was to be murdered. Mitchell made arrangements to meet two women at a local restaurant, Mr. T's. Johnston Sr., Mitchell, and the two women met at Mr. T's between 11:00 PM and midnight and stayed about an hour and a half. During the stay, Johnston Sr. disappeared to make a phone call. After departing Mr. T's the four went to another bar.

Johnston Sr. had his alibi for the night, Miller was murdered and his son shot.

The next day Mitchell said he met with Norman and David Johnston and the two brothers were arguing. "Norm Johnston kept on telling Dave Johnston, if he would have emptied his gun into Bruce Johnston Jr. he would be dead and he wouldn't have no trouble at all," Mitchell testified. "David Johnston said he always liked to keep a bullet in his gun."

In another conversation, according to Mitchell, Norman and David Johnston described Miller's murder. Mitchell testified, "Norman Johnston stated that he ran up in back of the car while they were smoking a cigarette. David Johnston stated he went up next to the car also on the passenger side. They started shooting Bruce Johnston Jr. It looked like Robin Miller ducked down. Apparently one of the bullets went clean through Bruce Johnston Jr. and killed Robin Miller."

When the defense attorneys had their turn to question Mitchell, they zeroed in on Mitchell's credibility beginning with some basic questions.

"Do you know what date today is?" Lachall asked.

"No, I do not keep track of time," Mitchell responded.

"Do you know what town you are in?" Lachall asked.

"I know what county I am in," Mitchell replied. Mitchell

then said Indiana County. He was in Cambria County.

Lachall continued to closely question Mitchell on his medical condition, memory, and details of his plea bargain. Under questioning from Goldberg, Mitchell read a statement he wrote to the Social Security Administration concerning reasons why he couldn't work. The statement said, "I have suffered severe multiple injuries in car accidents. I have epileptic attacks. I have damaged hearing in my right ear. I have a loss of equilibrium. I can't climb or stand on anything. I can't run, my left arm is weak. I have loss of memory from these accidents."

Mitchell certainly wasn't a typical paid murderer.

The defense attorneys pressed Mitchell on his statements to police and sought additional details. Many times Mitchell's response was either "I cannot state" or "That is possible." After being questioned for hours by the defense attorneys, Mitchell's core testimony that the Johnstons were guilty of murder stood.

WHILE MITCHELL WAS testifying he filed a federal civil rights suit against Delaware County Prison for withholding medical treatment from November 29, 1978, to December 24, 1978. The withholding of his medicine caused Mitchell to suffer a violent and severe epileptic seizure on Christmas Eve, the suit said.

WHILE MITCHELL'S TESTIMONY was disjointed at times, the next crucial prosecution witness, Leslie Eugene Dale, was more direct. On Valentine's Day, 1980, Dale recounted a conversation he had with Norman Johnston a few days after the shooting. Norman Johnston, according to Dale, told him that when Johnston Jr. was shot the victim would lean on the car's dash, be shot again, shake, and then shot again. Norman Johnston believed, according to Dale, that Johnston Jr. would die or have severe brain damage.

During a break in his testimony Dale confided to *Daily Local News* reporter Bruce Mowday that he was nervous about taking the stand against his former partners in crime.

Dale also told the jury that he was a murderer. In fact, he had killed two persons, Gary Wayne Crouch and Jackie Baen, and had made a deal with the prosecution for his testimony. Dale also admitted at one point he had agreed to kill Johnston Jr. Dale said he turned down Johnston Sr.'s first offer of $5,000 to commit the murder but later agreed to an amount of $15,000. The same $15,000 offer was made to Norman and David Johnston, Dale said, and David Johnston commented; "Now it is starting to get interesting." Dale said that on August 15, 1978, Johnston Sr. told him that when his son was released from prison they would go "after that s.o.b. and we will get him, too."

Dale also recounted a conversation he had with Johnston Sr. concerning the deaths of the three young gang members on August 16, 1978. Dale said Johnston Sr. told him that the victims were given Quaaludes as they were being lured to the execution site. "Them fools ate them like candy; they were like zombies. They were walking across the hill tripping over logs," Dale quoted Johnston Sr. as saying.

Norman Johnston told Dale that when victim Dwayne Lincoln saw the grave "he just jumped two feet closer to it, so we didn't have to carry him as far." Johnston Sr. admitted shooting his stepson, James Johnston, according to Dale. Johnston Sr. said he shined a flashlight into James Johnston's eyes, stunning the teenager, and then fired a bullet into his head. Norman Johnston said James Johnston was still "gurgling" when thrown into the grave.

Later, the Johnstons told him that they saw a groundhog with a letter in his mouth looking for the three young men.

The defense, especially attorney Lawrence Goldberg, hammered at Dale's credibility by going over in detail Dale's prior criminal history that included receiving stolen property, theft, interstate transportation of stolen vehicles, and conspiracy, besides murder. Goldberg kept pressing Dale, insinuating that Dale was the one responsible for all of the murders. At one point Judge Sugerman called for a recess to allow tensions to subside. His alibi for the night of the Miller murder was that he was out stealing a truck, a story that the prosecution verified but defense attorneys continued to attack. A wound on Dale's arm was made by a bullet fired during the murder of Robin Miller, according to the defense. Dale said his injury was caused by a fence on that night as he was stealing a truck.

Also on Valentine's Day the prosecution called Eva Saggese, a waitress at Mr. T's restaurant on Route 202 in Delaware County on the night Miller was murdered and Johnston Jr. shot. She testified Johnston Sr. gave her a $100 tip on a $33 bill. Another bar employee, Margaret Panichelli testified that Mitchell came into the bar the day after the shooting asking for Saggese and saying Saggese would be needed as an alibi witness for Johnston Sr.

THE THIRD MAJOR former gang member to testify against the Johnston brothers was James "Disco" Griffin. In her opening statement to the jury prosecutor Dolores Troiani called Griffin the "crux" of the case against the Johnstons. Griffin testified that in a lonely jail cell in Florida he turned to God and away from the Johnstons. "I put my future into the hands of God and I've become a born-again Christian," Griffin told the jury.

Griffin recounted conversations he had with the Johnstons, including one with Norman Johnston who said Johnston Jr. would never be able to identify them because they had worn ski masks. During a ride to Pottstown with David Johnston, he was told to "wave to your buddy Jimmy Sampson because Jimmy was buried on the hill."

After Johnston Jr. was shot the Johnston brothers continued to attempt to eliminate Johnston Jr., according to Griffin. Griffin said Norman Johnston admitted trying to attempt to break into the hospital where Johnston Jr. was taken and David Johnston had offered him $5,000 to locate Johnston Jr. after he was placed in the witness protection program.

"I wish I could find (Johnston Jr.)," Griffin quoted Norman Johnston as saying. "I would make sure I would blow out his brains this time."

Griffin also told the jury about an October 1978 conversation that involved the Johnston brothers. Johnston Sr. was upset over the botched attempt on Johnston Jr. "I could have done the job better myself," Griffin quoted Johnston Sr. as saying. Johnston Sr. also said, according to Griffin, "If I would have known my son was going to be a rat, I would have flushed him down the toilet."

Norman Johnston had said, "We hit him eight times, but you know how hard those rats are to kill." And David Johnston responded, according to Griffin, "This isn't the 30s anymore. You can't go around shooting federal witnesses and fifteen-year-old girls." David Johnston then warned Griffin not to repeat the conversation or he (Griffin) would be killed.

Griffin told the jury he used to be a professional burglar and admitted stealing between 100 and 150 tractors. He said he committed other crimes but was not a murderer and declined an invitation to take part in the killings. "Norman said they were going to bury some snitches and he asked me if I wanted some of the action," Griffin testified. "I said I'd rather not get involved."

One of the Johnstons' admitted fences of stolen property, Edward Otter of Boyertown, testified Norman Johnston didn't like using the young criminals for the theft of tractors. The young criminals smoked marijuana and "will get us in trouble one day," Otter quoted Norman Johnston as saying. "Norman said that Bruce (Sr.) shouldn't be horsing around with kids because the stuff they (the three brothers) were involved in was big-time stuff and you couldn't trust the kids."

Otter also said that after he mentioned that he had heard that James Sampson was in California, Norman Johnston laughed and commented, "Let's put it this way, Ed. You're never going to see James Sampson again. And you won't see the rest of the kids, either."

AS THE PROSECUTION was parading witness after witness against Norman and David Johnston, Bruce Johnston Sr. was appointed a new attorney, Anthony List of Delaware County, on February 20, 1980. Chester County Common Pleas Judge D. T. Marrone had searched for three weeks to find someone to take on Johnston Sr.'s case and finally went to a colleague in Delaware County, President Judge Francis J. Catania, for a recommendation.

List, a former assistant United States attorney, was in private practice with his brother. "I find it to be a professional challenge," List said at the time. "I feel that it's part of my professional duties to accept the case. I've read a lot about it. It's an interesting one. It's going to take a lot of effort. I will review all of the pre-trial motions, and that will be a good catch-up."

ONE PROSECUTION WITNESS, Sara Ranson of Lancaster County collapsed and had to be taken to the Coronary Care Unit at Miners' Hospital in Spangler. Ranson collapsed on the third floor of the courthouse. Ranson, who had open

heart surgery two years before testifying, recovered. Ranson
had been called to testify that Dale had rented a room at the
Oh Shaw Motel on Lincoln Highway on August 16, 1978,
under the name of Harry Landis. She couldn't identify Johnston Sr., who was with Dale at the hotel.

Dale testified he had checked into the hotel and had
James Johnston with him. Dale told the jury he had wanted
to take James Johnston out of harm's way but the youth refused. "My dad said I couldn't go nowhere," Dale said James
Johnston told him. While at the Oh Shaw Johnston Sr. gave
his stepson $15. Later, Dale said Johnston Sr. told him he
got his $15 back after murdering James Johnston. Johnston
Sr. said he took the $15 from the dead boy's pocket plus an
additional $2, a bonus, according to Dale.

Johnston Sr. asked Dale to take part in the murders but he
refused. "I didn't care to die that day," Dale testified.

ON FEBRUARY 22, 1980, Mitchell was recalled to the
witness stand, this time to testify about the murders of the
three young criminals, James Johnston, Dwayne Lincoln,
and Wayne Sampson. Mitchell said he didn't want to shoot
Wayne Sampson but did so after David Johnston pulled out
a .38-caliber pistol and threatened him. "I thought it would
be better for my health if I assassinated (Sampson)," Mitchell testified. Mitchell said he missed his first shot because
Johnston Sr. accidentally shined the flashlight into his eyes.
Mitchell's next two shots found their target.

Chester County Detective Larry Dampman then told the
jury that the most unpleasant job he ever performed as a
policeman was the digging up of the three young men killed
by the Johnstons. He told the jury about using spoons to
remove loose dirt from the corpses and about each body having to be carefully removed from the hand-dug tomb and
placed in body bags.

AFTER THREE WEEKS of listening to prosecution witness after prosecution witness give testimony against them, on March 3, 1980, Norman and David Johnston had their opportunity to present their defense. Defense attorney John Lachall's opening statement again pointed the blame toward Mitchell, Dale, and the defendants' own brother, Johnston Sr. The murders stopped, Lachall pointed out, after Mitchell, Dale, and Johnston Sr. went to prison. David and Norman Johnston didn't have a reason to kill the murder victims, according to Lachall, and barely even knew the victims.

David Johnston said he had only met Jimmy Johnston one or two times in his life and Johnston Jr. on just a few more occasions. He also said he didn't know Dwayne Lincoln or Wayne Sampson.

One of the first witnesses for the defense was Susan Johnston, Norman's wife. She testified she was with her husband, first at her mother-in-law's home and then at their apartment, on the day Miller was murdered and Johnston Jr. shot. She said she was with David Johnston until 11:00 PM that night and David Johnston left with his friend, Beryl Heaton. The two brothers spent the day of the shooting at a racetrack. Susan Johnston told the jury that her husband spent a lot of time at the racetrack but also did "do several things" to make a living.

The credibility of prosecution witness Leslie Dale was challenged by one defense witness, a former chapter president of the outlaw Pagan motorcycle gang, Jack Anderson. Anderson told the jury that Dale admitted killing James Sampson with the help of Mitchell and that Dale said he was going to kill Johnston Jr. Under questioning by special prosecutor Lamb, Anderson admitted he held a grudge against Lamb and Chief County Detective Charles Zagorskie.

Anderson was investigated by police for activities as a Pagan member and he blamed Lamb, Zagorskie, and others for causing emotional pain to his family. "They kicked me and my family to pieces," Anderson testified. "They ruined the lives of my wife and daughter. The man upstairs will take care of you people."

DAVID AND NORMAN Johnston had their day on the witness stand on March 5. The two men were polite and quiet as they testified in their own defense. They did not give the appearance of cold-blooded killers. The blame for the murders should be placed on Mitchell and Dale, they both testified.

Norman Johnston said he told Mitchell that the missing gang members would be picked up soon after a newspaper story reported them as being in Arizona. "Ricky said, 'no,'" Norman Johnston testified. "I said do you know these boys are dead. Ricky said, 'I don't think so: I know so.'" David Johnston recounted a conversation between Dale and his brother, Johnston Sr. "Dale said little Bruce (Jr.) had to go. Bruce (Sr.) said he didn't want little Bruce hurt, and he didn't want anyone hurt. Bruce (Sr.) said he put him on a plane and sent them away," David Johnston testified. "Dale said, 'Keep thinking like that and you and Sampson (James) will end up with a hundred years (to serve in prison).'"

Norman Johnston also had hard words for Dale. "I couldn't stand the creep," the murder defendant said. Norman Johnston also said Dale made obscene gestures to him every time they saw each other in prison.

In 15 minutes David Johnston gave the Cambria County jury his defense. For more than two hours Lamb hammered away at the defendant's testimony. When Lamb asked about testimony given by prosecution witnesses, David Johnston would conclude the witnesses were lying. Lamb completed his questioning by naming nine prosecution witnesses who gave testimony against David Johnston and asking if all of the witnesses were lying and only he was telling the truth. David Johnston said all the prosecution witnesses were liars.

Lamb also took hours on cross-examining Norman Johnston, poking at inconsistent statements and probing the defense story. At the conclusion of the testimony Norman Johnston proclaimed his innocence. "I've never shot anybody in my life, including Jimmy Sampson," he told the jury.

EVEN THOUGH BRUCE A. Johnston Sr. was a central character in the case against his two brothers, Norman and David Johnston, he never appeared as a witness. Johnston Sr. indicated a willingness to take the stand to help his brothers. "I know my brothers didn't do it. I want to take the stand because those people (the jury) want to hear from me," Johnston Sr. told a reporter. Johnston Sr.'s new attorney, Anthony List, advised his client against taking the stand because his testimony would be used when Johnston Sr. went to trial.

Defense attorneys wanted Johnston Sr. to be allowed to answer only selected questions, a tactic which Lamb argued against allowing. Judge Sugerman denied the defense's request and Johnston Sr. didn't testify.

Johnston Sr.'s wife, Carol, was also slated to be a defense witness but she wasn't put on the stand after she was taken to Lee's Hospital in Johnstown and then to Conemaugh Valley Hospital, Johnstown. Louise Johnston, the mother of the three Johnston brothers, said Carol Johnston was nervous about testifying. Johnston Sr.'s defense attorney, List, said he was staying at the Star Light Motel in Johnstown when he was summoned to Carol Johnston's room. "She was dressed in a nightgown and bathrobe, and wanted to go out in the cold and walk the streets of Johnstown," List said.

The defense also called Robert Proudfoot who testified that while at Chester County Farms Prison with Dale, Dale admitted committing four of the murders.

The defense's final witness was the defendants' mother, Louise Johnston. She testified she never heard any conversations at her home concerning murder and other illegal activity. Louise Johnston also said Beryl Heaton, David, Norman and Susan Johnston were all at her home on the evening Robin Miller was killed. When asked about contradictory statements she gave to police officers, Louise Johnston replied that she had been questioned numerous times and the interrogations "made me sick mentally and physically. I don't like talking to any of the police. They only lie on ya."

THE LONG TRIAL and strain was beginning to tell on all involved in the murder case. On March 9 an explosion near the car transporting the Johnston brothers to the courthouse was a breaking point. The explosion was believed to be a firecracker but at first it was taken for a gunshot and caused a number of well-armed state police to descend on the car. Chester County Detective Chief Charles Zagorskie was at the window of the prosecution's third floor office when the explosion took place and verified that it was a firecracker. The person who threw the firecracker was not found.

One of the state policemen guarding the courthouse expressed dissatisfaction with his assignment. "I'd rather be elsewhere," he told *Daily Local News* reporter Bruce Mowday. "I have a wife and kid at home."

Also during the trial a bomb was found outside the courthouse by police. On another occasion a possible escape attempt was foiled when somebody was surprised cutting a window near where the Johnstons were kept, according to Lamb. On another night two cars pulled up to the courthouse without lights.

The jury had been sequestered since the beginning of the

trial and steps were taken to give them some outings when not in the courtroom, including a tour of a spaghetti factory. "An overworked jury can be grounds for a mistrial," Judge Sugerman commented.

The attorneys and Judge Sugerman also had their moments in the courtroom during the later stages of the trial. One day, after defense attorney Lawrence Goldberg and Assistant District Attorney Dolores Troiani traded sharp comments, Judge Sugerman said, "I know tempers are short, including my own. We're a bit dragged out, beat up. Let's have no more demonstrations in front of the jury. Take a leisurely lunch." The leisurely lunch didn't work as the afternoon session began with Goldberg and Judge Sugerman hotly debating an issue.

AFTER THE DEFENSE completed its case, Lamb and Troiani called eleven witnesses in rebuttal to challenge statements made by defense witnesses. The testimony at one point was delayed for a day when a surprise snowstorm hit Ebensburg. Snow fell almost each day of the trial.

The prosecution wanted a surprise rebuttal witness—Carol Johnston, wife of Johnston Sr.—to testify for the prosecution. The defense asked for a hearing to see if she was competent to testify. A few days earlier a case of reported nerves led to her being hospitalized and not called as a defense witness.

Carol Johnston entered the courtroom on March 12 flanked by state policemen, FBI agents, and an assistant United States attorney; she immediately departed. "She came down, looked in the courtroom, and just ran out," Troiani recalled.

After being released from the hospital she told her husband's defense attorney, Anthony List, she wanted to go to her parents' home in Coatesville, Chester County. From there she contacted the District Attorney's office and was taken to

Ebensburg where she conferred with prosecutors. "This is an unbelievable twist in the case," List commented.

Carol Johnston never testified. She said she was afraid of retribution against her and her two-year-old daughter, Sharon.

Testimony in the six-week trail was then completed—after approximately 150 witnesses.

DEFENSE ATTORNEY JOHN Lachall, representing David Johnston, told the jury in his closing that his client and Norman Johnston were charged on the theory of guilt by association. "This is not what our system is based on," Lachall said. For two hours Lachall attacked the prosecution's case, especially the testimony of Mitchell. Mitchell, an admitted murderer, had made a deal with the prosecution, a deal giving Mitchell a chance of being released from prison. "Mitchell bragged about committing the three murders. He bragged, not lied. If ever there was a reasonable doubt, there is in the case of the three boys," Lachall argued.

When Lawrence Goldberg, representing Norman Johnston, had his turn to speak he pointed out that if Norman and David Johnston wanted to kill potential witnesses, Dale and Mitchell would have been at the top of the list. "They are alive and well," Goldberg said. "I have no doubt the boys were killed because they could testify. But I have great doubts the murders were planned as the prosecution witnesses said."

Three times during Goldberg's closing Lamb objected to statements and arguments made by Goldberg and the objections were sustained by Judge Sugerman. Goldberg apologized for his zealousness and told the jury, "I tend to overstate."

Lamb was also scheduled to give his closing on March 13 but another snowstorm stopped the afternoon session. He would have his chance the next day.

While Lamb was preparing his closing arguments *New York Times* reporter Ben Franklin paid a visit. "He told me that I was going to lose the case," Lamb recalled. "There is no way I was going to win this case. He was concerned about the polluted source issue, that our case involved deals with crooks and bums and murderers. We didn't have a priest, rabbi or minister. We had some major concerns about the issue. Basically we had a circumstantial case. One of the things that we had to impress on the jury was the thoroughness of the investigation. I also believe the jury had to be impressed with the cooperation of the various law enforcement agencies. We treated each other the same and we all had the philosophy of us against the world."

Chester County Detective Mike Carroll added, "When juries were out it was an anxious time. The Ebensburg jury didn't care about what took place in Chester County and really didn't want to be jurors. Every day we looked at the jury and tried to figure out what they were thinking. The jury didn't connect with us. They seemed to be more interested in the Johnston women."

Lamb completed preparations for his closing argument and was ready when Sugerman indicated he should begin. Lamb told the Cambria County jury that the Johnstons' code demands that police "snitches," even though they may be Johnston family members, must die. "We're not dealing with a regular family," Lamb said. "This isn't a family of love. This is a family of crime. These are the worst kinds of crimes imaginable. Not only is it murder, but murder for a purpose, murder to stop people from taking the witness stand and telling the truth."

For three hours Lamb addressed the jury. He described the murders and commented, "What a terrible price to pay for silence." The jury and spectators sat in silence listening to Lamb's speech and the prosecutor concluded by pointing to the courtroom's rotunda and booming out his final plea, "Let the word go forth to the world today, from this courtroom, that these defendants are guilty of murder in the first degree."

LAMB'S LAW PARTNER and former member of the District Attorney's office, James McErlane, attended portions of the trial. On one of his first visits he received a scowl from Zagorskie. "I came in through a side door of the courtroom and sat down next to some spectators. Zagorskie was glaring at me and I wondered what was bothering him. Then a man introduces himself to me. It was Passmore Peter Johnston. I had prosecuted him years before on a receiving stolen property charge. He also introduced his wife. The prosecution team was looking at me because I was sitting with the Johnston family."

JUDGE SUGERMAN BEGAN his legal instructions to the jury at 2:30 PM but halted at 6:45 PM after another snowstorm hit Ebensburg. He concluded his address to the jury the next day, March 15, a Saturday, and the jury began deliberations at 10:45 AM. The four alternate jurors were dismissed from service. Even though they wouldn't comment, the four jurors indicated two were for conviction and two undecided.

The deliberations stretched through the weekend and Judge Sugerman called for a rare Sunday session for deliberations. The jury had a few legal questions for Judge Sugerman and the attorneys. One dealt with corrupt and polluted sources, such as Mitchell and Dale.

Early in the deliberations a court official revealed the first vote by the jury was ten to two for conviction. The jury reportedly broke off deliberations when the accurate vote was reported to search their jury room, convinced the room was bugged.

"I don't know if I can take another day. My nerves," David Johnston said during the deliberations. "I would rather have them deliberate and come back with a verdict. Not guilty." The defendants spent the weekend in the courthouse waiting for the verdict, talking with friends and family.

Those guarding the Johnstons were still tense. Two hours after the case went to the jury an alarm went off in the court-room where the case was held. State police responded with weapons but it was determined an alarm had malfunctioned.

When the jury retired for the day on Sunday Judge Suger-man joined members of the press for a dinner at an Italian restaurant outside of Ebensburg. Reporters from the *New York Times*, Philadelphia *Inquirer*, Pottstown *Mercury* and *Daily Local News* joined the judge for a session where many questions were asked and Judge Sugerman judicially replied not revealing any legal secrets of the trial even though pre-dinner and post-dinner drinks were consumed along with wine at dinner.

While the trial was serious, there were breaks for the pros-ecuting team. During one long luncheon break, a member of the Cambria County Clerk of Courts' office helped host a meal at a relative's home that included Judge Sugerman, Lamb and Troiani, the prosecution attorneys, Chief County Detective Charles Zagorskie, other police officers, court of-ficials and a newspaper reporter, Bruce Mowday.

The jurors' contact with the outside world was limited but that didn't stop juror David Melnik from proposing to his girlfriend, Helen Sicilliano. Melnik asked Cambria County Deputy Sheriff Rita Burns to take his marriage proposal to Sicilliano. "Oh, yes," was the reply. "It was my most unusual request from a jury member," Burns said.

AT 9:30 AM on Monday, March 17, the jury was back in the courthouse deliberating. The jurors spent the day working through the murder charges against Norman and David Johnston. They concluded the day without indicating they had made a decision. Court officials indicated the count now was eleven to one for conviction.

Prosecutor Lamb said the lengthy jury deliberations caused him some anxious moments. "I would have shot myself if we had a hung jury," Lamb said.

The next day, March 18 at 11:00 AM the jury signaled, after 28 hours of deliberations they had agreed on verdicts. The attorneys were notified and all began assembling in the courtroom. Trial-watchers, prosecutors, defense, and police descended on the room and the crowd was six deep around the back of the courtroom. Reporters from the national media, wire services, and Chester County newspapers all notified editors to stand by for the verdicts. They then staked out aisle seats, so they could rush to waiting telephones to call in the verdicts.

The only member of the Johnston family present for the verdict was Susan Johnston, wife of Norman Johnston. "The waiting is really bad," she said minutes before the verdict was rendered while sitting in the courthouse cafeteria eating a candy bar. "That's the worst part, the waiting. I'm tired, the whole family's tired." As defense attorney Lawrence Goldberg walked into the room he commented, "I had a terrible feeling last night that it would be today."

At 11:26 AM the jury rendered its verdicts. Jury foreman Kenneth Kepler handed the verdict slip to court attendant Carl Harrison, who relayed it to Judge Sugerman. All eyes in the courtroom were on Judge Sugerman as he studied each page of the verdicts. The judge didn't give an indication of the jury's verdict and handed the slip back to Kepler. The jury members stood next to each other as the decisions were read.

Norman and David Johnston were found guilty of four counts of first-degree murder. The verdicts carried life imprisonment terms. The jurors found the brothers not guilty of one count of murder, the death of James Sampson, the victim whose body was buried in the Lanchester landfill and never found.

At the prosecution table Lamb, Troiani, and Joseph Carroll sat in silence. Dana Fernald, an investigator for David Johnston, called the reaction of the defendants as "an odd combination of grief and anger."

The reporters rushed to the doors to find telephones to call in the news to the waiting editors.

Judge Sugerman pronounced, "These proceedings are closed."

"THIS IS A proper verdict," Lamb said. "Miss Troiani and I have been saying all along this is a strong case. This establishes the strength of the American jury system." Troiani added, "It is a credit to the jury that they carefully considered the evidence. It is too bad the death penalty is not in effect. This is a highly appropriate case."

Defense attorney Goldberg's only comment to the press was: "All the thoughts I have about this case will be put in the motions for a new trial." Fellow defense attorney Lachall said, "The prosecution had a lot of evidence but I could never see it being enough to convict the defendants."

As the attorneys were making their remarks the giant metal detector on loan from an airline that had dominated the entrance to the courthouse was being removed along with other security equipment.

Everyone connected with the seven week trial seemed in a hurry to depart Ebensburg. Troiani did take home a trial memento; she was given the verdict slips from the jurors.

Attorneys for both the prosecution and defense thanked the jurors for their service and Judge Sugerman told the jurors, "go home and pick up the threads of your lives."

Lamb gave all of the credit for the convictions to the state police, county detectives, FBI, and other local and federal investigators. A number of courtroom observers also thought Lamb's dramatic closing argument helped gain the convictions.

"This investigation couldn't have been done without the people forgetting about themselves. They forgot about I, I and the glory. All they cared about was getting a conviction," Lamb said.

Zagorskie's comment was, "Too bad they couldn't get the chair."

CHAPTER FOURTEEN

Bruce A. Johnston Sr.'s Trial

"**O**ur first priority is getting Bruce Johnston Sr. convicted," Assistant District Attorney Dolores Troiani said immediately after the convictions of Norman and David Johnston on four counts of first-degree murder.

There would be no rest for the prosecution team in the months between the conviction of two of the Johnston brothers, Norman and David, and the trial of Johnston Sr. Troiani believed the trial of Johnston Sr. was much more difficult than the trial of Norman and David Johnston even though in many ways the trial was a rerun of the same witnesses and same defense and prosecution strategy.

"We had to keep Leslie (Dale) and Ricky (Mitchell) in line," Troiani said. "Leslie thought Ricky was getting too much attention and he wasn't getting enough. We prepared for the second trial by sitting down with (state policemen) Tom (Cloud) and Bob Martz and we read the trial transcripts. We took turns reading to each other. We commented 'this is good, this is bad, this is unclear.'"

A major change in the second trial that made it easier for all of the attorneys and witnesses in the case was the location of the trial, West Chester, the county seat of Chester County. On April 1, 1980, Pennsylvania Governor Dick Thornburgh signed into law a bill that permitted juries, in the cases of change of venues, to be selected in one county and transported to the county where the crime was committed.

"It was easier for us but harder for the jury," Troiani said. Jurors were selected in Erie County for the Johnston Sr. trial. Special prosecutor William H. Lamb said, "In a sense, the Erie trip was more fun because we were just picking a jury, not worrying about moving witnesses as we did in Ebensburg."

Having the trial in Chester County did pose at least one disadvantage. Troiani pointed out that in Cambria County the prosecution team had little to do but to prepare for the next day in court. In Chester County the prosecution team would return to their homes after the workday concluded.

Lamb said the Johnston Sr. trial was easier and "not nearly as exciting as the first trial." He said, "At the first trial we were together 24/7. We ate breakfast together and we had a system of having lunch in the courthouse while continuing to talk strategy and preparing witnesses. We ate dinner together. We were forced to think about the case 24 hours a day."

Security was still a concern and Troiani recalled an incident involving a legal assistant for Anthony List, Sheri Desaretz, who brought a gun to the courthouse. "She wanted to know if the gun was like the one used in one of the murders," Troiani said. "I told the sheriff deputies to take the gun away from her. Judge Sugerman was furious."

"Phil Perry was assigned to stay with Judge Sugerman the whole time," Zagorskie added. "Kill the judge and it would be all over."

AS THE PREPARATIONS for the Johnston Sr. trial continued other crime members had their day in court. Roy Myers,
brother-in-law of Johnston Sr., appeared for sentencing before Judge Sugerman in April. Chief Deputy District Attorney James P. MacElree II urged Judge Sugerman to give Myers a lenient prison term because of his cooperation against
the Johnstons. Defense Attorney David Wood said Myers
had been totally cooperative with prosecutors.

Myers had admitted to committing two burglaries in
Chester County and Judge Sugerman imposed a sentence of
11 1/2-to-23 months in prison and five years on probation.
The sentence was to run concurrently with other sentences
given to Myers by a judge in Lancaster County and federal
Judge Louis H. Pollak.

Martin Knecht, who also cooperated with the prosecution
and testified against Norman and David Johnston, was not
quite as lucky as Myers when he appeared before President
Judge D. T. Marrone in late April. Knecht, a convicted murderer, was sentenced for his escape from the Chester County
sheriff's office in 1979 and received a sentence of three to
seven years in prison. His attorney, Thomas Wilson, and
Troiani both asked Judge Marrone to allow Knecht to serve
his time other than in a state prison, fearing for his safety.

Judge Marrone said, "This man is going to be incarcerated
somewhere. His case has caused the public a great deal of
time and manpower. It is too grave an offense to give him
county time."

Knecht was a decent artist, according to Troiani. "My father died during the investigation. Marty did a card for me.
I had it for years."

One of the prosecution witnesses, Ricky Mitchell, found
Chester County Farms Prison to be an unsafe place. In
March four inmates jumped and beat Mitchell on his face
and body. Mitchell said he was in the prison's day room and

sat down at a picnic table. Several inmates were watching television.

"I had been there about a half minute and I catch a left hook and I go about six feet to the floor. And this guy, the biggest one of the bunch...he dances around the floor...I don't want to be struck again so I start walking towards the door. This time another man struck me in the back of the head also. And he drove me towards the man who was dancing. The man who was dancing gave me another left hook and I went down underneath a bench. And there was a man sitting on a picnic table right across from me.

"As soon as I went down, he came over and started to kick me in the face. And I tried to grab his leg and throw him down. While I'm doing that, the other two people come up and start kicking me also. And I thought I better come off this floor or I'm in trouble. So I start to get up. When I start to get up, a bench hits me in the back of the head. Bang. I fall back down on the floor. I see this young man with a bench. I see him. He's the only one sitting there, so he has to be the one to do it. I get hit again by the bench.

"After that I lost consciousness. After I hit the ground they kept kicking me and I lost consciousness. I don't know when I woke up. I could have been out as long as ten minutes. I don't know. I could have been out a half hour, I believe. I woke up and went to the door. I didn't look around. I wasn't interested in getting killed. My first thought was a hasty exit. Have you ever watched that cartoon on TV where he says exit stage right and exit stage left? Well, exit stage left is what I took."

Mitchell told reporter Bruce Mowday that he didn't know if the Johnstons were behind his being attacked and has not made an attempt to find out if the Johnstons were involved. "I mind my own business," Mitchell said.

Mitchell also took the opportunity to talk about his days

of crime with the Johnston brothers. Mitchell said the Johnstons invited him to be part of their gang. "They knew I was
good," Mitchell said. "I was a burglar. I borrowed things, like
green money. I don't like property; you have to sell it to others." Mitchell said he did honest work but could never earn
enough money to cover his expenses. He said some weeks he
committed three burglaries.

Being a victim of violence was not new to Mitchell as he
said he was shot seven times, including once in a card game
in Chicago. His wife had also shot him accidentally, he said.
Mitchell said the first time he was shot was when he was
nine years old. A farmer in West Grove caught him stealing a basket of peaches. "The farmer shot for my head but I
put the basket in front of my head. He ruined the peaches,"
Mitchell said.

Zagorskie recalled another incident involving Mitchell.
"Ricky was unreal," Zagorskie said. "Once there was a little
prison uprising, nothing overly serious, but inmates were out
of their cells, except for Ricky. When we asked why he remained in his cell Ricky said there was nothing to steal out
there."

THE CONVICTED JOHNSTON brothers didn't take long to
begin quests for new trials. In late April Norman Johnston
asked to have Goldberg removed from his case and have a
new attorney, Michael Barranco, appointed to represent him
on appeal. Barranco was a former member of the Public Defender's office who represented the Johnstons in previous
cases. Later in the year defense attorney Joseph Nescio was
appointed to take Goldberg's place.

New trial appeals would go on for decades in the cases.

Other cases involving the convicted Johnston brothers
were also finalized. David and Norman Johnston plead no

contest to two burglaries, the one at Longwood Gardens and the one at an A & P store in Caln Township, Chester County. They were sentenced to two-to-four years in prison.

Norman Johnston wasn't the only convicted murderer unhappy with his legal representation. In May Leslie Dale asked to have his attorney, Michael Kean removed from the case.

LEGAL MANEUVERING IN the Johnston Sr. case was ongoing from the conclusion of the Ebensburg trial. At a pre-trial hearing Johnston Sr. refused to sign a waiver of his speedy trial rights, resulting in the setting of a trial date of April 30. Since defense attorney List had only been assigned to the complex case for several weeks, he was not viewed as prepared to handle the defense and a built-in appeal was there if Johnston Sr. was convicted. Lamb called the defense stance "legal blackmail." Johnston Sr. eventually agreed to waive his speedy trial rights and the trial was scheduled to begin in September.

Several times List attempted to delay the trial beyond the September date. Judge Sugerman refused to grant the delay and List even asked to have Judge Sugerman removed from the trial of Johnston Sr. because of statements he gave in September 1978 to the *Daily Local News* in connection with the Miller murder. Judge Sugerman told List, "I have been assigned to try this case, and I fully intend to carry out that responsibility."

List lost his final attempt to delay the trial when Pennsylvania Supreme Court Justices Robert N. C. Nix Jr. and Bruce W. Kauffman refused List's request for a delay. Lamb argued against List's motion and pointed out 350 prospective jurors were to be in Erie the following week for jury selection and 130 subpoenas had been sent to possible prosecution witnesses.

When the argument before the justices concluded Justice Nix told List, "A good defense counsel never feels he has enough time."

IN JULY JOHNSTON Sr. became a victim of crime. Arson took place at his Maryland home on Blue Ball Road. Maryland State Police reported that someone entered the one-story wood frame home and set the blaze. Police didn't speculate on the motive for the fire.

THE PROSECUTION AND defense teams gathered in Erie to begin selecting jurors but the proceeding was delayed on September 25, 1980, as a prospective juror admitted researching the Johnston murder case. The juror said he went to a local library and read a magazine story on the Johnston brothers. The juror admitted she talked with other potential jurors. The magazine photographs were "so gory that she didn't think she could look at them if she were on the trial jury," the woman told attorneys. Judge Sugerman dismissed the remaining 60 prospective jurors and ordered new potential jurors to be in the courtroom the next day.

WHEN NOT IN the courtroom, the prosecution team played tennis matches. Joseph Carroll said, "I teamed with Tom (Cloud) and we kept winning. Lamb wanted me as a partner."

ON OCTOBER 1 the jury had been selected and was flown to Chester County. Six men and six women made up the panel along with four alternates, including three additional women. Judge Sugerman informed the jurors that the trial could last six weeks and arrangements had been made for them to stay at the Downingtown Motor Inn during the trial. A number of outings, including one to a professional football game, were also in the offing for the jurors. One of the jurors was dismissed before the trial began because of an illness of a family member.

As the Cambria County jury was told earlier in the year, the Erie County jurors were informed they were about to hear testimony from admitted murderers concerning the deaths of six people. In her opening statement on October 6, 1980, Troiani told the jurors the prosecution was going to "explore the evil motives" in the mind of Johnston Sr. Lamb added, "True, this is a complex case because of all of the characters, but the case is about this defendant killing witnesses to silence them. The purpose was the silencing of the witnesses against this defendant and his two brothers, David and Norman Johnston."

Troiani also took the opportunity to warn the jurors that Mitchell was an unusual witness. "Understanding Ricky Mitchell will be a very big difficulty," Troiani said since Mitchell suffers from a number of illnesses and had been involved in car accidents. Indeed Mitchell took the stand against Johnston Sr. and repeated the testimony he gave against Norman and David Johnston. List, as did defense attorneys for David and Norman Johnston, attacked Mitchell's credibility and Mitchell proved to be as combative with List as he was with prosecution attorneys at times. After Mitchell tried to ask List a question, Judge Sugerman interrupted and said, "Let's not get our roles reversed, Mr. Mitchell."

Johnston Sr. also had a few words for Mitchell after Mitchell completed his testimony. Johnston Sr. called out from the defense table, "Can you think of any more lies, Mitchell?"

Besides Mitchell, Leslie Dale, James Griffin, Johnston Jr., other former gang members and associates, family members of the victims, and the law enforcement officers all took the witness stand, as they had in Ebensburg, to testify concerning the six murders. Witnesses had told their stories numerous times under oath, including two murder trials, preliminary hearings, and pre-trial hearings.

One difference in the case was that Johnston Sr. faced charges of murdering police informant Gary Wayne Crouch. David and Norman Johnston weren't charged with Crouch's death. Delaware State Police Detective John Quigley told the jury Crouch had been cooperating with his department and on July 13, 1977, Crouch had given a statement implicating the three Johnston brothers in a number of crimes. Quigley also said Crouch was unreliable and was known to "play both ends (police and fellow criminals) against the middle." Crouch told Quigley just four days before his death that he was to meet with Johnston Sr. and Leslie Dale, who had admitted shooting Crouch on the orders of Johnston Sr.

"I put the gun behind Gary's head and shot him," Dale said when he took the witness stand. "Bruce's (Johnston Sr.) eyes got real big and he said 'look at the hole in the windshield.' Bruce got out of the car and ran around the front of it. I said, 'you dumb s.o.b., get back in the car.' Bruce said 'look at the blood coming out.'"

Dale said Johnston Sr. approached him on July 15, 1977, about making "big bucks" and the next day the two criminals discussed ways of disposing of Crouch's body. Dale testified they discussed getting a "chipper machine" that breaks up tree limbs and putting Crouch's body through the tool. Also, Dale said they discussed burying Crouch or putting the body in the Knickerbocker Landfill in Malvern. The two finally decided to bury Crouch in a grave they dug in a deserted section of Highland Township. "It took quite a while to dig.

I'm glad I don't have to do that all of the time. And it was hot too," Dale testified.

After shooting Crouch, Dale said he drove to the already dug grave and Johnston Sr. dragged Crouch's body from the car. "Bruce said, 'you rat'n s.o.b., I have something to talk to you about.' Bruce went through his pockets and gave me a handful of bills as a bonus," Dale testified. The money amounted to more than $80. Dale said he received an additional $3,000 for committing the murder. As Crouch was being thrown into the grave Dale said he noticed one of Crouch's eyes was open and said, "That s.o.b. is peek'in."

Actually, Crouch was alive when he was placed in the grave, according to testimony given by Dr. Halbert Fillinger, an assistant medical examiner from Philadelphia. Crouch was "alive and breathing" for at least a few minutes and maybe as long as a few hours after being buried. Fillinger found gravel in Crouch's lungs. He ruled the cause of death was a gunshot wound to the head with suffocation caused by the gravel a contributing factor.

Before covering Crouch's body, the two murderers took the stolen car used in the murder to a field and set it on fire. "I wanted to cover Crouch but Bruce wanted to get rid of the car because of the blood," Dale testified. After torching the car, the pair went back to the grave to finish the burial. "We hoped the s.o.b. didn't crawl out," Dale told the jury.

During cross-examination List pointed out that Dale had made a deal with the prosecution for his testimony and that at first Dale told police that Johnston Sr. was the one who pulled the trigger. Dale also said he had threatened Johnston Sr. in the past.

Additional testimony on the Crouch murder was given by James "Disco" Griffin. Griffin told the jury Johnston Sr. admitted taking part in the murder. "I gave him a new job, pushing up daises," Griffin quoted Johnston Sr. as saying. Also, during another conversation David Johnston said he wanted to dig up Crouch's grave and get rid of the bones. "Bruce (Johnston Sr.) said there was just dust left," Griffin testified.

Roy Myers, a gang member and brother-in-law to Johnston Sr., said Johnston Sr. also discussed with him the need to murder Crouch because Crouch was a police informant. An admitted fence of stolen property for the Johnstons, Ed Otter of Gilbertsville, recalled that Johnston Sr. was upset at Dale for talking about Crouch's death. "One of these days Leslie's mouth is going to get him blown away," Otter quoted Johnston Sr. as saying.

THE JURY SAW first hand the impact the deaths of the victims had on their families when the mothers of James and Wayne Sampson and Dwayne Lincoln testified on October 9.

Marie Ann Sampson of Havre de Grace, Maryland, dabbed at tears as she identified photographs of her sons, Wayne who was twenty at the time of his death, and James, age twenty-four. Amy Harris of Oxford, Lincoln's mother, didn't start to cry until after she completed her testimony.

Marie Sampson recounted a visit Johnston Sr. made to her home and a statement he made about Dwayne Lincoln. "If he squealed to police on me," she quoted Johnston Sr. as saying, "I'll kill the s.o.b. and your daughter too." Glenda Sampson Chamberlain was Lincoln's girlfriend at one time.

Glenda Chamberlain also played a central part in List's attempt to show that Dale had a reason for killing the Sampson brothers. During a hearing after the jury had been dismissed for the day, Marie Sampson testified that her daughter told her that Dale had beat and raped her. "The left side of her face was black," Mrs. Sampson testified. "It took a month to heal." She said her daughter was assaulted after she refused to go out on a date with Dale.

Judge Sugerman allowed List to question Dale about the rape allegation and before the jury Dale denied sexually assaulting the young woman. "She wanted me to pay her money," Dale testified. "She wasn't worth nothin'. She wanted $100. I wouldn't have minded paying her the $100 if she would have given $99 back," Dale said. Dale also testified that the woman's two brothers were present when the conversation took place. "How am I going to rape her with her two brothers there?" Dale asked.

Glenda Chamberlain had died within two months of the murders of her brothers. She was twenty-one years old on November 7, 1978, when she was found in a car with eighteen-year-old Willie K. Hutchinson Jr. in a secluded field in Lancaster County. The couple died of carbon monoxide poisoning. The vehicle was old and the exhaust system was in bad shape, according to a police investigation, but rumors persisted that Glenda Chamberlain's death was not an accident. One inmate, Richard Falasco, claimed Norman Johnston had taken credit for the couple's deaths.

Falasco, a convicted burglar, did take the stand against Johnston Sr. One day Falasco asked Johnston Sr. what it was like to murder a person. Johnston Sr., according to Falasco, said, "I have no problem. I can put my head on the pillow and go to sleep." From his seat at the defense table Johnston Sr. responded, "You lie." Another statement Falasco testified Johnston Sr. made was, "I may make a snitch but I make them tough." The statement was in reference to Johnston Jr.'s surviving numerous bullet wounds.

Falasco also quoted Norman Johnston as saying about the murder of Robin Miller, "'We filled the car full of holes. It was just like Bonnie and Clyde.'"

LINDA MILLER, THE mother of murder victim Robin Miller, was not only angry over the death of her daughter but she was also upset with the legal system. She was not allowed to watch the remainder of the trial after she had concluded her testimony. After she left the witness stand Miller took a seat in the spectator section of the courtroom and was asked to leave. Miller and Troiani had a heated discussion in the hallway outside of Judge Sugerman's courtroom with Miller saying she had as much right as any other person to view the trial. A sequestration order was in effect and the defense didn't want her in the courtroom. Miller would be a constant reminder to the jury of her murdered daughter.

After Miller's discussion with Troiani and Chief County Detective Charles Zagorskie, Miller was taken into Judge Sugerman's chambers for a meeting. Upon the conclusion of the discussion Miller left Judge Sugerman's office in tears and didn't return to the courtroom. Robin Miller's sister, Roxanne Miller, also wasn't allowed to stay to watch the trial after her testimony.

Roxanne Miller told the jury she returned home about an hour before Robin Miller and Johnston Jr. did and departed 15 minutes later because she saw a light in the cellar and was afraid.

Another prosecution witness, Edward Aldred of Oxford, testified that Johnston Sr. blamed Robin Miller for turning his son against him. A few days before the shooting, according to Aldred, Johnston Sr. said, "Robin has a big mouth." Aldred also said he was present when Johnston Sr. offered to pay Johnston Jr. $12,000 if he would stop cooperating with police.

THE PROSECUTION'S CASE against Johnston Sr. lasted 18 days during which Lamb and Troiani called 125 witnesses to the stand and used more than 300 exhibits. List was ready to begin Johnston Sr.'s defense which would take a lot less time than the prosecution's case. After the close of the prosecution's case List indicated that Norman and David Johnston were possible witnesses for their brother. Judge Sugerman informed the brothers that any testimony they might give could be used during their appeals of their murder convictions and their attorneys advised the brothers not to take the witness stand to help Johnston Sr. Norman and David Johnston were unsure if they would be witnesses as the defense began its case.

On Halloween, October 31, 1980, List began the defense's case by telling the jury that his client, Bruce A. Johnston Sr., neither "participated, planned, nor carried out" the murders of the six victims. List joined his fellow defense attorneys, Lawrence Goldberg and John Lachall, in blaming Leslie Dale and Ricky Mitchell for the murders.

The defense immediately suffered a setback. Two witnesses were called to prove that Crouch was alive after the date Dale said he and Johnston Sr. killed the police informant. A Wilmington, Delaware, woman, Helen Taylor, testified she saw Crouch after her baby was born on July 23, 1977. Taylor said she had previously seen Crouch with Dale. However, Taylor then twice failed to identify Crouch in photographic lineups. The second witness, Oxford policeman John Schaible, denied he ever said he saw Crouch in August 1977. Schaible said he saw a car that resembled Crouch's car but couldn't identify the driver. Schaible did say he heard Dale threaten Crouch. "Dale called Crouch a rotten fink. He said somebody should set him up and blow his fuckin' brains out," Schaible testified.

Additional defense witnesses testified they saw some of the victims alive after the time Mitchell said they were killed. Also, Mary Payne, brother of Johnston Sr., testified that Johnston Sr. was at her home swimming when Dale said Crouch was being killed.

One of the witnesses, gang associate James Ray Dotson,

was a reluctant defense witness. Dotson wanted to invoke his right against self-incrimination and not answer questions from List but Judge Sugerman, after a closed hearing, ruled Dotson had to answer questions concerning the murder but that his testimony couldn't lead to a charge of conspiracy to commit murder being filed against him.

Before the jury, Dotson, who was serving a term in state prison on burglary and escape convictions, invoked his right against self-incrimination 20 times, every time a question was asked about crimes he had committed with those affiliated with the Johnstons. When asked about the murder of James Sampson, Dotson testified, "I never wanted Jimmy Sampson killed." He said he was never asked to pay for having Sampson killed, as prosecution witnesses contended.

"Jimmy Sampson was a good friend of mine. I didn't dislike him. I wasn't in fear of him. When I was with Jimmy Sampson we stayed high. I'm not sure what I did when with Jimmy Sampson."

Judge Sugerman called for a special session on Saturday, November 1, to keep the trial moving. One of the witnesses for the defense was Marie Sampson, the mother of two of the victims. She testified Johnston Sr. was "like a father" to her family. Mrs. Sampson said Johnston Sr. gave them money for food, paid an electric bill when the power was about to be cut off and stopped her furniture from being repossessed. Under questioning from Troiani, the woman admitted that payments from the Johnstons were continuing and she had received $250 to help two of her children who were in trouble with legal authorities in Maryland. Mrs. Sampson also said Johnston Sr. wrote her a letter signed, "love always, Bruce."

THE FINAL WITNESS for the defense was Bruce A. Johnston Sr.

For a day and a half Johnston Sr. was on the witness stand answering questions directed to him by his attorney, Anthony List, and prosecutor William H. Lamb. Johnston Sr. portrayed himself as a ladies' man, a generous friend and a thief, but not a mass murderer. The first two and a half hours were spent answering questions from List.

The jury was told that Johnston Sr.'s former partners in crime that were now testifying against him were making up stories for various reasons and that the police had a vendetta against him.

To start Johnston Sr. told the jury two of the witnesses against him—Roy Myers and Jimmy Griffin—held grudges against him because he had sexual relations with their wives. "I was caught in an awkward position with his wife," Johnston Sr. said of his brother-in-law, Myers. "Myers wasn't such a good friend after that." Johnston Sr. and Myers were married to sisters.

"I used to have a lot of lady friends," Johnston Sr. testified. "I love women whether you know it or not." Johnston Sr. testified he stayed at motel rooms in the area when he was having issues with his wife Carol. He also said he didn't always use his real name because his wife had caught him coming out of one of the motels with another woman.

The reason Johnston Jr. said he began testifying against his father was the rape of his girlfriend, Robin Miller, by his father. On the stand Johnston Sr. denied sexually assaulting the girl. "I never raped Robin," Johnston Sr. said. "I viewed her as a fifteen-year-old girl. I was good friends with her. I considered her a little girl because that is what she was. It is disgusting to me that you even ask me about it. It never entered my mind."

Johnston Sr. then blamed the rape on James Sampson, one of the murder victims. Also, Johnston Sr. said James Sampson was one of his best friends. Johnston Sr. said he wasn't surprised that his son was upset about the rape allegations. "I would have probably done the same thing," Johnston Sr. testified. "He was in love with Robin and wanted out of prison."

The defendant said he wouldn't harm his son and Miller and would have stopped the ambush if he had been aware of the plan. At one point Johnston Jr. lived with Johnston Sr. The son was thrown out of the house when Carol Johnston, Johnston Sr.'s second wife, found Johnston Jr. with a needle in his arm. Johnston Jr. was a junkie, according to his father. Johnston Sr. then blamed the ambush on Ricky Mitchell. "There is no doubt in my mind Mitchell did it," Johnston Sr. testified.

Johnston Sr. also disputed Dale's testimony concerning the death of police informant Gary Crouch, saying he would never go out after dark in the woods with Leslie Dale, a known paid killer. "They used to call Dale 'Whacky.' I was scared of Dale. I knew his reputation." Dale was the cold-blooded killer, according to Johnston Sr., and had threatened Johnston Jr.

As for himself, Johnston Sr. said, "I was a thief." He said he hadn't had legitimate employment for the past four years when he had been a truck driver. Johnston Sr. said he would share the money he made through crimes with friends. "When I was growing up, I didn't have anything. I still don't."

Johnston Sr. said he had been a target of police ever since the murder of two Kennett Square policemen on November 15, 1972. Johnston Sr. had testified for the convicted murderer of the policeman, Ancell Hamm. Johnston Sr. said Chief Deputy District Attorney James MacElree told him, "Johnston, you're as guilty as Ancell Hamm."

"They hate me," Johnston Sr. claimed of Chief County Detective Charles Zagorskie and state policemen Tom Cloud, Robert Martz, and Gabe Bolla. Johnston Sr. then added FBI agent David Richter to his list of law enforcement officers he dislikes. The second day on the witness stand Johnston Sr. apologized for calling them dummies. "I guess I shot my mouth off when I shouldn't have. I was pretty mad at the questions they were asking me," Johnston Sr. said. He then added he still hated Zagorskie and he was sure the feeling was mutual.

Special prosecutor William Lamb wasted no time in pointing out discrepancies in Johnston Sr.'s stories. Before Lamb asked a question he walked out of the well of the courtroom and into the spectators' section. He stopped behind *Daily Local News* reporter Bruce Mowday and put a hand on Mowday's shoulder.

"Do you know this man?" Lamb asked.

"He's Bruce Mowday from the *Daily Local*," Johnston Sr. replied.

Johnston Sr. then said he had given Mowday an interview late the previous year. When Lamb pointed out differences in Johnston Sr.'s testimony and statements to Mowday, Lamb asked if Johnston Sr. made the statements to Mowday.

"If Mr. Mowday said I did, I did," Johnston Sr. answered.

Lamb also pointed out that multiple witnesses at a restaurant placed Johnston Sr. with Mitchell at the time Miller was murdered and Johnston Jr. shot. "How could Mitchell be responsible for the shootings?" Lamb asked. The testimony of the employees "fascinates me," Johnston Sr. replied.

For the homicide of the three young members of his gang, Johnston Sr. said, "I have no alibi. But I know one thing I wasn't out in the woods shooting them kids."

THE SUMMATIONS OF the attorneys weren't a surprise when they were given on November 13, 1980. Defense attorney Anthony List claimed Johnston Sr. was a victim of an elaborate frame and prosecutors William Lamb and Dolores

Troiani claimed Johnston Sr. was a vicious murderer.

For three hours List argued that Johnston Sr. was not the person responsible for the death of six people and that Leslie Dale and Ricky Mitchell were the murderers. "He told the most plausible story of all. He didn't commit those murders. This is his day in court. This is the day he has been waiting for since those charges were lodged," List said of his client. He then asked the jury to find Johnston Sr. not guilty.

Lamb had a different take on the defendant. Once the police net began closing on Johnston Sr. he knew he had to take action to escape prison and preserve his lucrative interstate burglary ring. Johnston Sr.'s motive was to stay out of prison, according to Lamb.

Such an elaborate conspiracy, as Johnston Sr. claimed, couldn't have been concocted, Lamb told the jury. "The commonwealth corroborated points made by the major witnesses, big points, little points, and obscure points. It is unthinkable the defendant was a victim of a mass conspiracy. To believe one took place you would have to believe the FBI, state police, county detectives, and the district attorney's office were involved. Give us a little credit, if we put it together, we would have done a better job. How can you rehearse someone like Ricky Mitchell?"

WHILE JOHNSTON SR. was on trial for attempting to kill his son, his son was undergoing abdominal surgery. He was admitted to Southern Chester County Medical Center in Jennersville and immediately transferred to another hospital. "We felt because of the sensitivities of the county at this time, it was better he was out of the immediate area," a hospital spokesman said. The surgery was successful. When released from the hospital Johnston Jr. was asked to leave the Federal Witness Protection Program. Johnston Jr. was considered a liability because he wouldn't follow the program's regulations and had a habit of returning to Oxford where he was in the most danger.

"I GUESS THEY didn't believe a word I said," was Johnston Sr.'s comment to his attorney after the Erie County jury spent less than six hours deliberating before returning guilty verdicts on all six counts of first degree murder. He was also found guilty of attempting to murder his son, Johnston Jr.

At 11:30 AM on November 15, 1980, the verdicts were given in the courtroom of Judge Leonard Sugerman. One juror, Dorothy Horn, said, "There was no question in anybody's mind. We agreed on the guilty verdict from the beginning. We just wanted to go over the material." Actually, the first vote was eleven to one for conviction. The one juror voting for acquittal had misunderstood the law. After a brief discussion the vote was changed to guilty.

Horn added that the jury wasn't impressed when Johnston Sr. called police names and tried to interject some levity into his testimony.

The jurors were dismissed from service and told they could return home. They had been away from Erie County for eight weeks. "We appreciate what you have done," Judge Sugerman told the jury. Lamb added, "We know how hard this has been and the sacrifices you made. You have the thanks of the Commonwealth."

Johnston Sr. didn't react to the verdict as it was read. As he was led from the courtroom by a cordon of law enforcement officers, he said, "I'm innocent." List said his client was in shock and later, in a lockup in the Sheriff's department, Johnston Sr. cried like a baby. "He's got six life sentences for crimes he still claims he didn't commit. Under the circumstances I think he has held up well. He's very upset, obviously," List said.

NO ONE WAS upset in the basement room of the Chester County Courthouse commandeered by the law enforcement team. While waiting for the jury's decision, Tom Cloud, Dave Richter, Charles Zagorskie, and the rest of the investigators remained in the courthouse. For decades, law enforcement officers had chased Bruce A. Johnston Sr. through back roads and fields of southern Chester County. Now, they were close to putting Chester County's most wanted criminal behind bars for life.

When the six guilty verdicts to counts of first-degree murder were finalized there was satisfaction for a job well done and some sadness.

"I feel relief," said Chief Chester County Detective Zagorskie. "But there can be no happiness when six people die. I feel very sorry for Mrs. Sampson."

State policeman Cloud placed a hand on the shoulder of Linda Miller, the mother of murder victim Robin Miller, and said, "It's satisfying but it's not a victory. You can't make it better for Mrs. Miller."

Miller, who had shown her emotions all through the trial, broke down in tears and was led from the room by Connie Noblet, the director of the Chester County Victim and Witness Assistance Agency.

Prosecutor William Lamb said, "It has been a long time. The wheels of the justice system grind slowly, but they do grind." Chester County Detective Sergeant Mike Carroll added, "The system does work." The system, according to Cloud, trapped Johnston Sr. "He didn't think it worked, until this point."

Lamb also had words of praise for the trial attorneys that

handled the defense, Goldberg, Lachall, and List. "Those guys did a good job. They did what they were supposed to do: represent their clients and give them a vigorous defense."

"I think the jury reached the proper verdict," Zagorskie said. "I think it also shows the effort made by the police agencies. Cloud agreed, adding, "I put in a lot of hours but so did a lot of other people. We had the right people involved in the investigation from all of the departments."

FBI agent Richter summed up the investigation, "Together, we did it." Richter and his family were also involved in a lighter moment. "My daughter Ashley was born at the end of the trial and the jurors heard about her birth and wanted to see the baby," Richter said. "Jayne (Richter's wife) brought her to the courthouse. Of course Leslie and Ricky wanted to hold Ashley as a newborn. I forget which one held her first, but the other one was upset as he was being outdone."

November 15, the date of Bruce A. Johnston's conviction, had a special meaning for many in the room. Eight years ago to the day they began investigating the murders of Kennett Square policemen Richard Posey and William Davis.

The belief had been strong that at least one of the Johnston brothers had directly aided convicted murderer Ancell Hamm in the murders of Posey and Davis. Lamb then summed up the feelings of the law enforcement team:

"This is poetic justice. It is eight years after officers Posey and Davis were assassinated in Kennett Square. There is no doubt in my mind that Ancell Hamm had help, and it came from one of these three defendants we convicted this year."

CHAPTER FIFTEEN

Escape and More Murders

Not by a long shot did the six first-degree murder verdicts
against Bruce A. Johnston Sr. conclude the cases of the
Commonwealth of Pennsylvania against Norman Johnston,
David Johnston, and Bruce Johnston Sr.

Chester County wasn't ready to relegate the Johnstons to
the history pages. In the future for the public and law enforcement team were decades of court appeals, a highly pub-
licized escape that put the county residents on edge for two
weeks and more murders. District Attorney Joseph Carroll
said he doesn't believe the appeals will end until the Johnston
brothers are dead.

Three decades after Leslie Dale placed his gun against the
back of the head of police informant Gary Wayne Crouch
and pulled the trigger the effects of the case are felt by those
involved in the investigation and trials, from the investigative team, to the families of the victims to the defendants.

AFTER THE GUILTY verdicts the professional lives of the
law enforcement team weren't the same. State policeman

Paul Yoder summed up the feeling by saying, "After the convictions there were a lot of changes. I went back on the road
as a trooper. I was burned out. I did a lot of other cases and
things quieted down. There were complaints on dog barking.
You were waiting for the next big case and there weren't any."

"What the hell do we do for an encore?" state policeman
Gabe Bolla remembers asking Assistant District Attorney
Dolores Troiani. "I was glad it was over but it made me sad."
Assistant District Attorney Joseph Carroll remembers that
many members of the law enforcement team were physically
tired at the conclusion of the trial.

Special prosecutor William H. Lamb said, "There was a
sense of relief when the trials concluded. I think there was
some mild sadness at not being together with police and the
other members of the team, but it was more relief. I'd fulfilled
my obligation and it was time to get along with my life. I've
been asked if I regret not being a District Attorney. I respond
by saying it was a great job but so was being Justice of the
Supreme Court of Pennsylvania. I've had a great career."

Tom Cloud said he didn't want to think about the number
of hours expended on the case. "It was almost every waking
hour. We had no social lives. We used to drink together but
I quit in 1978. I'd heard you could have two beers a day and
that is good for you. I figure my next beer will be in 2037."

The same sense of being lost held true for newspaper reporters covering the Johnstons. They were looking for the
next big story. One *Daily Local News* editor told Mowday
that for six months after the trials he wasn't worth anything
as a reporter.

State policeman Gabe Bolla remembers having arguments
with one of his state police superiors and Troiani during the
long investigation. "Dolores is now my attorney," Bolla said.
Bolla also remembers a rare time he was home during the
investigation and his wife lining up his children. "She said,

kids I want you to meet your father," Bolla recalled. "I would get home about every other weekend and bring home a bag of dirty laundry. I also had some bad timing on my part on another occasion. Larry (Dampman) and I were in Florida and I called my wife and she was outside chopping ice and snow. I said it was 80 degrees. She let me have it."

FOR YEARS CRIMINAL associates were herded into courtrooms in Chester County and Philadelphia to face charges on crimes committed with the Johnstons. A Downingtown couple, Janet and Frank Gazzero, pleaded guilty in United States District Court in Philadelphia to charges of receiving stolen property, $16,000 worth of stolen mushrooms. Johnston Sr. had stolen the mushrooms and sold them to the Gazzeros. The couple each received more than four years in prison but Frank Gazzero had his prison term suspended and was placed on probation.

In July 1987 during the Gazzero proceedings a startling disclosure was made in connection with a theft trial involving Johnston Sr. in the 1970s. Johnston Sr. was found not guilty of theft after a juror was given a bribe, a stolen tractor. The juror had since died and was not identified.

DAVID JOHNSTON APPEARED before Judge Sugerman on October 3, 1983, for his sentencing. As expected David Johnston received four consecutive life imprisonment terms from Judge Sugerman. One courtroom observer said the sentence is actually "forever."

Sugerman had carefully prepared his sentencing speech and read from the text. He said, "It falls to me to end at this level what began some years ago in this very courtroom. And I suppose one might characterize it as the culmination of a series of tragic events. Indeed, I reviewed the trial record and the pre-trial record in preparing for today's session. It reveals with clarity your life of crime. It appears to the court for years you have plied your nefarious trade in this county and elsewhere unmolested.

"Not content having to rob, pillage, and burglarize the good citizens of this county, you lured these three young men (murder victims Wayne Sampson, Dwayne Lincoln and Jimmy Johnston) into a life of crime and extracted the profits of their crimes as well. As if this wasn't sufficient to brand your actions as a scourge and blemish upon Chester County, when the noose began to close upon these young men you lured into this life of crime, you conspired with your brothers to assassinate them.

"Then in the dark of the night, your usual environment, you accomplished these assassinations, Mr. Johnston, by brutally murdering these people with malice aforethought. In spite of your protestations of innocence the jury found you guilty. Robin Miller, an innocent girl with her whole life in front of her, was also tragically killed in the attack on Bruce Johnston Jr.

"Fortunately this conduct was detected by superb police investigation through all the agencies involved. The county detectives, state police of Pennsylvania, FBI, and other agencies combined happily to stop this course of events that might have continued on as the trial record indicated.

"I say to you Mr. Johnston, personally and in behalf of those, for which I speak, your very existence in Chester County is an outrage and it falls to me, sir, to remove you permanently from this society from which you have fed so voraciously for so long."

David Johnston started to interrupt Judge Sugerman at one point, but Judge Sugerman said the defendant would be gagged if he tried to talk. Defense attorney John Lachall put his arm around his client and David Johnston remained silent.

JUDGE SUGERMAN SAVED a few choice words for John-ston Sr. at his sentencing session in March 1986. They were words Johnston Sr. cared not to hear. He called Johnston Sr. a "back-shooting, gutless child-killer." Johnston Sr. said he didn't want a lecture and Judge Sugerman said he was required by law to state the reasons for his sentence.

"Close your ears and bear with me," Judge Sugerman said.

"Indeed, crime was your life. For years you have plied your nefarious trade in this county and elsewhere, virtually unmolested. It would appear that the few short prison sen-tences you have served in the past were considered by you to be merely the cost of doing business, as a businessman pays rent or taxes. You have obviously learned nothing from those prison experiences, except, perhaps, to sharpen your skills in order to better conduct your criminal enterprise.

"Not content, however, to rob, burglarize, and pillage the good citizens of this county, you lured a number of young men into a life of crime, including your son, and then ex-tracted the profits of their crimes, as a modern-day Fagin.

"As if this were not sufficient to brand you and your broth-ers forever, when the noose began to tighten about these young men, the jury found that you conspired to assassinate them in order to maintain your murky secrets. Then, in the dark of night, your usual environment, you accomplished these assassinations, brutally murdering them, by your own hand or by the hands of others, with malice aforethought.

"As if to compound the enormity of your crimes, you caused to be killed Robin Miller, a perfectly innocent teen-age girl during the vicious attack upon Bruce Jr., your son.

We are all fortunate that superb police work, by all agencies, interrupted your dark schemes."

The *Daily Local News* of West Chester wrote an editorial on Johnston Sr.'s sentencing on March 7, 1986, that said, "It's a shame Judge Leonard Sugerman's eloquence was wasted on an unwilling and unrepentant audience."

FBI AGENT DAVID Richter was in his Delaware County office one day in the mid-1990s when he received a call from the Philadelphia office of the FBI. A man in Philadelphia wanted to see Richter. The man wasn't able to talk and Richter asked if the man could write his name; it was Leslie Dale.

"Leslie went to jail and he did about 16 years in prison," Richter said. I drove into Philadelphia to see him. Leslie had been released from state prison basically to die. He was full of cancer. He had throat surgery and lost his throat box and everything. He was waiting for a room to open up at the Brandywine Hospital because he still had family in the Coatesville area. I gave him some money and told him to let me know when he gets his room.

"I got word he was in Brandywine Hospital and Tom (Cloud), Charlie (Zagorskie), and I went to see him. He was in bad shape. He told us that when he was better he would be back and he would help us find the person who killed Dr. Kistler (an unsolved West Chester murder of a physician). He wanted to die on the good guys' side. When Leslie died there wasn't anything in the newspapers. Two months later there was an article and that was the first anyone here knew about his death."

The newspaper report in the Coatesville *Record* said Dale died on March 18, 1994, "alone and unattended he slipped into unconscious then death at Brandywine Hospital bringing to end one small chapter in what has become known locally as the Johnston Gang saga."

WILLIAM H. LAMB thought the case should be memorialized. Lamb didn't have *At Close Range* in mind, a Hollywoodized version of the story that depicts none of the police investigation and distorts the Johnston story, made in 1986 and starring Sean Penn, Christopher Walken, and Mary Stuart Masterson.

"It was just a tremendous team effort on the part of law enforcement to convict the Johnstons," Lamb said. "And then to see that stupid movie, *At Close Range*. Zagorskie and I and some others met with Sean Penn and the producer or director or someone. We were given a summary of the script and we read it. We were at the Downingtown Motor Inn. They were trying to decide if the movie was going to be made in Chester County or elsewhere and they were hoping we would become technical advisors. The story was a glorification of Bruce Johnston Jr. After we read the script we told them we wouldn't get involved."

James P. MacElree II, an assistant district attorney on the Johnston case who later became District Attorney and then a Chester County Common Pleas Court judge, said, "The movie was as bad as the script." MacElree was one of the ones to review the script. "They portrayed Bruce Jr. as some sort of hero with street smarts that had a sense of morality. They couldn't have been further from the truth. Bruce Jr. was a junior thief and nothing more. They tried to make him into a folk hero."

Zagorskie added, "The movie had nothing to do with reality. It might have been done for entertainment, but it sure didn't entertain me. It glorified things that shouldn't have been glorified."

As a final comment, Cloud said, "The movie, per se, stunk."

THE JOHNSTON CASE did become part of a book on mass
murderers by Northeastern University professors Jack Levin
and James A. Fox. "If this case took place in New York City,
it would have received nationwide headlines for months. The
importance of this case has been underplayed," Levin told
Daily Local News reporter Bruce Mowday.

The Johnston case was unusual, according to Fox, because
five persons were jailed for murder and usually mass murders
are done by only one or two people. Also, Levin said, "We've
seen communities paralyzed by fear, but it didn't happen here.
Most of the residents didn't identify with the Johnstons and
considered the case was either criminals killing criminals or
hillbillies killing hillbillies." Levin and Fox also compliment-
ed Judge Sugerman and the trial attorneys for their conduct
and not allowing the trial to become a three-ring circus. Too
many high-profile cases result in retrials, Levin said.

AS HOLLYWOOD WAS inventing its version of the murder
cases, the Johnston cases were winding their way through
the Pennsylvania appellate court system. Defense attorneys
continued to enter appearances while others withdrew. West
Chester attorney Sam Stretton, known for his vigorous representation of clients and a stickler for rules of law, took over
the Johnston Sr. defense. His appeal points included allegations that Tony List didn't provide a proper defense and that
the prosecution had committed violations of Johnston Sr.'s
rights. Albert P. Massey of Paoli, Norman Johnston's new
attorney, joined in the motions to dismiss.

In February 1992 the Pennsylvania Supreme Court upheld
Johnston Sr.'s conviction and six consecutive life imprisonment terms. After the ruling was issued, Judge Sugerman
said, "It's a relief to know the appellate courts agreed with
what we did here and properly affirmed our actions and kept
him behind bars."

As the twenty-first century dawned the defense attorneys representing the Johnston brothers were still attempting to have the convictions overturned. Defense attorney Vincent DiFabio filed a request in Chester County Common Pleas Court to have FBI surveillance reports released. DiFabio contended the reports could give the Johnstons an alibi for some of the murders.

AS THE YEARS passed the Johnston brothers were kept separated and they were shuffled from state prison to state prison to diminish the possibility of escape. In 1985 Johnston Sr. was housed in Western State Correctional Institution at Pittsburgh. With him were inmates Jose Lopez of Philadelphia and George Arms of Reading.

Arms, who was serving time for a third-degree murder conviction, needed to furnish his cell and picked the wrong inmate from whom to take some desired items. Johnston's radio, television and typewriter ended up in Arms' cell. On January 28, 1985, someone threw lighter fluid and then a match on Arms while he was in his cell. Arms suffered burns over 78 percent of his body. Arms died of his injuries on May 31 at the West Penn Hospital, Pittsburgh.

Lopez was charged with committing the murder at the behest of Johnston Sr. Prison officials said Lopez saturated the cell with a solvent and when Arms entered his cell he threw a cup of liquid on him along with a lighted match.

Before Arms' death Johnston Sr. wrote a letter to the *Daily Local News* proclaiming his innocence. "I just don't know how to put this, but it seems like trouble follows me."

In April 1986 Johnston Sr. and Lopez went on trial in Pittsburgh. The prosecution based its case on convicted criminals, including one eyewitness to the murder. Jury members said they couldn't believe any of the witnesses for either side and found both Johnston Sr. and Lopez not guilty.

The verdicts caused Judge John W. O'Brien to tell the defendants they had "beat the system." Judge O'Brien then commented he didn't know if the defendants believed in a superior being but they should get on their knees and stay on their knees for the next ten years out of gratitude.

"I'm sorry I have to display my emotions," Judge O'Brien said. "This case just upsets me."

Assistant District Attorney Gregory J. Nescott was more direct. He said, "Mr. Johnston is a butcher, and a convicted butcher. He really is a madman and a butcher."

In 1999, according to a prison guard at the State Correctional Institution at Graterford, Johnston Sr. admitted taking part in the murder of Arms.

AFTER TWO DECADES the memory of many events are gone and forgotten. For residents in southeastern Pennsylvania, Delaware, and Maryland and those who were members of the prosecution team, the Johnstons were never completely out of their minds. If for some reason the Johnstons were a distant, vague recollection, events in August 1999 brought the Johnstons' memories to vivid clarity. And those new to the Philadelphia region were about to be inundated with information about the murderous Johnstons.

Norman Johnston was being kept in the most secure section of the State Correctional Institution at Huntingdon, a prison about a two-hour drive east of Pittsburgh. He earned a cell in the restrictive unit after violating prison regulations. The cell was Johnston's home for 23 hours a day. He did get an hour for exercise and a shower. On Sunday evening, August 1, 1999, Johnston was in his cell preparing for his night's activities. Johnston had resided at the prison since April 1987. He would be gone from the prison by morning.

Prison officials began a manhunt after prison workers discovered a section of fence was loose and portions of Norman Johnston's cell window had been removed. Helicopters were used to search for Johnston but he had disappeared. A Land Rover car had been stolen from the prison grounds and prison officials believed Johnston had used it to escape. Johnston had been planning his escape for some time. Guards found an elaborate dummy, complete with human hair, on his bed.

Pennsylvania State Police Sergeant Tom McClung of the Avondale barracks said the forty-eight-year-old Johnston was to be considered armed and dangerous. Norman Johnston was described as 6 feet, 1-inch tall and weighing 180 pounds with brown eyes and hair, fair complexion, and a medium build. Police and citizens would have that description in mind for two weeks.

Those first receiving notification of Johnston's escape were witnesses against the Johnstons, family members of the victims, and law enforcement members involved in the case. Some were given police protection and some decided to leave the area until Johnston was captured.

William H. Lamb said he kept a low profile during Johnston's escape. "I've lived with this stuff for years," he said at the time. "Am I being careful and cautious in my movements? Yes. Do I take an extra look around the parking lot before I go to my car? Yes. But by and large, I don't let this stuff concern me."

At the time of the escape FBI agent David Richter said, "He's mad at a bunch of people who testified against him. I would hope no one gets hurt trying to apprehend him. He's been in jail for 20 years and is not ready to go back." Richter characterized the Johnston brothers as evil, clever, and violent. Prosecutor Joseph Carroll added, "He's proven he has no respect for human life, and he's going to be very desperate." Carroll also hoped that Johnston would value his freedom and not return to Chester County.

The FBI quickly joined the search for Johnston after a federal magistrate in Williamsport, Pennsylvania, signed an arrest warrant charging Johnston as an interstate fugitive from justice. Because of where Huntingdon was located, Baltimore, Pittsburgh, and areas in West Virginia were possible destinations for the escaped murderer. Presently, the area being considered was expanded to include New Jersey, Delaware, and all of Pennsylvania. The Johnston family's home town in Mountain City, Tennessee, was also searched.

Prison officials checked Johnston's visitors' log and conducted an internal investigation. Within three days of the escape two prison employees, a guard and nurse, were suspended after they admitted smuggling items into the jail for Johnston. The employees didn't check packages sent to Johnston and they said they believed the packages contained personal items, such as gum and cigarettes. In reality, the packages contained the tools Johnston needed to escape.

Sightings of Norman Johnston in Chester County were made almost as soon as word spread of his escape. Johnston was also reportedly seen in other states. "It's a manhunt, there's no question about it," Chester County District Attorney Anthony Sarcione said.

The manhunt was the lead story in many newspapers and television stations throughout the Philadelphia, Chester County, and Delaware region for days. Police were interviewed along with those involved in the trials, including the newspaper reporters who covered the trial. Bruce Mowday, who had left the *Daily Local News* two years before the escape, was interviewed by two television stations on air to tell the story of the Johnstons.

Throughout southern Chester County communities residents discussed Johnston, locked their doors, and in some cases even made jokes about the escape. One person taking the escape seriously was former Johnston fence Ed Otter. Otter kept a pistol at his side and a rifle with a scope in his room. "I wish he'd come up here right now," Otter told a newspaper reporter. "We'd get it over with."

As Johnston eluded capture the manhunt even made *America's Most Wanted* television show. After the show about 60 tips were given to police but none came from southern Chester County. A $28,000 reward, raised by the state police and private funds, was also offered for information leading to Johnston's capture. The amount was increased to $40,000.

One Oxford-based newspaper editor believed some people were turning him into a folk hero, the Hood of Nottingham. Nottingham is an area of southern Chester County. The editor told a *USA Today* reporter she had heard that some residents were rooting for Johnston to stay at large. Former prosecutor Dolores Troiani set the record straight in the same story. She said, "Norman Johnston is evil."

Law enforcement officers were closing in on Norman Johnston and they believed they had him in their grasp, twice. During the evening of Friday, August 6, park rangers Will Crouch and Robert Barker in West Nottingham saw Johnston. Nearby were members of the Delaware Astronomical Society setting up telescopes for an evening of watching the stars. Crouch grabbed Johnston by the shirt but the fugitive ran into the woods and eluded police by stealing two cars. A bicycle race at the park was cancelled the next day. Later, an unarmed University of Delaware guard also couldn't keep him in custody when he was spotted in Newark, Delaware.

Johnston was wearing a baseball cap, green T-shirt, and gray bib overalls. He was also reported to be clean shaven. "Somebody's helping him," Chester County Detective Ted Schneider commented. Some family members were indeed helping Johnston during his two weeks of freedom.

Two women who were at a fruit and vegetable stand in

Fair Hill, Maryland, just across the Pennsylvania state line, saw a man they believed was Johnston. The women were reading a newspaper that contained Johnston's photograph when the man fled into a field. The women called 911. The man was gone by the time police arrived.

The task force looking for Johnston expanded to 40 members by August 10. They had received hundreds of sightings and tips but had failed to corner Johnston. One sighting of Johnston near some homes in Cecil County, Maryland, sent state policemen to the location but Johnston wasn't found.

Persistence by police finally paid off as 10 Pennsylvania state policemen cornered Johnston and apprehended him at dawn on Friday, August 20. "You guys wouldn't quit," Johnston told a trooper after being arrested. Johnston was taken into custody in Pennsbury Township, only approximately a mile from where Norman Johnston took part in the murder of three young members of his gang.

The night before his capture Johnston was driving a stolen car when state policeman Louis Robinson spotted the fugitive. Robinson gave chase and as speeds reached 70 miles per hour Johnston turned into the Deerfield housing development in Mendenhall. "When he went in there I knew there was no way to get out of that development," Robinson said. Johnston jumped out of his car and ran as Robinson radioed for assistance.

Johnston eluded capture during the night but Ellen Baldo and Rick Mercurio, homeowners in the development, heard noises under their deck the following morning. They notified the police and were talking with police when Johnston started walking down the driveway. Johnston began to run but collided with a fence and was subdued by three policemen.

Johnston said his only mistake was not fleeing the area. He told police he spent days hiding and nights looking for food. He frequented convenience stores and spent one night at a motel but he liked camping out and looking at the stars. Family members contended Johnston escaped to uncover evidence that would clear him of the murder charges and revenge wasn't on his mind. Johnston indicated he wanted to visit prosecutor Lamb's office to find evidence that would clear him. Lamb labeled the excuse for the prison break as "just plain nonsense."

Norman Johnston missed a number of modern advancements during his twenty years in prison, including upgraded gasoline pumps. While trying to put gas into a stolen car he had to ask for help in operating the pump as he didn't know how to operate the automated pumps. The fugitive also passed up opportunities to steal ATM cards and cell phones as neither were available when he last had his freedom.

Norman Johnston did stand trial in Jefferson County on escape charges on July 10, 2000, and the jury after three hours of testimony convicted Johnston after 15 minutes of deliberations. Johnston blamed his escape on the strain of being locked in isolation for the better part of seven years. Johnston was then ordered to spend an additional 42 months in prison after completion of his four consecutive life imprisonment terms.

IN THE FIRST decade of the twenty-first century Norman and David Johnston and Ricky Mitchell were all still in prison, and Bruce A. Johnston Jr., who was the catalyst that began the killing spree of August 1978, had been in and out of prison on a 2003 theft conviction in Lancaster County and a December 2001 conviction in Chester County Court on burglary and drunk driving charges.

UPON THEIR BROTHER'S escape, Johnston Sr. and David
Johnston were placed in restrictive housing units at separate
state prisons. They were isolated from the rest of the prisoners and held in maximum security for months. Johnston Sr.
filed court papers saying he was being improperly held in
solitary confinements, a violation of his rights.

BRUCE ALFRED JOHNSTON Sr.'s appeals ended with his
death on Wednesday, August 7, 2002. He was sixty-three
years old and died of natural causes from a liver ailment,
prison officials reported. Two days before his death he was
transported from Graterford Prison, outside of Philadelphia,
to Mercy Suburban General Hospital. He was pronounced
dead at 4:45 AM.

At the time of Johnston Sr.'s death Chester County District Attorney Joseph Carroll called Johnston Sr. the most
notorious criminal in Chester County history. Johnston Sr.,
Carroll said, deserved the death penalty. "Unfortunately, we
didn't have one at the time. It is entirely appropriate he died
in prison," Carroll said. State policeman Tom Cloud added,
"He served his sentence."

BRUCE A. JOHNSTON Sr. served his life imprisonment sentence and he deserved the reputation as a butcher, madman,
and Chester County's most notorious criminal. Johnston Sr.
was convicted of six murders but many law enforcement officials believed he was involved in additional homicides, including the killing of inmate George Arms in Pittsburgh.

Johnston Sr. is also widely believed to have been a conspirator of Ancell Hamm in the murders of Kennett Square
policeman William Davis and Richard Posey. Prosecutor Bill
Lamb said at the conclusion of Johnston Sr.'s trial that there

was no doubt in his mind that Ancell Hamm had help, and it came from one of the Johnston brothers.

Roy Myers, Johnston Sr.'s brother-in-law, said he was told by two of the Johnston brothers that they were involved in the planning and carrying out of the policemen's murders. Johnston Sr. was driving the getaway car and the other brother was next to Hamm when the shots were fired, Myers said he was told. "Everything fell apart after the shooting," Myers said as he retold the story. "Bruce (Johnston Sr.) was to pick them up and when Bruce heard the shots he took off. They (Hamm and the other Johnston brother) ran off through the cemetery."

Myers also said Johnston confessed to another murder, that of a man outside of Coatesville in the mid-1970s. "Bruce told me they killed the gay guy," Myers said. "They were in a bar in Coatesville and Bruce picked up this guy who was dressed as a woman. He was giving Bruce oral sex when Bruce went to get a feel and found out he was a guy. Bruce also found out the guy had his hands in Bruce's pants and was lifting a wad of money from Bruce. Bruce shot him not because he was gay, but because he was stealing from him." Myers also said another gang member was involved in the murder. Pennsylvania State Police were told of Myers' story and began reinvestigating the homicide.

An unsolved murder took place in April 1977 when twenty-six-year-old Preston Frazer was found shot in Coatesville. He had a bra and skirt over his head, according to a police report.

Bruce A. Johnston's murder count appears to be at least 10: Gary Wayne Crouch, Robin Miller, Wayne and James Sampson, Dwayne Lincoln, Jimmy Johnston, George Arms, Preston Frazer, and Kennett Square policemen William Davis and Richard Posey.

Truly, the heroes in this mass murder were the members of the law enforcement team, the forces of justice. The law enforcement team brought Chester County's most notorious criminal, Johnston Sr., to justice and put out of business his vicious gang of criminals that for decades murdered, assaulted, raped, and robbed.

INDEX

Aberdeen, Maryland, 137
Adamstown, Pennsylvania, 77
Aldred, Edward, 225
Allen, Woody, 118
America's Most Wanted, 247
Anderson, Jack, 201, 202
Arms, George, 243, 244, 250, 251
Associated Press, 176
At Close Range, 241
Avondale Fire Company, 118

Baen, Jackie, 85-90, 93, 95, 101, 120, 183, 196
Baker, Earl, 68, 69
Baldo, Ellen, 248
Barker, Robert, 247
Barranco, Michael, 62, 87, 95, 217
Batty, Assistant United States Attorney Walter, 40, 56, 57
Blackburn, Joseph, 148, 149
Bloomsburg, Pennsylvania, 129
Bodnar, Albert, 131

Bolla, Gabe, 40, 41, 51, 53, 67, 74, 75, 88, 115, 141, 149, 154, 229, 236, 237
Booth, Gretchen, 88
Boothwyn, Pennsylvania, 39
Bosken, Ron, 71
Bove, Frank, 116
Brandywine Hospital, 240
Brandywine River, 79, 85, 89, 94, 102, 119, 120
Bronson, Charles, 52
Broomall, Pennsylvania, 86
Brown, District Magistrate Donald, 60, 62
Brown, Judith, 131
Bunjo, Raymond, 28, 29
Burns, Rita, 209
Bush, President George, 130

Caln Township, Pennsylvania, 100, 101
Cambria County Prison, 185

Campbell, J. R., 37, 48, 49, 56, 71,
83, 84, 91, 104-106, 121, 127, 137,
138, 153, 170, 171
Carroll, Joseph, 173-175, 211, 219,
235, 236, 245, 250
Carroll, Michael, 30, 34, 37, 39,
42, 45, 67, 96, 114, 116, 173, 207,
233
Carter, Frank, 33, 35
Cass, Julie, 176
Catanese, District Justice John,
60, 87, 149
Catania, Common Pleas Judge
Francis, 199
Chadds Ford, Pennsylvania, 46,
95, 117
Chamberlin, Glenda Sampson,
106, 223, 224
Chattanooga, Tennessee, 177
Chester, Pennsylvania, 80
Chester County Airport, 105, 173
Chester County Farms Prison,
24, 25, 36, 45, 62, 84, 94, 95, 120,
145, 149, 165, 166, 177, 182, 193,
203
Chester County Hospital, 97, 98,
165, 190
Clary, Truman Joseph, 28
Chicago, Illinois, 217
Clinton, President Bill, 130
Cloud, Thomas, 47-50, 52, 54, 56,
62-67, 70, 76, 77, 80, 84, 91, 236,
240, 241, 250
    Baen murder, 85, 90
    Crouch murder, 93, 97, 101, 103,
    105-107
    investigation, 170-173, 175
    Miller murder, 29, 46
    triple murder, 115, 117, 118, 122,
    127-130, 133, 137, 138, 142, 145,
    149

West Chester trial, 213, 219,
229, 233, 234
Coatesville, Pennsylvania, 37, 60,
85, 89, 97, 119, 205, 251
Coatesville Record, 160, 240
Cochranville, Pennsylvania, 78
Conemaugh Valley Hospital, 203
Cotter, Michael, 30, 96
Cow Town, New Jersey, 143
Crouch, Gary Wayne, 51, 92,
94, 95, 97, 98, 100, 101, 103, 104,
145, 153, 157, 169, 179, 183, 196,
221-223, 226, 229, 235, 251
Crouch, Will, 247
Cruise, Tom, 80

Dade County Jail, Florida, 142,
154
Dale, Leslie, 37, 38, 45, 46, 61-64,
84, 240
    Baen murder, 85, 86-90
    Crouch murder, 92-103, 105-107
    Ebensburg trial, 187, 188, 191,
    195-197, 200-203, 206, 208
    investigation, 170-172, 174, 182,
    183
    triple murder, 114, 118, 119, 121,
    124, 127, 133, 137, 148, 149, 153,
    158
    West Chester trial 213, 218,
    221-223, 226, 229, 231, 234, 235
Dampman, Larry, 30, 34, 37, 56,
84, 85, 96-98, 100, 101, 117, 118,
127, 145, 149, 154, 155, 157, 200, 237
Darrell, Bo, 49
Daull, Robert, 107
Davis, Charles, 35
Davis, Walter, 105, 106
Davis, William, 48, 51, 54, 172, 181,
234, 250, 251
DeBoard, Jacob, 30, 40

Delaware Astronomical Society, 247

Delaware County Prison, 115, 165, 195

Delaware State Police, 35

Dempsey, David, 108

Denken, Barry, 59

Desaretz, Sheri, 214

Des Moines, Iowa, 90, 91

Dickerson, Bernard, 28, 148, 164

Dietz, Vernon, 100

DiFabio, Vincent, 243

DiFilippo, District Magistrate Eugene, 38, 84, 87, 144, 147, 157, 158

DiMaio, Dr. Dominic, 85-87

Donnell, Richard, 37, 85-90, 153

Dotson, Jimmy 49, 55, 63, 106, 107, 110, 133, 162, 164, 165, 177, 226, 227

Downingtown, Pennsylvania, 84, 85, 101, 105

Duchemin, George, 48, 49

Duffy, John, 59, 110, 112, 139, 140

East Nottingham Township, Pennsylvania, 23

Ebensburg, Pennsylvania, 69, 167-169, 173, 175-177, 180, 182, 184, 185, 205, 208, 211

Elkton, Maryland, 35, 39, 75, 92, 102, 108, 159

Erie, Pennsylvania, 218, 219

Esquire magazine, 160, 176

Evans, Denise, 42

Exton, Pennsylvania, 143

Fair, Francis, 140

Fair Hill, Maryland, 247

Falasco, Richard 224

Fernald, Dana, 211

Fether, June, 186

Fillinger, Dr. Halbert, 97, 104, 118, 120, 222

Fox, James, 242

Fox, Wilson, 145

Fragale, Anthony, 162

Frame, Thomas, 36, 75, 76, 165

Franklin, Ben, 207

Frazer, Preston, 251

Freeman, James, 167

Gap, Pennsylvania, 37

Gavitt, Michael, 35

Gawthrop, Common Pleas Judge Robert, 96, 155, 156

Gazzaro, Frank, 237

Gazzaro, Janet, 237

Gittings, Ray, 185

Glenwood Memorial Garden Center, 86

Goldberg, Larry, 156, 157, 169, 180, 181, 187, 188, 192, 195, 197, 205, 206, 210, 211, 217, 226, 233

Gordon, Jeff, 174

Griffin, Jimmy, 31, 102, 103, 110, 126, 133, 142-144, 149-155, 157, 165, 183, 187, 188, 191, 197, 198, 221-223, 228

Hamilton, Denise, 111

Hamm, Ancell, 49-53, 68, 78, 93, 128, 143, 229, 234, 250, 251

Hamm, Jimmy, 49, 63, 162, 164, 165

Hamm, Raymond, 35, 49, 63, 128, 143

Hand, Ned, 53

Hanney, Vicki, 42

Hannum, John, 78

Harris, Amy, 223

Harrisburg, Pennsylvania, 53

Harrison, Carl, 178, 210

Harrop, Dr. Donald, 98
Haskell, Harry, 117
Heaton, Beryl, 201, 204
Hersheypark, 23, 26, 27
Highland Township, Pennsylva-
nia, 97, 221
Homeville, Pennsylvania, 188
Hommas, Richard, 111
Honey Brook, Pennsylvania, 193
Horn, Dorothy, 232
Houpt, Debbie, 161
Howell, Ken, 51, 76, 142, 154
Hutchinson, Willie, 224

Irving, Dana, 61

Johnston, Jr., Bruce A., 24, 25, 33,
    34, 36, 41-43, 58, 60-62, 74, 76,
    83, 84, 117, 123, 128, 133, 145, 159,
    169, 182, 238, 239
    Ebensburg trial, 188-191,
        193-197, 201, 202
    Federal Witness Protection
        Program 26, 28, 90, 91, 96
    Robin Miller murder, 27-29,
        31, 46, 59
    West Chester trial, 221, 224,
        225, 229, 231, 232
Johnston, Sr., Bruce A., 26, 41,
    42, 51-53, 55, 57, 60, 61, 64, 66, 73,
    75, 78, 79, 81, 82, 94, 235, 237, 239,
    240, 242, 249-252
    Crouch murder, 92, 101, 102,
        105-108
    Ebensburg trial, 189, 191, 193,
        194, 196-203
    investigation, 159-161, 163, 165,
        168, 169, 172, 177, 178, 180-184
    Miller murder, 29, 34-37, 40,
        45, 46, 59
    Miller rape, 25

prison murder, 243, 244
triple murder, 109-114, 117,
    122-126, 131-134, 139, 141-144,
    146, 148, 150, 153, 156, 157
West Chester trial, 213-215,
    218-220, 222, 223, 225-233
Johnston, Carol, 39, 40, 78, 112,
    113, 161, 203, 205, 206, 228, 229
Johnston, David, 50-53, 64. 66, 73,
    80-82, 94, 105-107, 235, 237-239,
    249, 250
    Ebensburg trial, 185-190,
        193-204, 206, 209-211, 217
    investigation, 161, 169, 172, 175,
        177, 179, 181, 182
    James Sampson murder, 134,
        135
    Miller murder, 29, 40, 41, 46
    triple murder, 109, 110, 113,
        122-127, 129, 131, 133, 143-146,
        150-153, 155, 156
    West Chester trial, 213, 215,
        220-222, 226
Johnston, James, 34, 35, 40, 91, 95,
    114, 116, 120, 123, 126-128, 132, 145,
    146, 162, 163, 189-191, 193, 196,
    200, 201, 238, 251
Johnston, Jenny 75, 145, 146, 163
Johnston, Louise, 41, 50, 53, 73-75,
    122-124, 126, 127, 133, 141, 152, 153,
    155, 172, 203, 204
Johnston, Manuel, 151, 152
Johnston, Norman, 53, 55, 66, 73,
    79, 81, 105-107, 218, 235, 242
    Ebensburg trial, 185-190, 193,
        194, 196-199, 201-204, 206,
        210, 211, 217
    escape, 244-249
    investigation, 161, 168, 169, 175,
        177, 180, 182
    James Sampson murder, 134

Miller murder, 29, 35, 40, 41,
    46
triple murder, 109-113, 122-127,
    131, 133, 137-140, 142, 143, 146,
    148-153, 155-157
West Chester trial, 213, 215,
    220, 221, 224, 226
Johnston, Passmore, 74, 75
Johnston, Pete, 111, 208
Johnston, Susan, 40, 41, 74, 81,
    111-113, 115, 131, 137, 161, 201, 204,
    210
Jones, James, 27, 28
Jordan, Barbara 78

Kauffman, Pennsylvania Supreme
    Court Justice, Bruce, 218
Kean, Michael, 95, 96, 149, 156,
    172, 173, 218
Kennett Square, Pennsylvania,
    48, 75, 77, 124, 143
Kepler, Kenneth, 210
Kerr, Wayne, 67
Kesler, Jim, 52
King Ranch, 85
Knecht, Martin, 172, 177, 178, 215
Kneff, John, 76
Knickerbocker Landfill, 221

Lachall, John 156, 169, 179, 180,
    181, 192, 194, 195, 201, 206, 211,
    226, 234, 238
LaCorte, Bennie, 81
Lake George, New York, 150
Lamb, Justice William, 53, 67, 69,
    70, 73, 76, 236, 241, 245, 249, 250
    Baen murder, 85, 86, 88, 90
    Crouch murder, 93-96, 98, 99,
        100, 102, 104
    Ebensburg trial, 187, 201-212

investigation, 166-168, 174, 175,
    180-182
triple murder, 118-121, 139, 145,
    157
West Chester trial, 214,
    218-220, 225, 228, 230-233
Lancaster County Prison, 25, 193
Landchester landfill, 140, 211
Landis, Robert, 41, 59, 61, 62, 107,
    114, 119, 147, 184
Leomporra, U.S. Magistrate
    Tullio, 110, 112
Levin, Jack, 242
Lewisburg Federal Prison, 87
Liddy, G. Gordon, 179
Lincoln, Dwayne, 35, 46, 83, 95,
    114, 116, 120, 126-129, 145, 150,
    180, 200, 201, 223, 238, 251
List, Anthony, 199, 203, 205, 206,
    242
    West Chester trial, 214, 218,
        220, 222-224, 226-228, 230-234
Longwood, Gardens, 81, 218
Lopez, Jose, 243, 244

MacElree, James, 43, 62, 65, 66,
    145, 215, 229, 241
Maksymchock, Gerald, 37
Manheim, Pennsylvania, 77
March, George, 119
Marchinisiani, Nick, 91
Mark, Jim, 76, 77, 81
Marrone, Common Pleas Judge
    D. T., 156, 160, 184, 199, 215
Martin, Sarah, 162, 190, 191
Martz, Robert, 37, 56, 57, 64, 66,
    108, 118, 122, 128, 133, 138, 144,
    149, 153, 168, 171, 173, 213, 229
Masciantonio, Jean, 142, 155
Massey, Albert, 242

Massorotti, Anthony, 30, 33, 36, 37

Matherly, Frances, 52, 79, 154

Mayberry, Richard, 94

Maxwell, William, 177, 178

Media, Pennsylvania, 85

Melnik, David, 209

Melvin, Michael, 111

Merrick, John, 87

McClung, Tom, 245

McCorkle's Rock, 85, 89

McDevitt, Brian, 52

McDevitt, Larry, 99, 100

McErlane, James, 111, 208

McGinty, Frank, 35, 43

Mehn, Karl, 51, 66

Melvin, Michael, 34

Mendenhall, Pennsylvania, 248

Mercurio, Rick, 248

Miami Beach, Florida, 144

Michner, Paul 110

Miller, Linda, 24, 190, 224, 225, 233

Miller, Robin, 24-31, 33, 42, 43, 45, 59, 61, 75, 83, 84, 90, 94, 95, 105, 106, 114, 117, 127, 128, 132, 144, 145, 150, 157, 159, 180, 182, 188-190, 193, 194, 197, 204, 224, 225, 228, 229, 238, 239

Miller, Roxanne, 43, 225

Miner's Hospital, 199

Mitchell, Ray, 134

Mitchell, Ricky, 63, 64, 95, 249
    Ebensburg trial, 187, 188, 191-195, 200-202, 206, 208
    investigation 161, 168, 170, 171, 174, 175, 182, 183
    Miller murder, 35, 39, 45, 46
    triple murder, 114-119, 121-127, 129, 133, 134, 137, 140, 144, 145, 148, 150-153, 155, 157, 158

    West Chester trial, 213, 215-217, 220, 226, 229-231, 234

Mitchell, Ruth 119

Mitman, William, Jr., 87

Modena, Pennsylvania, 102

Monroe, Leslie, 154, 155

Montgomery County Prison, 87

Mountain City, Tennessee, 73, 246

Mowday, Bruce, 86, 88, 93, 98-100, 104, 118, 165, 166, 169, 172, 174, 176, 182, 196, 204, 209, 216, 230, 236, 242, 246

Mr. T's restaurant, 194, 197

Murphy, John 107

Myers, Roy, 35, 41, 63, 65, 75, 78-82, 145, 158, 159, 162, 215, 223, 228, 251

Nescio, Joseph, 217

Nescott, Gregory, 244

Newark, Delaware, 37, 39, 247

Newcomer, U.S. District Court Judge Clarence, 162

Newtown Square, Pennsylvania, 55

New York Times, 160, 176, 207, 209

Nix, Pennsylvania Supreme Court Justice Robert, 218, 219

Noblet, Connie, 233

O'Brien, Common Pleas Judge John, 244

O'Donnell, Patrick, 69

Oh Shaw Motel, 127, 200

Otter, Ed, 101, 106-108, 110, 111, 128, 132, 141, 159, 198, 199, 223, 247

Oxford, Pennsylvania, 43, 47, 56, 60, 80, 91, 95, 104, 132, 188, 247

Oxford Diner, 182

Panichelli, Margaret, 197
Parkesburg, Pennsylvania, 97, 102, 164
Payne, Mary, 59, 74, 164, 226
Pease, Barry, 106
Penn, Sean, 241
Pennsbury Township, Pennsylvania, 117, 247
Pennsylvania Correctional Institution, Huntingdon, 244
Pennsylvania Supreme Court, 160, 168, 180, 242
Pennypacker, Paul, 52
People magazine, 176
Perry, Phil, 37, 214
Philadelphia Bulletin, 160
Philadelphia International Airport, 83, 113, 135
Philadelphia Inquirer, 160, 176, 209
Phoenixville Hospital, 97
Picciotti, Anthony, 156, 160, 165, 181, 183, 184
Pinkerton, Nancy, 176
Playboy magazine, 172
Pollak, U.S. District Court Judge Louis, 158, 160, 215
Posey, Richard, 48, 49, 51, 54, 172, 181, 234, 250
Pottstown Mercury, 160, 176, 209
Powers, U.S. Magistrate Richard III, 59, 113
Presley, Elvis, 155
Proudfoot, Robert, 203
Pugh, John, 104

Quigley, John, 221

Ranson, Sara, 199, 200
Rapone, Thomas, 165
Reading, Pennsylvania, 111, 113, 161

Reading Fairgrounds, 112
Rebert, Tom, 128, 129, 143, 162
Reeves, Joseph, 83
Reighley, Alan, 111
Reinert, Frank, 110, 111, 126
Richardson, Doug, 56-59, 107, 112, 132, 145, 158
Richter, David, 54-57, 66-68, 71, 90, 92, 245
    Crouch murder, 101, 107
    investigation, 171
    Miller murder, 29, 30, 43
    triple murder, 110, 113, 129-133
    West Chester trial, 229, 233, 234
Ricketts, Estelle, 109
Robinson, Louis, 248
Rome, Italy, 184
Rought, Walter, 37, 38

Sacred Heart Hospital, 119, 122, 165
Sadsburyville, Pennsylvania, 105
Saggese, Eva, 197
Sampson, James, 35, 46, 61, 83, 91, 92, 95, 106, 107, 114, 117, 120, 133, 134, 140, 141, 145, 159, 180, 183, 189, 198-200, 202, 203, 211, 223, 227, 228, 238, 251
Sampson, Marie, 120, 223, 227
Sampson, Wayne, 35, 46, 83, 91, 95, 106, 114, 116, 120, 126-128, 140, 141, 145, 150, 180, 193, 200, 201, 223, 238, 251
Sandell, Mike, 131
Sarcione, Anthony, 246
Schaible, John, 226
Schneider, Ted, 56, 71, 168, 173, 247

Schonely, David, 106-108, 110, 111, 132, 141
Shultz, Clayton, 88, 90
Schuylkill County, Pennsylvania, 160, 168, 169
Sicilliano, Helen, 209
Slauch, John, 29
Smith, George, 61, 176
Solt, Ray, 37, 64, 65, 76, 77
Southern Chester County Medical Center, 28, 33, 231
Stauffer, John, 70
Steffy, Kathy, 34
Steffy, Harriet, 34, 163, 190
Stottsville, Pennsylvania, 97
Stottsville Inn, 100
Stretton, Sam, 242
Stowe, Pennsylvania, 107
Sturges, Helen, 26, 27
Sugerman, Chester County Common Pleas Judge Leonard, 25, 64, 70, 139, 140, 160, 165, 169, 172, 174, 175, 179-182, 184, 197, 237-240, 242
  Ebensburg trial, 185, 186, 191, 192, 203, 205-212
  West Chester trial 214, 215, 218, 219, 224, 225, 227, 232
Swarthmore, Pennsylvania, 74

Talerico, John, 107, 184
Taylor, Helen, 226
Thompson, Joe, 70, 97, 100
Thompson, Nancy, 70
Thompson, Robert, 68, 70, 100, 179
Thornburg, Richard, 214
Thorndale, Pennsylvania, 84
Time magazine, 154, 160, 176
Torrance, Ted, 100
Toughkenamon, Pennsylvania, 87
Towber, Wasyl, 94, 119, 120

Troiani, Dolores, 53, 66, 67, 236, 247
  Baen murder, 85-87, 89
  Crouch murder, 93-96, 98
  Ebensburg trial, 186, 187, 192, 193, 205, 209, 211
  investigation, 168-172, 175
  triple murder, 114-116, 122, 138, 139, 145, 149, 155, 157
  West Chester trial, 213-215, 220, 225, 227, 230, 231
Tucson, Arizona, 159

United Press International, 176
United States Marshals Service, 90, 91
United States Witness Protection Program, 26, 28, 231
Unionville-Chadds Ford School District, 47, 74
Unionville Community Fair, 48
USA Today, 247

Valley Township, Pennsylvania, 84

Walken, Christopher, 241
Wandishin, Ed, 40
Warner Theater, 118
Weimer, Richard, 29, 30, 35, 87, 99, 112, 129, 130, 145, 147, 160, 171
Weiniger, Walt, 101, 106
Welch, Neil, 55
West, Sandy, 39
West Chester Daily Local News, 86, 93, 104, 118, 119, 160, 165, 166, 169, 174, 176, 182, 196, 204, 209, 218, 230, 236, 240, 242, 246
West Chester, Pennsylvania, 94, 96, 102, 118, 144, 156, 166, 176, 214
West Grove, Pennsylvania, 76, 217

West Marlborough Township,
  Pennsylvania, 100
West Penn Hospital, 243
Western State Correctional
  Institution, Pittsburgh, 243
WCOJ, 88, 160
Whalen, Bill, 133
Wilmington, Delaware, 35, 162,
  164, 173
Wilmington *News Journal*, 160
Wilson, Laura, 42, 43
Wilson, Thomas, 215
Wood, David, 158, 215
Wood, Lawrence, 179
Wooden Shoe Inn, 92, 104, 183
Woodward, Kenneth, 28
Wright, Common Pleas Judge
  Robert, 86

Yoder, Paul, 40, 41, 56, 121, 128,
  137, 138, 144, 145, 159, 236

Zagorskie, Charles, 51, 54, 56, 63,
  66, 67, 70, 240, 241
  Baen murder, 88, 90
  Crouch murder, 93-96, 98, 99,
    103
  Davis-Posey murders, 50, 52
  Ebensburg trial, 201, 204, 208,
    209, 212
  investigation, 170, 174
  Miller murder, 35, 36, 38, 43
  triple murder, 115-117, 119, 122,
    138, 139, 141, 142, 149, 155-157
  West Chester trial 214, 217, 225,
    230, 233, 234
Zagorskie, Frank, 54
Zinn's Diner, 101
Zizzo, Michael, 131

OTHER BOOKS IN OUR BARRICADE CRIME SERIES

Human Sacrifice: A Shocking Exposé of Ritual Killings Worldwide
Jimmy Lee Shreeve
Human sacrifice still goes on today, and uncomfortably close to home. Jimmy Lee Shreeve paints a horrifying picture of ritual killings around the world.

$15.95 • Paperback • 1-56980-346-3

The Jews of Sing-Sing
Ron Arons
Besides famous gangsters like Lepke Buchalter, thousands of Jews committed all types of crimes--from incest to arson to selling air rights over Manhattan--and found themselves doing time in Sing-Sing.

$22.95 • Hardcover • 1-56980-333-1

The Mafia and the Machine
Frank R. Hayde
La Cosa Nostra reaches right into the heart of America. Nowhere is that more evident than in the "City of Fountains," where the Mafia held sway over the political machine.

$22.00 • Hardcover • 1-56980-336-6

Black Gangsters of Chicago
Ron Chepesiuk
Chicago's African American gangsters were every bit as powerful and intriguing as the city's fabled white mobsters. For the first time, Ron Chepesiuk chronicles their fascinating stories.

$22.00 • Hardcover • 1-56980-331-5

The Silent Don
Scott Deitche
A follow-up to Deitche's best-selling *Cigar City Mafia*, *The Silent Don* exposes the life of one of America's most powerful and feared mob bosses, Santo Trafficante Jr.

$22.00 • Hardcover • 1-56980-322-6
$16.95 • Paperback • 1-56980-355-2

Blood & Volume
Dave Copeland
Ron Gonen, together with pals Johnny Attias and Ron Efraim, ran a multi-million-dollar drug distribution syndicate in 1980s New York. But when the FBI caught up, Gonen had to choose between doing the right thing and winding up dead.

$22.00 • Hardcover • 1-56980-327-7

Gangsters of Harlem
Ron Chepesiuk
Veteran journalist Ron Chepesiuk chronicles the life and crimes of Harlem's gangsters, including "Nicky" Barnes, Bumpy Johnson, and the notorious Frank Lucas.

$22.00 • Hardcover • 1-56980-318-8

Cigar City Mafia: A Complete History of the Tampa Underworld
Scott M. Deitche
Prohibition-era "Little Havana" housed Tampa's cigar industry, and with it, bootleggers, arsonists, and mobsters—and a network of corrupt police officers worse than the criminals themselves. Scott M. Deitche documents the rise of the infamous Trafficante family,

ruthless competitors in a "violent, shifting place, where loyalties and power quickly changed."

$22.95 • Hardcover • 1-56980-266-1

I'll Do My Own Damn Killin'
Gary W. Sleeper

A detailed look into the life of notorious casino owner Benny Binion, which looks into his life in Dallas before his infamous Las Vegas days.

$22.00 • Hardcover • 1-56980-321-8

Thief!
William "Slick" Hanner & Cherie Rohn

The true story of "Slick" Hanner and how he gained insider access to the Mafia, starting out as a Chicago street tough and workin his way to a friendship with Tony Spilotro, the Outfit's notorious frontman.

$22.00 • Hardcover • 1-56980-317-X

Gangster City: The History of the New York Underworld 1900–1935
Patrick Downey

From 1900 to 1935, New York City hosted more than 600 mob-land killings. No other book delivers such extensive detail on the lives, crimes, and dramatic endings of this ruthless cast of characters, including Jack "Legs" Diamond and the sadistic Dutch Schultz.

$23.95 • Hardcover • 1-56980-267-X
(coming soon in Paperback, March 2009)

Il Dottore
Ron Felber

By day, he was Dr. Elliot Litner, respected surgeon at Mount Sinai Hospital; by night, Il Dottore, a sex and gambling addict with ties to New York's reigning Mafia Dons. But when Attorney General Rudolph Guiliani stepped in, Litner had to decide where his loyalties lay: with La Cosa Nostra, or the Hippocratic oath.

$24.95 • Hardcover • 1-56980-278-5

Murder of a Mafia Daughter
Cathy Scott

Not until college did Las Vegas native Susan Berman learn her father had been a notorious leader of the local Mafia. Her life took an even more bizarre turn when the wife of her college friend, real estate heir Robert Durst, disappeared, leaving Durst a murder suspect. When Berman was found dead, shot execution-style, investigators wondered if she knew more about Durst than he could afford.

$23.95 • Hardcover • 1-56980-238-6

The Life and Times of Lepke Buchalter
Paul R. Kavieff

Lepke Buchalter had a stranglehold on the New York garment industry, rising from small-scale push-cart terrorism to leadership of Murder Inc.'s staff of killers-by-assignment, until an obscure murder ended his reign as America's most ruthless labor racketeer.

$22.00 • Hardcover • 1-56980-291-2

The Purple Gang
Paul R. Kavieff

This is the hitherto untold story of the rise and fall of one of America's most notorious criminal groups. The Purple Gang was a loosely organized confederation of mobsters who dominated the Detroit underworld and whose ten-

tacles reached across the country.
$15.95 • Paperback • 1-56980-281-5
Hardcover

The Violent Years
Paul R. Kavieff
A follow-up to Kavieff's best-selling *The Purple Gang*, this book delves deeper into the Prohibition-Era gangs of the Detroit area.
$22.00 • Hardcover • 1-56980-210-6

The Rise and Fall of the Cleveland Mafia
Rick Porrello
From obscurity, the Cleveland Mafia rose rapidly to power and position, taking its place as the third most powerful operation in the country. But the city's crime syndicates nearly decimated themselves during the Sugar War—"Big Ange" Lonardo's vendetta-driven play to control the lucrative bootleg liquor production racket.
$15.00 • Paperback • 1-56980-277-7
Hardcover

Lucky Luciano
Hickman Powell
Written by a top investigative reporter who covered Luciano's trial from beginning to end, *Lucky Luciano* is a detailed account of Luciano's intriguing life.
$23.95 • Hardcover • 1-56980-163-0

Mala Femina
Theresa Dalessio with Patrick W. Picciarelli
Theresa "Terri Dee" Dalessio was a Mafia daughter, pregnant teenager, barkeeper, heroin addict, murder witness, and twice-divorced mother of three. For a start.
$24.95 • Hardcover • 1-56980-244-0

COMING SOON!

Balls: The Life of Eddie Trascher, Gentleman Gangster
Scott M. Deitche with Ken Sanz
For 50 years, Eddie Trascher stole from mob-owned casinos, scammed gangsters, and was one of the top bookies in the country. He capped his career as an informant for Florida enforcement to get inside the Trafficante Mafia family.
$24.95 • Hardcover • 1-56980-366-8
APRIL 2009

A Cop's Tale
Jim O'Neil and Carmelo Fazzino
Focusing on New York City's most violent and corrupt years, the 1960s to 1980s, this book delivers a rare look at the brand of law enforcement that ended Frank Lucas's grip on the Harlem drug trade, his cracking open the Black Liberation Army case, and his experience as the first cop on the scene at the "Dog Day Afternoon" bank robbery.
$24.95 • Hardcover • 1-56980-372-2
JULY 2009